St. Francis Receives The Stigmata

"Francis was kneeling outside his hut. His prayer quivered in the silence of the night. Dawn was near. It was bitingly cold, and the stars were shining brightly in the sky. And then, as the first glimmer of light appeared in the dark, what he had lived for all his life happened.

"All of a sudden there was a dazzling light. It was as though the heavens were exploding and splashing forth all their glory in millions of waterfalls of colors and stars. And in the center of that bright whirlpool was a core of blinding light that flashed down from the depths of the sky with terrifying speed until suddenly it stopped, motionless and sacred, above a pointed rock in front of Francis. It was a fiery figure with wings, nailed to a cross of fire. Two flaming wings rose straight upward, two others opened out horizontally, and two more covered the figure. And the wounds in the hands and feet and heart were blazing rays of blood. The sparkling features of the Being wore an expression of supernatural beauty and grief. It was the face of Jesus, and Jesus spoke.

"Then suddenly streams of fire and blood shot from His wounds and pierced the hands and feet of Francis with nails and his heart with the stab of a lance. As Francis uttered a mighty shout of joy and pain, the fiery image impressed itself into his body, as into a mirrored reflection of itself, with all its love, its beauty, and its grief. And it vanished within him. Another cry pierced the air. Then with nails and wounds through his body, and with his soul and spirit aflame, Francis sank down, unconscious, in his blood."

—*From* THE PERFECT JOY OF ST. FRANCIS

THE PERFECT JOY
OF ST. FRANCIS

Felix Timmermans

TRANSLATED FROM THE FLEMISH
BY RAPHAEL BROWN

Image Books
A DIVISION OF DOUBLEDAY & COMPANY, INC.
GARDEN CITY, NEW YORK

Image Books edition 1955
by special arrangement with Farrar, Straus & Young, Inc.
Image Books edition published March, 1955

ISBN: 0-385-02378-2
Copyright, 1952 by L. A. Aspelagh

Printed in the United States of America

Contents

Benediction

The sun had glided down like a goldfish. Suddenly a lovely subdued melody floated through the forest above the solitary and forsaken little chapel of Our Lady of the Angels, just when a shepherd who was passing by with his sheep was going to play a tune on his horn in honor of Mary. The shepherd turned pale and looked up at the fallen-in roof, but there was nothing to be seen.

"Have they got an organ now?" he wondered. He pushed the little door open. All was dark and still within. "So it must come from outside," he said. The sheep too were listening now. Overhead the music was becoming more and more heavenly, as a hundred golden voices seemed to mingle in counterpoint.

"Lord, how beautiful! It's enough to make one want to die, it's so beautiful! I'll have to tell the priest about it!" he thought, for he was so moved that he could not utter a word. His heart told him what was happening; taking off his hat, he knelt down and stammered: "A—A—Angels! Angels!"

The sun had vanished behind the distant mountains. The valley with its rivers and vineyards had turned dark blue. But half way up the hill the little white town of Assisi with its black cypress trees was still rose-tinted.

Such an unbroken silence filled the countryside that it seemed as though everyone were waiting for a concert to begin. Wondrous events often occur in such moments. Just then a tall lean man came in through the city gate. On his bare body he wore only a tattered sheepskin. He held one arm out straight, like someone

7

who is preaching. And with a smile on his lips he shouted, amid the silence of the town: "Peace and all that's good are coming now! Peace and all that's good are coming now!"

Thus he went up through the little streets and squares, past the fountains and past the churches. People came running out of their houses. But the tall lean man did not look back. He went right on up the hill until he disappeared over the top—still singing.

Later, about the time when people put off lighting their lamps for a while, a little old man dressed as a pilgrim emerged from a dark alley. He was blind, and only the whites of his eyes were visible. Yet without hesitating, like someone who could see, he crossed the small Piazza of the Holy Spirit and headed straight for the house of the cloth merchant Pietro di Bernardone, who last year had married a noblewoman from the south of France. It was a fine rich business house with small columns.

The pilgrim knocked on the door, and held his hand out like a beggar. The maid, a plain fresh-complexioned country girl, hastened to open the door. But before she could utter a word, the blind man said: "Tell Signora Pica that she must go to the little stable. The child can only be born there. Our Lord so wills it!" And off he went, with the whites of his eyes raised toward the sky.

Five seconds later the servant girl was upstairs, gasping for breath and announcing ecstatically that a little blind monk—with a halo of light around his head—had come to say on behalf of Our Lord—that the baby must be born in the little stable!

Everyone in the room, that is, the doctor, the midwife, some women friends, and the Signora, who had already been suffering so long in bed, immediately felt a sudden and profound awe for what the maid told them. For they were all good Catholics and believed in

8

miracles. "To the little stable!" they exclaimed, one after another.

"Yes, to the stable," moaned Signora Pica, "because I dreamed something like that . . . Didn't the little monk have wings?" she asked.

"Very likely he did," said the maid, "but I didn't see them."

Then with great care the doctor and the midwife helped the Signora to go down the stairs. Her friends followed, carrying towels and jugs of warm water, and after them came the maid with a holy water basin. They went through the house and crossed the little garden, which was bright with September roses. And there in the stable, on a bundle of fresh straw, by the light of a candle, the child was born. And the birth went as smoothly as a popular tune. The baby was a tiny thin creature.

"I ask you, was it worth getting so excited?" said the midwife as she washed the child and wrapped him up. Then she put him in a small crib next to his mother, who had fallen asleep from fatigue and relief.

They all gazed admiringly at the scene.

"Wonderful! Wonderful!" said the doctor.

The maid laughed and exclaimed: "It's like the Stable of Bethlehem!"

"But without the ox and without the ass," snickered the midwife.

"Still, there was an angel," said the maid indignantly. "And he spoke to me and not to you!"

The Troubadour

Francis and his friends were singing as they returned by moonlight from a village fair. Francis was riding a horse and playing his mandolin, while two men with torches went ahead. When they entered the sleeping little town they again started to sing very loudly some satirical songs against Perugia, a city two hours away that had long been stirring up a quarrel with Assisi.

Francis motioned for silence and cried out: "No more war songs! This is the time for love. Let's serenade all our sweethearts. We'll begin with Andrea's Marietta!"

They all cheered the idea. Andrea was a poor painter, and Marietta was the daughter of a sculptor of religious objects. Her home was on a narrow little street, directly opposite a convent garden.

Still on horseback, Francis slowly sang and played a French love song which he had learned from his mother. His clear voice rang out high above the roof tops. All of a sudden a window was flung open, and Marietta's father roared: "See here, my fine 'Lord' Bernardone, just let your wretched friend speak for himself! Then I'll teach him how to paint black eyes! Buffoon—actor—clown—sissy! Tomorrow I'll drag you and your dainty friends into the police court!"

The boys began to jeer and hoot, until suddenly a bucketful of water came pouring down upon them. Just then the night watchman hobbled into sight, and they all ran off and scattered into nearby alleys. Francis could hear his friend Theodore still shouting in the distance:

"Let's go to the Rose Tavern! They have strong wine and lovely girls—we'll bust up everything in the place, like last week!"

"And I'll pay the bill, as usual," thought Francis.

He let them go, and rode homeward. He had had enough for one day: they had drunk, danced, and flirted. Tomorrow he was going hunting with some noblemen. Day after tomorrow there was to be a fencing contest at Arnaldo's, with a first-class banquet. On Sunday he was giving a party at which he was going to read aloud some of his latest poems, and in the evening there would be a mid-lenten fancy dress ball. And on Monday he was due to leave on a two weeks' trip to Florence with his father. Nothing like being young!

He doffed his cap to a Madonna painted on a wall, and stopped a moment to gaze at it. A little bouquet of flowers was lying in front of the Madonna. Francis had no flowers with him. However, he broke the white ostrich-plume off his cap and tossed it beside the flowers. "Ah, to love—to love!" he murmured as he rode on. "When will I too ever feel a love that will tear me away from my parents, from my friends, and even from myself? A love that devours and burns . . ."

He meant to say a lot more, but he had reached home. He looked up at the moon, gleaming high in the sky. "I love the moon!" he said. "I love the unattainable!"

He wanted to sing a serenade to the moon. But he gave up the idea on account of his father, who laughed at such things.

On the yearly fair-day the town was teeming with people. Scented with fresh nutmeg perfume and wearing several gold rings, Francis was working behind the counter in his father's store, measuring damask linen. Several customers were standing around, waiting their turn. A servant boy and Francis' younger brother

11

Angelo were helping to unpack and lay out the goods.

His father stood outside the front door, where more cloth was on display on shelves. He was talking with two wool dealers, making forceful gestures and laughing like a trumpet. With his big hands he often thumped the men heavily on the shoulders, and each time their legs sagged a bit.

Francis enjoyed hearing his father talk like that. But just now he had no time to listen. He still had to go and get some fresh trout for tomorrow's little party, which he had to give because he had lost a bet: he had not managed to put away two pints of wine and twenty-four oysters without stopping. "I must hurry up and get through with these customers," he thought, "and then ride down to the fishers along the riverbanks."

Out in the streets there was a lot of noise. People were talking gaily of the impending war against Perugia. There were swarms of beggars. One simply could not give something to each and all of them. Now here was one more of them coming into the store: a poor devil, half naked, hairless from head to foot, nothing but a pack of bones and muscles, leaning on a heavy cane. His unwashed body and clothes filled the room with a sewer-like stink.

"For the love of God—" he begged.

But before he could hold out his hand, Francis, who was overcome by the smell and in a hurry to get the fish, snapped at him: "I'm too busy!"

The beggar limped away, and the customers immediately began to discuss the beggar problem: "They're all loafers and spies!" . . . "They're making the cost of living go up!" . . . "They're to blame for the war . . ."

"I'm going to war too!" Francis exclaimed. He raised his fist as though he were grasping a sword, and his dark eyes flashed like the gems in his rings. He was no longer listening to the talk. His thoughts kept going back to the beggar, and he began to regret bitterly not having given him something. "Maybe he is hungry—I'm going to eat trout, and I'm sparkling with jewels," Francis thought. "If he had come on behalf of a Count, I would have helped him at once. But he came in the name of God—and I drove him away!"

His remorse became so intense that he could no longer restrain himself. Suddenly he snatched a small purse from a drawer, exclaimed to the customers, "Just a minute—!" and ran out after the beggar, but he did not find him.

"I won't go home until I find him!" he decided, and questioned every acquaintance that he met. All morning he searched up and down the streets, in the churches and the shops, and among the cows in the cattle market. Finally he caught sight of him. The beggar was standing eating a piece of stale bread which was so hard that he had to dip it into a fountain in order to swallow it.

Francis gave him the purse and said: "Here is your alms, with interest," and very courteously he asked the beggar to forgive him.

The poor wretch was struck dumb by this unexpected good luck. But as soon as Francis had gone, he quickly glanced into the purse and began to laugh like a child. "What a fool! What a fool!" he shouted. "But that's his business!" Then he dropped his big stick and pushed his way into a first-rate inn, to round out his slack belly with a leg of mutton.

Happy again, Francis hurried home in order to go and get the trout. And he resolved never again to refuse something to a poor man.

On the great square another beggar pushed his way through the crowd toward Francis. He was a hairy little man, a sort of hermit from the caves. His long robe was stiff with dry mud. Stretching out his arms, he planted himself in front of Francis like an immovable rock. Then he threw his tattered cloak onto the ground, as though it were a carpet for a prince to walk on.

13

Francis hesitated to step on it, and said: "I've just given away all I have."

"I'm not asking for anything," replied the little fellow. "I'm doing this to honor you. For soon you are going to accomplish great things which will be talked about until the end of the world!"

Francis was thrilled, and stepping out into the sight of all the crowd, he proudly walked on the rags.

The little streets resounded with the grinding and sharpening of swords and pikes. Then one morning, when a rose-tinted sunrise crowned the mountains like an altar, the long lines of troops paraded out through the narrow city gate, with armor flashing and banners floating, while trumpets blared.

Down in the valley the Perugian army was also advancing. The two forces took up positions, then, like two walls, the armies fell upon each other with a deafening crash.

Francis fought his way right into the middle of the bloody carnage. He raised his sword to hack a Perugian officer in two. But just then he received such a powerful blow on the neck that he tumbled unconscious from his staggering horse . . .

He awoke in a dark dungeon, to find himself sitting among some knights and noblemen of Assisi. Had he been taken for a knight too? His friends Arnaldo and Theodore were also there. They told him that Andrea had been killed by an arrow in the heart, and that Assisi had lost the battle.

All the prisoners sat around looking as gloomy as a November day, and for a few days Francis too was depressed. But then a ray of sunlight came into his melancholy. "What a pity I haven't got my mandolin," he said. "I'd sing some songs."

But he acted as if he had it, and while he sang, he pretended that he was playing a mandolin. He sang

14

about Roland and his horn, about Tristan and Isolde, and all the songs he had learned from his mother and from the French troubadours.

A thickset old knight with a bloody cloth over his right eye told him to keep quiet. "Are you crazy?" he barked at Francis. "This is no time for singing! Nobody sings in a cemetery!"

"I do!" exclaimed Francis, "if only to entertain the dead!" and went on singing.

The knights were angry at first, but Francis sang so beautifully, with so much heart and feeling, that he stirred them all, and soon tears were running down their unshaven cheeks. The old knight's good eye sparkled, and he joined in the chorus with all the eagerness of a bumblebee. Soon they were all singing together, and one of them kneeled down and hid his face in his hands.

In that moment Francis realised more clearly than ever that he was destined to become a troubadour and to spread joy everywhere, like the famous Italian troubadour Divini. Every morning thereafter he sang a "reveille." During the day he amused his companions with droll stories, and they no longer went to sleep without singing an evening prayer together . . .

Their clothes wore out but not their hearts, and so after a year of songs and stories, one day an officer came in and read an announcement on a parchment roll: a peace treaty had been signed and they could all go home!

"Let's not enter the city with our heads hanging!" shouted Francis when they approached the walls of Assisi. They were long-haired, gaunt, and ragged, but they marched in through the gate singing a gay tune. The townsfolk cheered and wept . . .

At home Francis found the dining room table loaded with plump pullets and other delicacies. While he was embracing his mother—his father happened to be away on a trip—and as he was sobbing on her breast, suddenly his knees gave way. His accumulated fatigue made him collapse like a house of cards.

They carried him up to bed. Thick candles were lit before the Madonna's shrine. His mother prayed. And his father, when he returned, took two rolls of his costliest scarlet cloth to His Excellency the Bishop of Assisi. Falling on his knees he begged pitifully: "Please, Excellency, I'll give you my whole store—just make him well! He is the dearest thing I have—he is all my hope and all my pride!"

"We will pray for him," said the Bishop. After all, what else could he say?

The doctor, the same who had delivered Francis, but whose head was now snow-white, said with firm confidence: "Just leave him in God's hands. I may be wrong, but I still think it was not for nothing that God caused him to be born in a stable."

Francis recovered slowly. With the mild and clear weather he was able to go outdoors for the first time. He had had a new suit made to order for the occasion: it was yellow with a purple sheen, and when he went out, he looked like a rainbow.

How eager he was to be outdoors, out in the country, in nature, which he had been forced to miss for so long, and which would completely cure him, so that at last he could become a troubadour. People were really glad to see him again. They joked with him and told him to eat a lot and get his strength back, because without him Assisi was dead.

He was glad now that he did not meet any friend who, out of politeness, might have come along with him. He wanted to be alone, all alone, in order to enjoy perfect solitude. Tired yet happy he reached the other side of the hill, over near the dilapidated little church of St. Damian, where the town was completely out of sight. And there before him, as far as eye could see, lay all the beauty of nature in the spring. But Francis' arms hung motionless beside his body. With a sigh of disappointment he lay down in the grass.

He gazed at that nature for which he had longed so intensely during his imprisonment and illness. There it was in all its fresh beauty: the young shoots in the vineyards and the daisies at his feet, and far, far in the distance, like mother-of-pearl seen in a dream, the snow-covered peaks of the Apennine mountains. He watched the birds fly and listened to their chirping, and he smelled spring in the air, and he looked at the castles on the hills. Everything was bathed in bright sunlight. He saw and he smelled and he heard it all—but his heart remained unmoved.

It was just as though scales had fallen from his eyes. All of a sudden everything looked different to him, as if it were inside-out. Everything he saw seemed empty and hollow. His longing for distant horizons had vanished. And as always happens, the death of one desire dragged others down with it, and within a quarter of an hour all that had filled his life with song and joy meant nothing to him.

He felt ashamed of himself for having been a playboy who had lived for pleasure and for the good things of this world. Did they really have any importance, these expensive clothes of his, these gold rings, these jewels, the parties and poems and friends and music? They were nothing but illusions to gild the emptiness and vanity of the world! Can a man not be just as happy in a woolen shirt as in a silk one—or even without any shirt at all?

He sat there weakly gazing at the glorious sunset. Later he looked up at the stars, and then he thought of God.

"God is the only thing that counts," he sighed, but the thought came and drifted away again, like a whiff of

17

scent. For, of course, he was not used to thinking of God. "Why am I here?" he wondered.

Listless and spiritless, he got up and slowly strolled back to Assisi. When he came home, he pushed aside the cakes and sweet wine which his mother gave him.

"You look exhausted. Are you feeling worse?" she asked.

"No, Mother," he said, "I'm just terribly sleepy . . ." and went up to bed. He wished that he could sleep and sleep on and on and never think another thought.

The Call of God

Francis felt crushed and hunted, as though something were on his heels, something that he could not see. At times he liked to be all alone in the silence of the mountains; then he could creep into a cave and hide from whatever it was. But it followed him wherever he went.

At other times he threw himself again into going to wild parties with his friends. Then he took up cloth selling with all his energy. And when he tired of that, he wrote poems. But soon he let his pen fall. And he always sighed the same complaint: "What's the use?"

He was tired of living, without knowing why, and afraid of something, without knowing what. And besides he could not sleep.

He never said a word about it to anyone, only saying that his stomach was bothering him. But his mother, like all mothers, knew very well that her boy's heart was troubled. To all her cautious questions—for he was very moody—he gave only evasive replies. When she mentioned it to his father, he said: "If you ask me, he's trying to act like a saint. You spoiled him too much when he was sick. The right kind of girl will cure him. I'm going to find one for him!" So the mother had to worry all by herself.

But one day about nightfall the father came home from a trip with the big news that there was going to be a war. Walter of Brienne, a famous knight of the Pope's party in Rome, was taking up arms against the German Emperor. All the nobility and everyone else who amounted to anything were arming also.

"Because," thundered the father, "the whole world is interested in this great conflict! The war between Assisi and Perugia was only a cat fight. But this one— why, I've heard very important men say that whoever comes home alive from this war will have his name written in letters of gold and will be made a baron or a count!" And placing his big hairy hands on Francis' thin shoulders, he said: "Young fellow, let's see if you still have my blood in your veins! Give me the thrill of being the father of a baron!"

Francis was killing time by carving a bird from a little piece of wood, and only shrugged his shoulders and did not reply.

Then his father flared up and snarled bitterly that Francis was good for nothing but squandering money, that he was too lazy ever to accomplish anything, too vain to work, that he acted sick to make himself interesting, and that if he went on that way, he would end up as a regular tramp.

As Francis still said nothing, the father grew even angrier and began to blame his wife for being the cause of it all. The mother wept, and Francis said: "I'm going up to bed."

"That's all you're good for!" his father shouted after him. And to calm his raging temper, he went out to a nearby inn.

The mother took up her prayer book and began to pray.

Strangely enough, that night Francis slept like a log. And he had a very remarkable dream: he dreamt that his home had changed into a great palace, but instead of linen and cloth, it was filled with fine shields, armor, swords, banners—and on all this war equipment glittered a red cross. As he wandered through the halls, a beautiful poorly-dressed girl appeared and clasped his hand tightly and said to him: "Francis, my beloved, all

20

this is for you and for your companions. Take up your arms." Then he awoke. It was just dawn.

Dreams can have a profound influence. Sometimes they completely upset men's plans. This dream aroused Francis' vanity again. He began to imagine himself fighting beside the famous Sir Walter. He never missed a blow. He hacked away and cleaved and thrust so fast and furiously that the pieces flew into the air by the basketful. He was the winner! Olive branches were presented to him, while trumpets blared long and loud before him . . .

He got such a thrill from these figments of his imagination that as he was going downstairs to join the others at breakfast, he cried from the top of the stairs: "Father, I'm going to fight in the big war! I want to become a famous knight—and I will!"

"Aha!" shouted his father, springing to his feet with arms outstretched and his mouth still full of food. "Then you will also be dressed like the richest knight in the whole country—even better; I'll get you a new horse—a white one! And when you come home, there will be a feast—a great feast!"

Turning to his troubled wife, he exclaimed: "And you were always dreaming that he was going to become a monk! What do you think of your monk now?" He was weeping as he hugged Francis against his stout body until he almost broke the boy's bones.

The mother turned as white as a candle. Of course she was glad to see her son so full of life again. But fear gripped her heart when she heard the word "war."

His brother Angelo, from near the door—to avoid a slap from his father—said to Francis mockingly: "A fine hero you'll make! I bet you let yourself be taken prisoner again!"

The bright sun made the scene doubly magnificent: all the knights had assembled on horseback in the big

21

market place, ready to march off. But the finest of them all was Francis. He sat there proudly on his white horse, looking like a golden beetle, with copper rings and scales and plates, with plumes on his helmet and black inscriptions on his armor and shield and precious stones on his sword. His face was shining with pride and courage.

The noblemen remarked among themselves that it was a disgrace that the son of a merchant should be more handsomely equipped than they were, but Francis' father had never known a happier day. He tried to restrain his tears while he kept kissing his son's hands. When the warriors left, he went to church and dropped some money into the poor box.

As they rode over the mountains, the noblemen would not say a word to Francis. They avoided him, but he was so happy with his daydreams that he did not notice it.

Once in a while, near a castle or a village, some more riders joined them. At a crossroads they encountered a knight whose appearance was very shabby. It was the old one-eyed officer who had been in prison with Francis and who had at first been so angered by his singing. He went over and shook hands with Francis, and they rode on together. The knight began to talk about the significance of the war.

But Francis was not listening. All the joy had vanished from his heart when he saw the worn-out clothes and weapons of the old knight. He felt ashamed—not of his companion—but of himself. He began to contrast the knight with himself. He, the son of a linen merchant, was dressed as if he were the noblest of the aristocracy, while this great knight, who had gradually been ruined by all the wars in which he had fought, had nothing but rusty iron. Francis simply could not stand that—no matter what it cost him!

Suddenly he decided to do something about it. He let the others go on ahead, and when they were far enough away, he exclaimed: "Please forgive me, noble knight, but I have not been listening to you, because we are both ridiculous. The servant is dressed like the master, and the master like the servant . . . We're going to exchange clothes and armor right here. You're just about my size, so everything will fit all right!"

The knight's one eye blinked with surprise. He objected and flatly refused the offer.

Francis flared up excitedly. "I insist!" he cried out. And using his teeth and hands he violently tore his gorgeous silk cloak in two. "Even if I have to go without a shirt, I will not ride to war dressed like this!"

The knight could not resist such sincerity and such a strong will, and then too he preferred being well-dressed to looking contemptible. So each of them went behind a bush and tossed his clothes to the other.

They had hardly arrived in the little town of Spoleto, where many soldiers were already waiting, when Francis felt so sick and exhausted that he had to go to bed. He seemed to be about to die. People said that the noblemen had made him sick in order to be rid of him. But then people say so many things.

It was a bitter blow when one morning he heard the blare of the trumpets announcing the troops' departure, while he who was so eager to go with them had to stay there in bed. Francis cried like a child.

Now that the soldiers had left, a great silence fell over the little town. Thereafter he too made frequent attempts to leave. But every time he got up and fastened on his armor, he collapsed from weakness and had to crawl back to bed on hands and knees. He lay there moaning, and at times in his fury he bit his fingers. But one day, toward dawn, in a dream he heard a mighty Voice and he saw a great Light above a pointed rock.

Yes, that was the Voice! And he heard the Light say: "Francis, what is better: to serve the master or the servant?"

"The master," Francis stammered.

"Then why are you working for the servant?"

Francis could not answer. But all of a sudden he felt as though the Light was shining right through his body.

The Light was God.

He kneeled down, and with his head on his knees he asked: "Lord, what must I do?"

"Go home. There you will be told what to do. You misunderstood the dream about the weapons."

The Light stopped speaking and slowly vanished as in a mist.

Francis woke at once and jumped out of bed. He had forgotten that he was sick. "Home!" he cried.

Then he saw the armor which he had taken in exchange for his own. Supposing he went to war first and then returned home? Now that he was wide-awake, he did not feel like trusting the dream. He slowly got dressed, took his horse from the stable, and rode out through the city gate. He stopped at a crossroad. One way led to the war—the other toward home. In one direction lay the rank and title of a baron and a life filled with honors and glory. In the other direction, ridicule and a dark future—all for a voice heard in a dream!

God had called him. Why had God called *him?*—he who had never bothered much about God: no more than just going to a late Mass on Sundays, eating no meat on Fridays, and receiving Communion every Easter.

He had to choose between God and the world.

Sitting on his horse, he shut his eyes and clenched his fists. He was torn between God and the world. He realised very clearly that for years the sweet sound of the Voice had been whispering in a corner of his heart, in his longing for far horizons, in his greed for life. A yearning for the unattainable came over him, and in its grip he cried out: "God!"

Then he opened his eyes and shouted exultantly: "God! God!"

At the sound of that word, his heart nearly burst with joy and light, and he recklessly galloped off toward Assisi.

Oh, how they were going to laugh at him and make fun of him! He could already foresee how his father would give him a doubly good thrashing, and he could already hear his fat brother's mocking laughter. Yet he felt as if he were returning from a ride among the stars in heaven! He had become indifferent to the scorn of others. And he rode through the busiest streets of Assisi, slowly and defiantly, as though he were following a procession.

An extraordinary peace had come over Francis. Now he was often seen gazing at the Blessed Sacrament for hours at a time. He was no longer fastidious about his clothes, and he, the proud Francis, was sometimes seen strolling around and conversing with the filthiest beggars. He gave money away right and left. People said of him: "Either he's crazy or he's going to become a monk."

Francis anxiously tried to figure out the meaning of his dream. He sought it in church, in silence, in solitude. He sought it in the words and gestures of children and beggars, especially beggars—for was not the maiden who had called him also poor? He sought it in the clouds . . .

His father was heart-broken and spoke to him only in curt snarls, but his mother's heart beat faster for joy. His friends sought him out, some because they really liked him and others only to make him drunk. He went along with them, thinking that he could find the key to his riddle that way just as well as any other. They made him drink, and he drank. They made him celebrate, and he celebrated, but his heart was no longer in it. Sometimes it even happened that he, the guest of honor, suddenly collapsed in the middle of all the carousing.

Theodore kept reminding him of the feast he had promised to give to celebrate his home-coming. In a moment of despair, Francis exclaimed: "All right, I'll give the party! Next week you'll have it—and myself too!" and his friends cheered and threw their caps in the air.

No matter how hard it was for him, he was determined to be the same Francis as before. The key to the riddle had not yet appeared—it was only a dream. So it was that he ordered a more elaborate feast than any his friends had ever seen before. He had a new costume made to order for himself. It was flaming red, the color of life. He put new strings in his mandolin. His father, seeing all this, rubbed his hands.

On the night of the party Francis sat at the head of the beautifully decorated table. He was covered with ribbons and plumes, jewels and lace. His hair was arranged in curls under a crown of red roses. On the table there was an enormous cake, and a boy of four or five, dressed as a little cupid, came skipping out of it.

But Francis found no amusement in all this. He acted as if he were somewhere else. He got up to leave. His friends went out too, with torches and music. They wanted to carry Francis on their shoulders, as in the old days, but he would not let them. He followed them by himself and took advantage of the darkness to let them go on without him. He stopped at some stairs, leaned against the iron railing, and watched his friends as they disappeared down the street.

When they were out of sight, he looked up at the stars. "God! God!" he murmured beseechingly, and he repeated the word "God" many, many times. He felt as though drops of fire were falling onto his heart one by

26

one, and it was a fire that did not burn but intoxicated. His heart was bursting with fire. His arteries were like a burning bush. And he felt himself lifted up into a great Light. He was aflame with God . . .

His friends began to miss him and hunted for him. And when in the light of their torches they caught sight of him standing on the stairs holding out his arms, they shouted: "Bravo! You're saved!"

"He's in love—he's cured now!"

Their yelling dragged him down from the realm of light and back to earth. Now they seemed to him like vile muck in human form, and he suddenly exclaimed: "Yes, I am in love! Forever! Yes, now I am sure of it. And my beloved, in all her poverty, is lovelier and richer than you can imagine!"

"Bravo! Bravo!" they yelled. "Where does the lady live? We must serenade her!"

They came gaily running toward him, but the closer they approached, the more sharply did he feel the distance between them and him. He threw his mandolin to them, snatched off his crown of roses, and suddenly ran away through the narrow streets until he reached home.

It was several days before he was seen again.

This time love had pierced his heart: he had fallen in love with God. He felt disgusted with himself, unworthy and ashamed before God—and yet he also longed to lose himself in God. When he remembered his past, he felt impure, worried, and dejected. What should he do in order to be freed from his former life and from his sins? What was his calling and his duty?

He wandered in the mountains and went to pray in the small churches and chapels of the region. He went to the little church where the angels had sung on the day when he was born, and especially to the Chapel of St. Damian with its beautiful crucifix. Often he crawled

27

into a grotto and lay there in the dark, praying out loud: "I love You, my Lord and my God—and You alone! Please come and console me! No—don't come, I don't deserve it. My blood still thirsts for sin. But for the love of You, I am going to tame my body as if it were a donkey! Lord, give me peace, and take this fear from my heart. Make me whatever You want—a beggar, a leper. Break my bones. But please take this fear away! And forgive me my sins!"

When he came out of the cave, sweat was dripping from his hair, and there was a wild light in his eyes. At home he tried to hide his inner turmoil. His father, who was often away on trips at the time, noticed nothing. But his mother guessed it all, though she did not show it.

Francis spent much time bent over religious books, but he dreamed more than he read.

One day as Francis was leaving the cave at twilight, someone stood before the entrance: a plainly dressed young man with a black beard and big round eyes. The youth gave him a friendly nod. Francis suddenly felt embarrassed, and said apologetically: "I'm hunting for a treasure."

The young man replied: "So I have heard. You will find the treasure all right, if only you dig deep enough. The Gospel says: 'Knock, and it shall be opened unto you.'"

Francis was astounded. The youth knew what he was doing! He understood him. "Who are you?" he asked. "I do not know you."

The other answered: "I live over there, beyond the mountains."

The young man was so overflowing with kindness and confidence that Francis, in his great need, could not restrain himself, and with tears in his eyes he asked: "What must I do? What must I do?"

"Dig deeper and deeper," said the youth with a smile. "Read a lot—here, read this little book of the Gospels. And then listen to the silence and the suffering of men. Great sorrow is hidden beneath men's laughter. Then you will certainly find the treasure."

"You—you can help me," Francis sobbed.

"No," replied the young man. "I cannot help you. Everyone's heart is his own. And no one else can dig your treasure up for you. I can only pray for you."

Henceforth the two were often together. Francis was drawn to the youth because he said little, never asked questions, but always answered them in a way that was filled with profound mystical meaning. Francis looked forward to the hours they spent together. And while he prayed for mercy in the cave, the youth remained standing at the entrance, smiling like an angel who knows all.

One day Francis said to his friend: "Suppose I go to Rome, to the Tomb of the Apostles, for inspiration in my treasure-hunting?"

"Go ahead," said the young man, "and God go with you!"

They were silent as evening approached. Down below in the town a bell was slowly tolling. The friend took Francis' hand and said: "Look how beautiful Nature is: the corn is growing, and the clouds are making rain for it. A tree honors God by giving its shade and fruit. It lets God work in it. Whoever honors God wants nothing. Whoever owns nothing can give most of all to God. Poverty is the pearl of the Gospel."

The day's end, the twilight, and his friend's words were filled with beauty. Down in the valley all the colors were fusing into a purplish blue. How still it was, how utterly still! They sat there together, hand in hand. A bit later they perceived the silver rim of the moon. "It's like the Word of God," whispered the friend.

"Is there any human being who has such peace?" Francis asked cautiously, and he pointed to the beautiful scene before them.

"Yes," said his friend, "those who do not fear but love God: the saints."

After a long pause Francis said: "Tomorrow I'm leaving for Rome."

By his third day his knees felt numb, he had prayed so much at the Tomb of the Apostles, but God remained silent.

Sometimes Francis tried to read men's hearts. But he did not find love—nothing but selfishness. Their money meant more to them than their souls. They gave almost nothing to the beggars. Yet how ostentatiously the rich tossed a few pennies onto the Apostles' Tomb! It made Francis' blood boil. Suddenly he took a little purse containing silver coins and emptied it over the Tomb.

When he came out and saw the swarms of beggars on the steps, he was sorry that he had no more to give them. All his money was gone except for a small amount which he kept for a day's lodging and for his provisions on the way home. He was surrounded by beggars and cripples. They clustered around him, holding out their hands and lamenting loudly. Some of them wore scapulars, while others had religious medals. All of them spoke of God.

"These are the real friends of our dear Lord Jesus Christ," thought Francis. It was all very fine for him to go around with the poor and eat with them and give them money. He had listened to their hearts, so to speak. But all that is easy when you have all you want at home. "To be poor yourself, to live with the body and soul of a poor man—that is really something!" his thoughts continued. "To be a beggar one's self!"

No sooner said than done. He sought out the most

ragged wretch of the lot. "Come with me," said Francis to the beggar. "I've got something fine for you!" When they were alone in an alley, he said: "Sir, would you mind changing clothes with me until this evening? I'll pay you well."

"Are you going to kidnap someone or do some spying?" asked the beggar. "But what do I care? It's all right with me."

"Where can we undress?"

"There's a ruined tower over there."

They went to the tower and undressed. Francis was the first to strip to his shirt—the other had none. Then he had to put on the beggar's trousers, which were stiff with dirt. He could feel how they scratched his legs. He wanted to push his shirt into the trousers—but who ever heard of a beggar with a fine shirt! He took it off and gave it to the beggar. Next he put on a jacket that was much too big and had a nauseating smell. Then came a tattered coat, a scapular, and finally a greasy cap. Francis shuddered and trembled with revulsion, but he gritted his teeth and went through with it.

He looked himself over: now he was really one of the poor and a friend of Jesus Christ.

Suddenly from behind a pile of stones the beggar came dancing out, dressed in Francis' brown velvet suit. Francis just stood, amazed at himself. His courage began to sink, but he roused himself and stepped out into the sunlight . . .

Later he was sitting by the curb on a bridge among other beggars. He held out his hand and cried: "For the love of God—" He wanted to eat bread which he had begged himself. But no one gave him anything.

Next to him sat a little old blind woman who also got nothing. Francis wanted to give her some money—but he remembered that he had left his purse in his belt. "It's better this way," he thought, "because a rich beggar is no beggar."

31

People passed by, rich and poor, young and old—but no one gave anything.

"Are you hungry?" asked the old woman.

"A bit," Francis replied.

Whereupon the old woman gave him a piece of hard bread without butter. His hunger made it taste delicious.

That evening he went back to the ruined tower. Naturally the beggar never showed up! After a long wait Francis fell asleep in his malodorous clothes. Hunger woke him early the next morning. There was still no one there. "The fellow must have forgotten," he said to himself.

When he was again sitting among the beggars, he caught sight of the man wearing his velvet suit and singing drunkenly in the streets with two other beggars. "Now I'm a real beggar," Francis said with satisfaction, and then he too earnestly begged for a bit of bread, driven on by a real hunger that tied knots in his stomach. So this was how it felt to be poor and scorned and rejected! He felt that he was more a friend of God than before.

This lasted for two days more, and then he went home, still as a beggar. He slept in barns and begged for his food on doorsteps. Here and there on the way he had to sing a song in order to get something. But often too he sang songs to thank God for his poverty.

No one could say how it happened, but before Francis got home everybody already knew that he had been living as a beggar in Rome. Although he changed his clothes in a nearby village where he was known, as soon as he opened the door, his father knocked him into a corner.

His mother was trembling as she murmured: "You really should not have done it, child. But you won't do it again, will you, child?"

But his mother's words only made matters worse.

The father then began to make more and more noise, pounding on the table and roaring: "What a fool—what a crazy fool! He could have become a baron! But he goes and throws himself into the gutter—all for a dream. He had the best future in the world, and he throws himself into the worst rabble in the slums. I'd rather drive you out of this house than let you stay as you are. And you"—turning to his wife—"you're in it with him! Now you're wailing and feeling sorry for him. But behind my back you've been encouraging him in his madness—all because you mistakenly dreamed that he would become a monk, because some mystic lunatic came and said that he had to be born in a stable—oh, that stable! To do what he does, he really must have been born in a stable—he stinks of it! It should have been a pigsty. I don't dare show myself in public any more. I come from an honorable family, one of the best in the Province! We have always helped the poor secretly—without any show. And I insist that we continue doing it that way. If you really want to be a monk, then go right ahead! But you're too lazy and too cowardly to do that—then people wouldn't pay any more attention to you or talk about you. But from now on, you're going to work, like your brother and me—or else you're going to get out of here!"

Francis looked at him sadly. Every word his father said broke the branch that much more from the tree.

His mother tried to comfort him. "Child, you can do more good by giving to the poor than by being poor yourself. It's no help to break your leg because someone else has broken his."

"That's right," exclaimed the father, "—if only you had always talked that way!" And suddenly he bellowed: "I don't want to hear another word about it—not another word! It's finished! I'm the boss! He'll do what I say—and if anyone dares to mention it again, I'll break him in two!" And he ran into the store.

When Francis went up to his room, he fell on his knees before the crucifix and sobbed: "My Lord and my God, I cannot turn back to what I used to be. I am a prisoner of Your invisible power. You have wounded me with Your Light—and yet I wander in the dark and do not find You. I am so afraid and so lonely. Wound me again and again, so that I can know that You are near me. Forgive me for all the wrong that I have done—it is burning within me! Put it out with Your fire! My Lord, my Lord . . . !"

His mother was listening at the door with a bowl of milk in her hand, but she did not dare go in.

Francis was walking over the mountains, leading his horse by the bridle. He was returning from the market in a small town of the district. His father and a servant had gone ahead with the wagon and had left him far behind. Francis was searching for his friend, whom he had not seen for two months, since his trip to Rome. He needed his friend so much, to pour his heart out to him, because it was full to overflowing!

Francis had recently been behaving very differently. After the big quarrel he had secretly gone to see the Bishop and told him some of his troubles. His Excellency, who had an understanding heart and a keen knowledge of human nature, had advised him: "Act as if nothing had happened to you. Don't pay any attention to externals. Shut yourself up in your heart—that's where our greatest strength lies. That way you won't disturb your parents. And if it is really the Holy Spirit that is working in you, then your time will certainly come. Meanwhile pray a great deal in silence."

Francis did so, and waited for the Holy Spirit.

Now, so as not to stay too far behind the others, Francis rode ahead rapidly over the monotonous sand path. Suddenly his horse sprang aside and stood stock-still. A leper was standing in front of him!

The leper was bald and covered with sores. His chin was eaten away, and his nose was a red hole. A dark stream of blood was running down from his left eye, which bulged out like a frog's. Only one finger was left on his right hand. The leper looked up at Francis with infinite sadness.

Francis felt his hair standing on end from horror. Fear of infection gripped his throat. He quickly gave his horse the spurs and galloped away. He did not dare to look back. His hat fell off, but he paid no attention. Yet as he rode on, he remembered the message of Christ's Gospel: despise all that you formerly desired, and cherish all that you formerly despised.

Then he said to himself: "You actor! You are moved to tears when you read the Gospel—but when you meet someone whose suffering is the truest continuation on this earth of Our Lord's Passion, you are so selfish that you run away!"

He felt intensely ashamed of himself. So that was the kind of knight he was! Suddenly he turned his horse around and rode back.

The leper was still standing there. His stench nearly made Francis faint. Nevertheless he dismounted and bowed to this man in whom he saw an image of Jesus Christ in all His sufferings. All concern for his own life had vanished. All he felt was love. And he kissed the man on his cleft lips.

The leper wept, and his tears mingled with the stream of blood on his cheeks. His jaws moved as he tried to say something. But he said nothing. He no longer had any tongue.

The next day Francis rode to the little leper colony that was located in an isolated section of the country. As he rode, he thought of the Bishop and of his father, but only vaguely and remotely, without being influenced by such considerations. When he entered the lepers' building and saw them cowering there like stray dogs in the stench of their sores and pus, he had a moment of physical revulsion. But his love and his will power were stronger.

How astounded the patients were that such a rich and healthy young gentleman should suddenly appear and kiss their hands! They looked upon him as an angel from heaven. Among them were fathers and mothers whose children had driven them from home with sticks, and boys who had been dragged away from their parents. On the filthy walls were stains made by their bleeding hands. And flies, millions of flies, were swarming back and forth between their wounds and their food. And the demon of the flesh still throbbed in the poisoned blood of many of them.

Such was the hell into which Francis came. No wonder the lepers kneeled and wept. But Francis was the happiest of them all, because he had overcome the dictates of his physical nature, of his "Brother Ass," as he later called his body.

All through the following winter, whenever his father was away, he secretly went out to the leper colony. He gave them his affection. He put oil and new bandages on their sores. He washed them. And he read the Gospels to them or told them beautiful stories.

One Sunday after High Mass, Francis stayed in the church, praying. He was listening to God. There was no one else in the church except a blind man smiling at the altar. Francis' mother came running in; pale and upset, she tapped him gently on the shoulder. "Child, come home right away. Is it true that you have been visiting the lepers? Oh, your father is beside himself with anger! Come quick, otherwise he might even drag you out of church . . ."

The father was standing there like a bear, legs apart

and hands ready to tear down pillars of stone. "Is it true?" he roared.

"Yes, Father," said Francis calmly.

Instead of seizing him, the father began to yell and shout: "You're a stinking hypocrite! I don't dare knock you down for fear that some of your filth might stick to my hands. First you'll get washed in the rain barrel before I thrash you!" But suddenly he gripped Francis firmly and shook him back and forth. "Are you going to do it again?"

"I only brought them a little happiness."

"—and misfortune on us!"

"Father, if you were one of those unhappy people, wouldn't you be glad if someone came to visit you?"

The father was panting like a horse. "What a question! I—I don't want you to go there!"

"But if God wants me to . . ."

"How can you talk of God, you hypocrite? You act as if you were a schoolmate of God. You've already forgotten the loose life you were living only a year ago, when they had to carry you home!"

Francis was speechless: it was true. What right had he to speak of God? He was not even worthy of pronouncing God's name. He let his father talk on, while he looked at his mother, who was so frightened that she could not pray a whole "Our Father." Things could not go on like this—it was unbearable for him and for his parents. Some solution must be found. "If only I knew what God wants me to do," he thought.

Again his father loomed up before him saying: "Are you going to do it again?"

"I can't answer now," Francis replied.

The father began to give him one blow after another. His mother screamed, and Angelo was so frightened he hopped onto a chair. As he drove Francis out the door, the father shouted: "Come back when you have had a bath and when you know the answer! Tomorrow you're going on a trip with me."

Out in the street, people, his former friends, laughed. Burning with shame, Francis ran up an alley and fled to the hills. Then for the first time he went back to the cave. He did not come out till dawn the next day, looking as if he had been sick for a year. He stayed in the mountains, wandering around aimlessly.

"God! God!" he cried, and the mountains sent back a triple echo: "God! God! God!"

He came to the dilapidated little church of St. Damian and went in, as he had done so many other times, to pour out his troubles before the crucifix. The pastor, a little old man, was sitting out in the weak February sunshine with his hood over his head, reading a small book before lunchtime. He looked just like St. Antony the Abbot with his little pigs, except that he had bees instead of pigs. Right in front of him were two hives, and the bees were walking over his hands and beard and flying around his head. Though he lived in a small barn, he was quite happy living there with his bees near his little church. What more does an old man need, especially a priest, than honey for food and wax for candles? He was a bit deaf, but he saw Francis approaching.

"It's a fine day," Francis exclaimed.

"Ha! Ha!" said the little priest. "When the wind blows from the west, I can't hear well."

"This is the east wind from over the mountains," Francis said in his ear.

"Ha! Ha!" laughed the old man. "Then I hear even less." What did he care if he was deaf? He had his honey-making bees and his little church, and he listened to the voice of God in his heart.

Francis motioned that he was going to pray a bit. When he was inside the church, he fell on his knees and held out his arms toward the crucifix. He could not say a word. He gazed at the crucifix, on which was painted a gentle-looking Christ who just stared back, with saints and angels on each side. Francis gave himself up to Jesus with all his soul as he looked deep into His eyes. He opened his hands and his heart to receive the light for which his whole soul was longing. Jesus too was holding His arms out, and He seemed to be embracing the whole world with them.

The crucifix was made of wood and paint, and Francis was made of living flesh and blood. Between the crucifix and him there was air and the dim twilight. Yet between them there was also love, which is invisible, and all the prayers of the old priest and the peasants, and the prayers and tears of all mankind and of the whole of creation.

Silence. Francis was crying. And in the silence, the crucifix spoke.

It spoke. Jesus moved on the Cross. His body quivered. He raised His head. His eyes became animated, like those of a living man. His mouth moved, His lips parted, and then in a melodious voice He said: *"Rebuild My Church. It is falling down."*

He repeated these words three times, then His head dropped again. The light in His eyes went out. And again there was the wooden crucifix.

But Jesus had spoken! By speaking, Christ had come down from His Cross. His love and Francis' love had met and mingled. A rose of bleeding light blossomed in the heart of Francis. "Jesus! Jesus!" he cried. "I am no longer myself. I am You!" And he fell prostrate on the ground, sobbing and trembling with happiness . . .

Some time later the old priest tapped him on the shoulder. Francis sprang up, kissed his hands, and thrust his purse into them: "This is for oil for the altar lamp," he shouted in the little priest's ear. "I want to rebuild your church!"

"How's that?"

39

"I want to rebuild your church!"

"Ha! Ha!" laughed the priest. "You want to do some building? A fine bricklayer you'll make!"

"I'm going to make your broken-down chapel into a beautiful little church!"

Francis had to shout all this into his ear.

"Ha! Ha! With your fine clothes—you, the son of such a proud family! You're joking . . ."

"I'm going to get money to buy tools and wood and stone—"

And Francis ran off. "Jesus! Jesus! Now I know it!" he shouted again and again. "Jesus! Jesus! Now I know it!" And he danced along as he said it.

"Where is Mother?" Francis asked his brother.

"In bed—you've made her sick . . ."

But Francis was already running upstairs. His mother was lying in bed with a wet cloth on her forehead. When she saw him come in, looking so happy and excited, she was startled and sat up straight.

"Mother! Mother! I'm going to rebuild St. Damian's church!"

"Why didn't you come home last night? Why are you hurting your father so much? You know how he blames it all on me. He even threatened to hit me if you go out again. Make up your mind, child. If you want to be a monk, then go to a monastery. But what did you say about St. Damian's?"

Angelo burst into the room and said: "Don't make Mother worse. Just wait till Father comes home—he'll teach you a lesson. Because he has sworn that he will change you."

Francis looked at his brother and then at his mother. In his heart he heard the Voice of the crucifix, and he said: "Tell him he needn't bother. I'm leaving."

"Child! Child!" cried his mother, holding out her arms.

40

"Don't cry, Mother," said Francis. He ran to her and kissed her. "Don't worry, Mother—it's the only thing for you and for me . . ."

"Where are you going, child?"

"I'm going to rebuild St. Damian's church. Our Lord has inspired me to do it."

She looked at him with raised eyebrows. Such wonderful things had already happened in his life. "How about your board and lodging?" she asked anxiously.

"Our Lord will take care of that all right, Mother," he said as she sobbed on his chest. "He takes good care of the sparrows and the rabbits. Goodbye, Mother."

He left. After taking his horse out of the stable, he loaded it with some silk and velvet, and said to Angelo: "Tell Father he can deduct this from my inheritance later on. And now goodbye!"

"You're a thief," yelled Angelo. "I'll tell Father on you—you thief!"

The neighbors came out of their houses while Francis calmly rode off without once looking back. His mother stood watching him at her window, wearing a black veil over her head. Francis reverently raised his hat to her, as before an image of the Sorrowful Mother.

As he rode toward the market at Foligno, it began to rain.

That evening Francis returned to St. Damian as wet as a fish. He had sold his horse and the cloth.

The little priest was milking his goat. For he had a goat too, and he also had two rabbits, white ones with red eyes. And what else did he have? Some seed for flowers and radishes, because he had a small garden, about as big as an apron. One of these days he was going to plant the seeds. And then he also had some jars of salve, a good salve for wounds and bad burns. The peasants could tell marvels about this wonderful salve! And he had some books too, four or five entirely hand-

41

written books full of learned subjects and beautiful stories. And he also had a marvelous view of the distant horizon and the sky. In all his poverty he was a rich little priest. When people told him that it was a pity that his hearing was not so good, he often answered: "Ha! Ha! A deaf man hears no evil."

Francis saw him sitting there in his patched gray cloak, with his hood up, milking his goat and smiling at the little stream of milk that spurted from the udder into a small bucket—swish, swish! The goat was eating a handful of grass and acting exactly as though it was not she that was being milked.

Francis said to himself: "He's smiling at the milk. I'm going to make him smile at all this money . . ." He tugged the priest's coat, and after they had exchanged smiles he shouted in his ear: "Here is some money for your church," and he emptied his purse into the old man's lap.

"Ha! Ha! That's fine. Where did you get it?" Francis told him. "Then you've taken it from home," exclaimed the old priest in fear. "And one of these days I'm going to have your father after me. No, no, boy! Here is your money. Take it right home."

"I'm not going home any more," cried Francis.

"How's that?"

"I'm not going home any more."

"Not going home again?"

Francis nodded.

"And why not?"

Francis cupped his hands around the old priest's hairy ear and told him why he was not going home any more. He told him everything. It was the first time since the beginning of his soul struggle that he told the whole story. He told it in a few words but so well that the hermit could see into his thoughts as clearly as Francis himself. It took a long time, so long that first they had to put the goat back in her stable and light the clay lamp.

Then Francis went on. He told about his longing for God, his friend, Rome, the leper, his mother and father, and the crucifix that had spoken to him. At times tears came to his eyes, and then they could hear the rain on the mountains.

Anyone who might have seen the little priest sitting there, old as he was and too deaf to hear a cannon shot, would have felt sorry for him and given him a coin. But this little priest really had a very good head on his shoulders. Actually he was a well-educated man. He had an insight into many matters of which other people could make neither head nor tail. He had the gift of reading men's hearts like a book. If his hearing had been good, he would long since have been a bishop.

When Francis had told him everything and was crying on his knees before him, the old man said: "You are right. You cannot serve two masters."

Francis was happy to hear that, especially from a priest! And then the saintly old man said (for he was a saint): "You can stay here with me. There's enough room in my little barn. I haven't got too much food, but we'll manage. You're going to begin a fine spiritual life—wait and see! As to building, that won't go so well. We have no money. And this purse does not belong to us. You can go in for building later on. Meanwhile you'll find something to do here all right. And I'll go see the Bishop so he can make you a Deacon. Now let's just say a little prayer and then go to bed."

They said a little prayer together and then went to bed, but first Francis took the money and went outside. What should he do with it? Throw it away in the grass? No. He left it on the window ledge of the church and went in. The little priest gave Francis his blessing, the way a father blesses his son. Then he blew out the light and stayed on his knees for a long time in front of his bed, like a sack full of hay. He thanked Heaven for his little honeybees and for the goat's milk and for the rain, and for this boy that he felt would be a saint. And Francis too kneeled for a long time in front of his bundle of straw, and he thanked God for the Voice of the crucifix and for the little priest and for his mother. And he prayed for his father and for his brother.

That night the rain kept pouring down, and the straw roof leaked, but under it slept two happy men.

They lived through some wonderful hours at St. Damian's. Francis was sexton and altar boy, as well as assistant gardener in the little garden that was no bigger than an apron. He milked the goat, collected stones into small piles, and pulled grass out of the roof. With a home-made broom he swept the little church clean, and he polished the two copper candlesticks with sand and a dash of vinegar. And he planted radishes.

Not everyone knows how to plant radishes. The old priest showed him how: "You've got to do it this way. Hold the seed lightly in your fist, then turn your fist around and let the seed slip into the ground. And later on, radishes will sprout from these tiny seeds. There are seeds like beechnuts, for instance, from which trees grow to be as big as a church."

"How beautiful is a seed!" exclaimed Francis. "O God, how beautiful You have made everything!"

He had also found another cave. It was hidden behind thorny bushes, and he had to slide in sideways, and not a glimmer of light could get in. In that cave, which not even a devil could ever find, and in that pitch darkness, more and more love and light were infused into his soul every day. And Francis could not resist singing—he was so happy.

When his father came home and heard that Francis had run away, he lost all self-control. He cursed and wept. Waving his arms, he blasphemed. Then he sat down and rested his head on a table and sobbed. His wife kept quiet, though she cried and bit her handkerchief. And when she tried to say something, he sprang up in front of her and shouted: "Silence—or else there'll be a tragedy here!"

He simply had to make a row. He kept it up when they went upstairs and while he was undressing, and he was still roaring when he got into bed. But then he began to say things that froze her heart with terror.

"Tomorrow I'm going to get him out of that stinking hiding-place! I'll take the whole town with me. We'll get him and drag him out. And I'll give him a good thrashing right in public, in the market place! We're going to see something that people will talk about for years! My honor must be redeemed. You're trembling? Just keep on trembling! It's your fault too . . . Tomorrow—tomorrow is going to be a great day for me!"

The next morning she got up first. She went to Mass at St. Nicholas Church on the market square. She spoke to a beggar and gave him something. And a little later the beggar went off on his crutches toward St. Damian's.

After the father had swallowed a bit of bread—for he could hardly eat a thing—he sent Angelo and the maid to call his friends and those of Francis. He told them his plan, and they approved. As respectable middle-class citizens, they thought it was a fine idea. When a child revolts against his father, the father must punish the child.

But Philip, a friend of Francis who enjoyed humiliating people, suggested that they should not harm Francis physically: "Rather let's take him along, get him drunk, and carry him around town like before, like a King of the Feast. The wine will make him sing and dance the way he used to do, and then when he's sober again he'll be too ashamed of himself to act like a saint any more.

45

The only way to bring him back to his senses is to humiliate him and make him completely ridiculous—I know him!"

"Fine!" shouted the father, and the others agreed.

"Let's have a flag and some mandolins!" cried Philip.

When Francis' mother heard this, she went out the back door and found a little old woman sitting on the doorstep of a gloomy little hut. After the mother had spoken to her and given her some money, the old hag put on her cape and hobbled off in the direction of St. Damian's.

When the small procession got there, the little priest was walking up and down near a stream while his goat was feeding on some fresh grass. Francis' father came forward out of the crowd, holding a stick in one hand and a rope in the other. "Where is my son?" he snapped at the priest.

"What did you say?" asked the little priest, stretching his head forward.

"Where is my son?"

"I don't hear well . . ."

"My son!"

"Oh, your son?"

"Yes."

"You're looking for your son?"

"Of course I am—for whom else?"

"Of course."

"Where is he?"

"What?"

"Where is he?"

"Yes, yes. But you mustn't get so angry. I'll understand if you don't make quite so much noise. But this east wind . . ."

The father's anger was boiling over. He put his heavy hand on the little priest's shoulder and roared: "You've got to show me my son!"

"At first I thought you came to find a bull," said the priest. "One blow from that stick would kill your son! Has he done anything wrong?"

"He's stolen! He's a thief!" yelled Angelo.

"Have you come after the money for the horse?"

"For the money and for my son!" shouted the father.

"The money is lying there on the window sill."

Angelo went and got it.

"The money doesn't mean a thing to me," exclaimed the father. "I want my son." Still, he put the money in his pocket.

"What did you do with my son?"

"We ate honey together."

At this, the father cursed and shook the little priest back and forth, bellowing: "My son! My son!"

Someone quickly restrained him, saying: "Calm yourself, Peter, my friend. Remember, he is a priest. Besides, he won't tell you a thing. Let's start searching for him."

And they began to search. "He has been here," shouted the father. "His hat is hanging there!" He threw the hat away scornfully. "He is here. We must find him!"

They searched through the church, the barn, the bushes, and behind the rocks. They climbed up the hill and went into the woods. Angelo shouted: "Francis, this is Angelo. We're not going to hurt you, but Mother is sick and wants to see you before she dies."

The others shouted the same thing. The father bellowed with his trumpet-like voice: "If you don't show up, I'll strike you dead!"

Meanwhile the old priest just sat there calmly reading his little book. But Francis was not to be found, and the men who had come along began to complain about wasting their time and so they quietly went home. The father suddenly turned to the little priest and said angrily: "Are you going to bring him out—yes or no?"

"I want to tell you about something that happened when I was young . . ."

"I'm not interested in your stories. But I'm going to tell the Bishop about this!"

"So am I."

"What do you mean?"

"That the Bishop is a holy man."

The father was trembling with rage. "We'll be back!" he shouted. "Tell him that we'll be ready for him."

"I'll tell him."

The others acted as if they did not belong to Bernardone's unsuccessful expedition. His friends slipped away by a short cut and left him alone with a few prominent citizens. And when he returned to Assisi with his rope and stick, lots of people had a good laugh, and some of them asked whether he had stuck Francis in his pocket . . .

What had really become of that bad boy, Francis? Jesus Christ, his Lord and his God, had spoken to him personally from a wooden crucifix. Such a grace was enough to inspire a man to achieve the impossible! And yet, there he sat, trembling with fear, hiding like a fugitive for days at a time in a hole in the ground— all because he was afraid of his father, afraid of being laughed at and scorned. That was certainly weak and cowardly on the part of someone to whom Christ Himself had spoken!

But Francis could not rid himself of his fear, even by prayer. It was like a nightmare. And in his imagination he could hear the songs and mandolins of his former friends. He felt faint when he thought of the trick they wanted to play on him. And yet, in spite of all his fears, his soul was gaining a deeper and deeper insight into the great truths of the Christian religion. He began to feel and to perceive their beauty, their truth, and the harmony of all things in them. He would have lost himself in fervent meditation, if only that fear were not gripping his soul.

"That fear of yours—it's the Devil trying to hold you back," said the little priest, who had been bringing his meals to the cave in the evenings. "If you can pass this test, Our Lord will win out in the end."

Day and night Francis prayed against the evil power that wanted to keep his soul plunged into spiritual darkness . . . And one day while he was again thinking over the sufferings of Christ, how He had been ridiculed and how He had endured it all in such holy meekness, a ray of light seemed to fall upon him. "I want to imitate Jesus in His poverty!" was the cry that came from his heart. And then he shouted: "And also in His humiliation!"

Suddenly he felt new strength within him. He stood up in the bright light. All his fears had vanished. He fell on his knees and sang a prayer of thanksgiving.

Then he ran out of the cave. The sun was high in the sky, and the birds were chirping. As he stood there in the sunlight, he felt suffused with the light within him. His heart was overflowing with joy. He kissed the earth and kissed the flowers. He ran to the little priest and kissed him on his gray beard. "I've been freed! I'm free! Free! Now even lions can't scare me," he shouted. "Give me your blessing."

"What a beautiful soul he has," murmured the little priest as he turned his face away to hide his tears.

With firm steps Francis strode toward Assisi. His clothes were torn and dirty. He was unshaven, his hair was long, and his face was pale and sickly. But joy and elation blazed in his eyes, and he was singing.

It was a quiet afternoon in the little town. Only sunlight and some chickens were in the streets. In the silence the water could be heard splashing in the fountains. Peter Bernardone was sorting out materials in his store. He who never used to stop talking now did his work without saying a word. He was as silent as a wall. There were deep furrows on his brow and secretive lines around his mouth.

Angelo really felt sorry for his father: what a pity that such a good and likable and gentle man should have to waste away on account of the sorrow that his son gave him. But while Angelo pitied him, he also hoped a bit that Francis would persist in his folly, "for then," thought Angelo, "the cloth business will be all mine."

The mother had gone to visit a sick friend. One could feel that the house was filled with sadness.

Suddenly there was a noise outside and shouting in the distance. "Something is going on," said Angelo. Holding the scissors in his hand, he went to the door, and looked out. "I think it's some kind of a lunatic they're making fun of," he called back. "Look—they're throwing mud at him and kicking him, the poor devil . . ."

The father kept working fiercely at his accounts. A man passed by and said something to Angelo. The father heard Francis' name. The blood rose to his head, and with a wild look in his eyes he listened. Angelo, his face pale, came in, quickly shut the door, and gasped: "Father! Father, it's Francis. Our Francis is coming! Oh, I'm so ashamed . . . Don't let them see you!"

"What? It's he?" bellowed the father, springing from behind the counter. "Get out of my way," he roared, pushing Angelo aside. He groped for the door latch, but in his haste and anger he could not find it. "Damnation!" The latch of his own door! In his rage he kicked at the door . . .

Francis was walking in the middle of a mob of big and small street urchins who were hooting at him, spitting on him, and pulling his hair and tattered clothes. Francis was calm, even rather solemn, with a beautiful light shining in his eyes. A butcher with whom the Bernardones did not deal was just going to throw the guts of a newly slaughtered goat into Francis' face, when the door burst open and the father appeared, massive and fierce. The butcher immediately let the tripe drop from his hands, and suddenly the crowd became silent. But Francis went straight toward his father, and the father went toward him, slowly, with clenched fists and hunched shoulders, trembling and white with hatred.

They stood facing each other. The father looked down at his son, and the son looked up at his father. Francis wanted to say: "I have been washed in the light of God." But before he could utter a word, two fists as big as hammers struck him to the ground. Blood streamed over his face. Then his father grabbed him by the hair and quickly dragged him into the house. As the door slammed, the crowd surged forward like an ocean wave onto the window ledges and onto the shoulders of the men in front, and they fought to get a peep through the keyhole.

Suddenly they all made way for someone. It was Francis' mother, with the maid supporting her. No one was in the store. The father was standing in the living room, leaning against the table, with his hands behind his back. He was panting, and there was sweat on his forehead. He glanced scornfully at his wife as she came toward him sobbing: "Our child! Our child!"

Without changing his position he said curtly: "He's in the wine cellar."

She cried out and tried to run past him, but he held her back with one hand. "No, you don't," he said.

"Besides I have the keys. From now on he will have to deal only with me."

To her, these words were like prison walls. She sank onto a chair and buried her face in the folds of her cloak.

A few days later the father had to go off on a trip with Angelo. Francis' mother had been longing for this moment. She had kneeled at her husband's feet and begged him to let her see Francis, but he had pushed her away with his foot. One night she had tried to get the keys from his pocket while he was sleeping. But when she was searching for them in his pockets in the dark, he had said: "Stop it!"

She had cried so much that her eyes were red and swollen. Before he left, he said to her: "Here is the key. Take him some food twice a day—no more! I've still got another key here—the one to the wine cellar. I'm not giving you that one. I don't trust you."

He looked at her stricken face, and with sudden emotion he took her hand and said helplessly: "You must think I'm cruel, dear. I'm not. It hurts my heart to have to punish him so severely, but it's for his good, Pica." He took her other hand. "If he doesn't change, I'll be dead and buried in two months. Oh, it hurts me so much here—it hurts me so much that I'm going crazy! I can't think of anything else. God, sometimes I would rather be dead. This has made me twenty years older . . ." Tears were running down his red cheeks. He kissed her hands. "Pica, you try now. Maybe he'll listen to you. I no longer have any influence on him. Still—" and he shook his fist—"if he doesn't give up his plan, I'll kill him!"

"I'll try," she said impatiently.

He gave her another kiss on her white brow, and climbed onto his wagon. She stood with the key in her hand. It felt like holding a burning coal. She listened, and when she could no longer hear the wagon, she ran down to the cellar. She had forgotten to take a candle, and she had to feel her way in the dark. "It's your mother," she said. "Your mother."

"Mother! Mother!" cried Francis.

She touched the bars and felt his arms, and they kissed each other through the bars.

"Mother!"

"Child!"

Then, all at once, this gentle lady began to act like a savage. "Out of here!" she screamed. "Even if your father beats me to death, I won't let my children be treated like animals. Out of here!" She tugged at the iron bars. The door clattered, but that was all.

"A file!" she cried, and ran upstairs, holding her skirts in her hand. "A file! A file!" she shouted to the boy who was serving customers in the shop. He had to let the customers wait, while he went to look in the storeroom. He had never seen her act this way. It was frightening. But there has to be a file before you can find one.

"Here's a chopping knife," she cried. "We'll hack it open!" While the boy was still searching, she ran back to the cellar. And she began to strike the lock with the chopping knife. This well-born lady, this gentle mother hacked away at the iron with the chopping knife in her delicate hands.

A mother will run into a fire for her child. A mother will jump into the water for her child. A mother will break through iron for her child. Soon Francis was trembling on his mother's sobbing breast. She took him upstairs into the light of day. He sat on the floor in front of her, and she held his head in her hands. She had not seen him for over a month! Now she noticed

53

the dark circles around his eyes, the wounds on his forehead, his colorless lips and drawn cheeks and dishevelled hair. All that was missing was a crown of thorns.

Her tears dropped onto his face.

It was twilight when Francis was ready to leave, dressed in a black velvet suit, with a package in his hand. He had told his mother everything. Her heart thrilled with joy when she heard it. Her dream was coming true. He said: "Mother, I'm going back to St. Damian's."

She replied: "Do what Our Lord inspires you to do."

"And what about Father?" he asked, fearing for her.

Proudly she said: "There isn't a cellar deep enough to prevent me from getting you out."

That is how mothers are: if one of their babies has to be buried, they dress it in woolen socks and a little flannel nightshirt. Francis was enthusiastically taking up voluntary poverty, but still he could not deny his mother the pleasure, which she so charmingly requested, of seeing him leave wearing a good suit and taking along a baked chicken, a small flask of old wine, and some money—for himself, for the old priest, and for the latter's church. Francis could not help smiling: a pauper with a baked chicken! Would she also give him a silver platter and a gold spoon?

"I'm leaving, Mother," he said. "Pray for me a lot."

"That's all I'm going to live for now."

They were silent a moment. Behind the slightly open kitchen door, someone could be heard breathing. It was the maid, listening.

"I'm going now, Mother." He kissed her.

"God is going with you, my child." She bit her lip, then she gave him her blessing and turned her face away.

54

Francis ran off, and went to knock at the door of the Bishop's residence.

The large hall of the Bishop's palace was crammed with people: there was going to be a session of the Episcopal Court, and the Bishop was to act as judge in a trial between a father and a son. Rich and poor, noblemen and bourgeois, lower-class people from the alleyways and knights from the castles, monks and priests—all were standing in their assigned places according to rank, completely filling the long room.

The green windowpanes did not let in much light, and so some candles were burning, most of them near to where the Bishop was sitting on his throne. He was wearing his gold-embroidered cloak and white miter. Near him was a shining golden cross, and a tapestry of the Last Judgment was hanging behind him.

Francis stood at one side, and his father at the other. The crowd surged and pushed, until suddenly an attendant holding a staff with a silver top shaped like an apple shouted: "Silence!"

The Bishop stood up—he was a tall dignified man with hard eyes—and told the father to state his grievance. Then he sat down again.

Peter Bernardone greeted the Bishop, swallowed once or twice, and said in a voice that trembled: "I brought my son to be judged by you, because you conferred Minor Orders on him. I need not describe his conduct now. The whole town is talking about it as a scandal—even other towns have heard about it. I ask these honorable gentlemen present to put themselves in my position. They too have children. Now, with their income and property, would they want their son to associate with the scum of the town and squander their money on them and play around with lepers, bringing danger of infection into their homes—and then steal from them and deceive them into the bargain?"

There was some murmuring in the room, and it was obviously in the father's favor. This encouraged him, and he launched into a list of all Francis' misdeeds. "But I'll forgive him all that," he went on, "if he stops his disgraceful behavior. He can even come home, and he need not work! He'll have money to give to the poor. He can go on pilgrimages and hear as many Masses as he likes, as long as he behaves decently. What more can I offer?"

"You're right!" they shouted. "Well said, Bernardone!"

The Bishop had let him talk himself out, and now he said: "But this is a question of disinheriting him . . ."

"Yes, I disinherit him," cried the father, "if he intends to keep up that kind of life!"

The Bishop turned to Francis: "In that case, I advise you voluntarily to give up your rights."

"So you have planned this together—it's a trick!" shouted the father.

Francis stepped forward, thin and pale: "Your Excellency, I want nothing from my father, neither gold nor property. All I want is to be allowed, under your protection, to live in poverty and to follow Jesus Christ. The decision rests in your hands."

The crowd thought that was fine. They craned their necks and stood on tiptoe.

The Bishop said: "It is a good sign that you have so much confidence in the authorities over you. The path of poverty is a beautiful one, but it is covered with thorns, and sometimes the human spirit weakens."

"Yes, Your Excellency, men do weaken. Jesus fell under the Cross three times, but His Father stayed with Him. I am relying on the same Father—otherwise I would not be here."

You could see the priests telling one another that what he had said was impressive. The Bishop seemed to think so too, for he asked: "Do you give up your inheritance of your own free will?"

"Yes!" Francis' reply came like a pistol shot.

A murmur of surprise ran through the hall.

The father was relieved to know that he could keep his money, but he could not stand that giving it up did not hurt Francis, and suddenly he shouted: "You've got to give me back every last cent of that money you took from home . . ."

"Mother gave it to me for the priest and the church."

"It's my money!"

Then the Bishop said: "Give the money back, Francis. God does not want His work to be advanced by money that may have been badly earned."

The father foamed with rage and waved his arms in the air. Francis tore the purse from his belt and tossed it at his father's feet. "There you are. Whatever is missing has already been given to the chapel."

"Thief!" shouted the father as he picked up the purse. "I want it all—every last cent!"

Confused cries came from the crowd. Some were for him, others against him. No matter how often the attendant with the silver apple yelled: "Silence!" there was no silence.

Then the Bishop stood up, and the people were silent. "Has anyone anything else to say?" he asked, and he looked at Francis, the father, and the whole room.

Francis had shuddered with indignation when he saw how his father clung to the money. That was the last blow of the axe that cut the branch from the tree. "Just a minute!" he cried excitedly to the Bishop, and he ran behind the tapestry screen, which began to move and shake. Everybody stared at it, even the father and the Bishop.

There was complete silence in the hall. The screen shook. The Last Judgment scene moved: the dead, the angels, the devils trembled. So did Christ on His cloud. Then, all of a sudden, Francis came out stark naked— he had a small, lean body—holding his clothes on his arm. And he dropped them at his father's feet, saying: "You're getting my clothes too. Here I am the way I was born. Now we are even!"

The crowd shrieked and screamed. They shouted enthusiastically: "Bravo! Bravo! Bravo for Francis!"

The Bishop quickly went up to Francis and drew him under his cloak. A sacred cloak decorated with gold and precious stones quickly covered his naked-ness and poverty. The father was so upset that he picked up the clothes without being able to say a word. He could not manage to utter the curse he had in his throat, but it blazed in his eyes. His cheeks were quivering.

Francis thrust his head from under the gilded cloak and cried in a loud voice: "Listen to me, everybody! Until today I have called Peter Bernardone my father. From now on, I'm no longer going to say 'Father Peter Bernardone', but 'Our Father Who art in Heaven'!"

And from under the cloak he held his bare arms out toward the golden crucifix. The crowd cheered wildly. The Bishop put a forefinger up to his hard eyes, and went into another room with Francis under his cloak, while the people shouted: "Bravo for Francis! Bravo! Bravo!"

"Drive him out!" These last words were for the father, who ran out of the hall, boiling with rage. In the street he realised how ridiculous and hateful he looked with his son's clothes in his arms. Scornfully he threw the things into the gutter and stamped upon them, like someone trying to put out a fire. Then he fell weeping into the arms of a dignified gentleman, one of his friends.

A French song rang out clearly over the hills and through the woods. Francis was singing as he set off. He was so happy he hardly knew what he was doing, for on this day he had taken Lady Poverty as his bride, and now he was going on his honeymoon trip with her. So he sang as he walked along. Where to? He had no idea. Anywhere. He just had to walk and sing, as a lark has to fly through the air and sing for pure joy.

The sky was filled with larks, for spring had come with its fresh surge of life throughout nature. Spring was making the snow melt in the crevices of the rocks. And here and there it offered the delight of cold, clear water, which Francis enjoyed drinking, using his hands as a cup. Is there anything better than a drink of running mountain water, as clear as crystal and as fresh as early morning?

Francis was dressed like a scarecrow in a tattered gardener's outfit, with sleeves that were too long and trousers that fell in folds like an accordion, for he was just a little fellow. His hat hung down over his ears. And he also had a torn old cloak, on the back of which he had chalked a large white cross. That is the way he went singing through the dark woods for two days. He slept under the stars in heaven.

All of a sudden, in the solitude of the mountains, three fierce bearded men with knives sprang up before him. They were bandits, the lords of the forests, who made their homes or dens there, like bears, and attacked anyone who ventured to pass through.

Who was this who dared to come and disturb them by singing like that? It was all right for a man to whistle in the dark from fear. But to sing so gaily in the robbers' own territory—well, they thought that was pretty bold, especially coming from such a puny little fellow!

The biggest bandit asked: "Who are you?"

"It doesn't matter who I am," said Francis. "But since you want to know, I am the Herald of the Great King." And he pointed toward heaven.

So the little sissy dared to tell them that it didn't matter who he was, and then even made fun of them? Smack! Francis received a blow that knocked him flat on the ground. Then they jumped on him and beat him and shook him until his bones nearly broke. They tore his clothes off, threw his hat into a tree, and pushed him into a crevice that was still filled with deep snow. Thank God for the snowdrift! Otherwise every bone in his body would have been smashed.

As he lay in the snow, wearing nothing but an old shirt, he heard the men go off, laughing. And with great difficulty he managed to climb out in the opposite direction. What should he sing now? The same song!

The cold air of the forest blew against his bare flesh, and the wind made his shirttails flap like a flag. So he tied them together under his legs, and set out, singing. He caught sight of a fox that at first stared at him for a moment and then ran off. "Little fox," he called after it, "you needn't run away from me. I'm just as poor as you are and not a bit better. I'm your brother!"

But the fox kept on running. It was not convinced.

Francis came to a glade which he remembered from the times when he used to go hunting. It was here that they had once caught a deer. And nearby there was a small Benedictine monastery—that's where he would go! Men who had also given up everything for Christ lived there. Ah, how wonderful it would be to spend some time in that atmosphere of prayer and Christian brotherhood! With awe and longing, he knocked on the door.

The Abbot, the Fathers, and the Brothers all came to open at the same time, out of curiosity, because they

hardly ever had any visitors. They looked at him sus-
piciously.

"For the love of God," said Francis, and he briefly
told them his story and asked whether he might stay
there a few days.

The Abbot was a plain outspoken man. He preferred
to send Francis away rather than to let him in. The
others also looked glum. But they allowed him to come
in because their Rule stated that they should give
shelter to travelers and see Jesus Christ Himself in
beggars.

"But you've got to work," said the Abbot, and the
cook exclaimed: "If you think you're going to sponge
on us, you're very much mistaken!"

Francis worked like an ox. They made him do the
dirtiest jobs: cleaning up, washing the dishes, and tend-
ing to the swine. He slept on some straw and ate the
leftovers.

It was a monastery without much discipline. All the
monks gave orders to one another. Everyone acted as
though he were the Abbot. The prolonged isolation
had made them irritable and rude. But they were not
able to drive the sun out of Francis' soul. He remained
obliging, gay, and polite. They could not stand that,
and after a week or two for a mere trifle the cook sent
him away, still dressed in rags.

He wandered on, but not very far because that heart
of his, that warm human heart, also had ideas of its
own. The spring with its flowers and all its fresh green
coloring was very lovely. But it was far lovelier in
Assisi! Ah, that was where the spring was really beautiful! And that was where there was such a good little
priest, and a small church to be rebuilt, and a crucifix,
a holy crucifix, and lepers, and a mother. They were all
waiting for him. He kept thinking of them.

He was no longer singing. As he walked on, he felt

61

a painful yearning for that town, for that countryside, for those people. And what can a man do against homesickness? It was as if he were walking in a prison, a nice big prison, as big as the world, no doubt—but still a prison all the same. He stopped. He was in a broad peaceful valley. A bird flew over him, heading south.

"Me too!" Francis exclaimed, and he turned around and headed south.

He began to sing again, and two days later when, from a hilltop, he caught sight of Assisi clustering on its slope, all white in the sun, he stretched out his arms like a child to its mother, and cried out: "That's the garden I must work in!"

Lady Poverty

Under a baking sun Francis was going to Assisi, wearing shoes that were too big for his feet. Everyone else sought the shade, but he walked right in the sun. At the market place he went straight to the Greek temple and climbed onto the base of a column. Holding onto the pillar with one arm, he raised the other and began to sing. His voice echoed clearly over the little square, against the houses opposite him. Beggars and idlers stirred in the shade, and people came to their doors. The stillness that had been hanging over the countryside had penetrated even into the town, and now Francis' song filled the silence like the sound of a bell.

"Who is it?"

"Why look! It's Francis, who used to be admired as a hero!"

"Look! He's back. What kind of foolishness is he up to now?"

One by one they went toward him, half mockingly. Francis kept on singing, and when there were enough people around him, he said: "And now—the Song of Parsival, who started out as a crazy young man and became a holy knight!" And when he was through, he said: "Do you know why I'm standing here singing?"

"To sell your sweat!" shouted someone. It was his brother Angelo.

"You couldn't pay enough for it," Francis replied. "I'm selling it to Our Lord. He gives what it's really worth."

Angelo made a face and ran off, ashamed, and

Francis spoke to the crowd again: "Well, I've become the repairer of the broken-down little Church of St. Damian. It's got a beautiful crucifix. Whoever prays in front of that crucifix will be heard. Isn't it a shame that such a beautiful crucifix has to hang in a dilapidated church? You live in your homes, and when there's a leak in the roof, you fix it. But we let the House of God fall to pieces. That's wrong of us. He came and died for us. Let's repair His House. You all have your jobs, so I'll do it for you. But you know that the priest of St. Damian is poor, and I live there with him on the crumbs of his poverty, and I'm very glad to do so. And now I have come to ask you, in the name of the Lord, to provide me with stones, mortar, a trowel, a plumbline, and such things. You mustn't give it to me for nothing. I'll sing songs for you and pray a lot for your salvation. If you give one stone, you'll get one reward from God. If you give two stones, you'll get two rewards, and so on. Since you haven't any stones in your pockets, you can give me the money for them, and I'll get them from the contractor. You can also give him the money directly. Now first we'll have another song, and then I'm going to take up a collection!"

Suddenly the greedy corner grocer shouted: "You won't get even half a stone from me!"

"Of course not," said Francis, "because then you would have to split your heart in two!"

"Bravo!" cheered the crowd. "He had it coming to him!"

The grocer walked angrily away.

Francis sang a romantic popular song, and many people were actually moved to tears by the sight of this young son of rich parents standing there dressed like a peasant, with worn shoes, singing so fervently for some stones and mortar! They gave and gave until he could hardly hold all the money in both hands together.

"Thank you! Thank you!" he exclaimed. "When the stones are all gone, I'll be back!" and followed by a number of children, he went to the building contractor.

Later he came out, curbed under a sack of mortar and with an old trowel tucked in his belt. The children were glad to help carry the stones. Some took three stones, others four—and they really were big stones too! Francis and his first little companions . . .

It was no joke suddenly to become a mason. He had to have a ladder, some scaffolding, ropes, buckets, a spade, a plumbline, and so on. To get all those things together by singing for them was quite a job!

Early the next morning he was hard at work, whistling and singing. There was an opening in the wall, caused by an earthquake. The old priest sometimes went in and out through it, in order not to have to push the door open, as it was stiff. Francis began by closing up this opening. He had to split up the stones, prepare the mortar, cut and assemble beams from the woods, and put up the scaffolding. Three days later his hands were scratched and caked with dust and mortar. He worked from dawn to dusk, as if he were being paid by the hour. In the evenings he was completely exhausted. Then it did him good to read some prayers with the little priest and to raise his heart to God with him.

Those were wonderful days! Francis even found time to help out here and there, milking the goat and doing other menial jobs. And twice a week he went to visit the lepers.

The little priest wanted to lend a hand by giving Francis the stones and doing other odd jobs. But Francis said: "Don't. Just pray that the stones keep coming in!"

The stones did keep coming in. Mostly it was children who brought them, with their parents' greetings and a request for prayers, and from time to time the contractor's helper came with a whole wheelbarrow full of stones, tiles, and mortar.

"But who keeps sending all that?" asked Francis.

"Someone who doesn't want to be known," said the boy.

Francis thought it must be his mother. He inquired at the contractor's, and from a beggar who worked there part-time he found out that it was Bernard of Quintavalle. Who would have guessed it? Bernard was a quiet rich young man of Francis' age who had never been one of his friends, but whom he knew fairly well from the times when they had studied under the priests together. Now when Francis met Bernard, he greeted him as before and pretended that he knew nothing about the stones.

It was a beautiful summer—at least that was the way it seemed to Francis and the little priest. Actually there was quite a lot of rain and thunder and wind. On weekdays when the priest did not say Mass, Francis always went to hear a Mass in town. And before and after praying, he carefully glanced around to see if his mother were there.

He did not see her. In fact, they had not seen each other again since she had let him out of the cellar. Yet he wanted so much to know what she thought of him now. Often in the evening when he was sitting with the little priest looking out over the valley, he grew sad, and he would say to the old man: "Let's pray a bit for my mother . . ."

And then they prayed quite a bit for his mother.

One morning Francis saw that he had no more mortar. He waited three days but none came, so there was nothing left for him to do but go to the market place and sing for it. On the way he met Father Silvester, the pastor of St. Rufinus' Church.

"How is your chapel coming along?" asked the priest.

"Fine, Father. I'm just going to sing for some more mortar."

"Oh, please don't do that," said the pastor. "People are beginning to laugh about it. They're already calling you the street singer of Assisi. You are making our holy ministry ridiculous. The Bishop must put a stop to it!"

"He won't do that," said Francis, "because he enjoys listening to songs very much. But if you give me some mortar now, then I won't have to go and sing."

"I should give you something? Not on my life!" exclaimed the priest. "My own church needs repairs."

"I'll fix it for you with my singing!" Francis suggested.

"I don't need your help. I'll take care of my church all right without you!"

"But I can't restore mine without you—unless I sing songs."

They continued to argue that way for a while, until finally the priest said: "Get a sack of mortar and charge it to me. But you've got to pay me back!"

"How? God doesn't pay me with money."

"Then work for it! How else? Do you promise to pay me back?"

"I promise," said Francis. "God will provide somehow all right."

They shook hands. And Francis went and charged a sack of mortar to the pastor of St. Rufinus' Church.

"Tomorrow is the Feast of Our Lady's Assumption," said the little old priest. "And there's no oil left for the altar light."

No oil? They looked at each other. There was not a penny in the house!

"Just give me the oilcan," said Francis. "I won't come back till I get some!" And he walked to Assisi in a pouring rain. Where was he to get the oil? From

67

somebody who had some. Surely he would be given some sign as to where to go.

He was soaking wet when he passed by the home of his former friend Theodore. The latter was fat and gluttonous, but still he had a good heart. He certainly would not refuse to give some oil for an altar light.

Francis let the knocker fall on the door. Then he began to think that Theodore would laugh at him. He was about to go on when the door opened. "May I speak to Theodore?" he asked the servant girl.

"I'll go call him," she said, and she ran off, giggling. Obviously she thought her master would be delighted.

She opened another door leading into a brightly lighted room in which a number of Francis' old friends were sitting around a richly laden table. Suddenly they began to shout, and he heard them call out his name. He felt that they were going to make fun of him, and he wished he could sink into the ground. He was so ashamed he intended to run away. He grasped the doorknob.

"Come here! Come here!" shouted Theodore. His mouth was full, and he held half a young pigeon in his hand. Francis was dragged into the banquet hall.

"I'm getting married!" Theodore exclaimed. "So now I'm giving my last party as a bachelor!"

The maid snickered and cackled like a hen and they all yelled: "Hooray for Francis! He's come back! Hooray for our prodigal son! Bring in the fatted calf and the oldest wine! Give him a new costume with ostrich plumes! And a mandolin! Let's have a song in honor of Theodore's farewell to bachelorhood!"

Francis looked at them sadly. Mockingly, they offered him wine, meat, and cakes. And Philip, the envious one, tossed a half-eaten leg of meat at him. Francis felt very depressed as he reflected that he used to be like that too. Then he became angry and gazed at them fearlessly.

Meanwhile Theodore snatched at the oilcan in order to fill it with wine, but Francis held it firmly. He waved his hand, and they were all silent as he said: "I haven't come to eat, and forgive me if I've disturbed you. I've just come for some oil for the altar lamp at St. Damian's —that's all."

With that they became more cordial. "Come on. Sit down and have something to eat. You'll get some oil. Why not? But first tell us all about yourself, please."

"All right, I'll tell you about myself. Just now when I saw this door open, I was ashamed to come before you like this. In my shame I intended to run away. That was very wrong of me. It was the spirit of pride. I want to humiliate myself by confessing it to you. And I want to be proud of being able to beg oil for Jesus."

His friends were as silent as codfish.

"Come with me," said Theodore, and he took Francis into the hall and sent the maid to fetch some oil from the cellar.

One day the old priest was counting his money, and Francis heard him saying to himself: "—and sometimes he likes to eat a strip of bacon, and bacon costs a lot. But still he must eat well, otherwise the skinny little fellow will collapse, what with all his praying and fasting. How shall I go about getting him a strip of bacon for Sunday? I'll just eat a bit less myself. And then too, there's no more flour for bread . . ."

Francis said nothing, but went away and beat his forehead with his fists. "What a fool I am! I've become wedded to Lady Poverty—and I'm living off someone! That's over now! Everybody has got to earn his own living."

The next day he was sitting by the stream cleaning out the mortar bucket. "You're making it so clean you'd think you were going to eat out of it," said the little priest.

"That's right," shouted Francis in his ear. "I want to earn my living. I'm going to beg!"

The old priest objected: "Don't do that! I have enough to eat. Don't do it—for your mother's sake . . ."

"Our Lord did it first, and it's no disgrace to follow His example!" said Francis, and off he went to Assisi.

Still, his heart was thumping in his throat. Where should he start? Where better than among the poor? The open door of a poor hut seemed like an invitation. He went up to it and said: "For the love of God, give me something to eat."

A woman with a child in her arms came to the door. "Why, aren't you the rich young man who decided to live like the poor?" She drew back in amazement. "Sir," she said. "I have nothing you would like. I can't give you a thing. We're so poor ourselves."

"Just give me something all the same. The least bit will be quite all right."

The embarrassed woman poured into his bucket some leftover stringbeans and a crust of black bread. "God will reward you!" said Francis, and he went on.

Where next? To that big rich mansion over there which belonged to friends of his parents. He went up the steps. The maid opened the door, and he asked for something to eat.

The maid did not come back, but the master of the house himself appeared. He was a handsome man with white hair, and his wife came out of a room to watch. "You should be ashamed to disgrace your honorable father this way," sneered the old gentleman. "You're a lazy loafer, a black sheep, a bad son! Get out of here— or I'll send my hounds after you!" And he slammed the door shut.

"God reward you!" said Francis to the door.

Where next? To the grocer across the street. There the whole family came to the door. None of them said a word, but they gave him a slice of bread and some remnants of salted meat. They went to the door to watch him walk away, and then they ran to tell the neighbors.

Francis deliberately walked past Sir Bernard's home. And then he came to the house of Marietta's father. How the latter laughed and laughed! He had to hold his sides. So this was the brave troubadour of not long ago! Now the chicken had come home to roost!

"Give you something? With the greatest pleasure! Such a poor devil, who is too dirty to be touched with pincers! With the greatest pleasure! Marietta, give him the red cabbage we had day before yesterday—it's probably turned black, but when a fellow is hungry, what's the difference? Come back every day—I'll make you fat!"

Marietta obeyed unwillingly, but Francis said to her with a smile: "Just give it to me, Miss. It's better to have something black in one's stomach than in one's soul."

He went on to several other doors, but received only insults and ridicule. Someone said to him: "You say: 'God reward you'—yet you get nothing."

Francis replied: "God will reward you for humiliating me, because I need it more than I need your bread."

He knocked at the palace of the well-known aristocratic Scifi family. A footman opened the door. Just then a slim girl with blond hair and blue eyes came running into the richly decorated hall with her younger sister. The two children stood gazing at the beggar. "That's Francis, who became poor for Jesus' sake," said the girl to her little sister. They stared at him with amazement.

"Please come back tomorrow," said the footman. "Tomorrow is the day when the Scifi family gives alms to the poor."

Francis was about the leave, but the young lady exclaimed: "No. Give the gentleman something. Wait— I have something myself!" She ran into a room and came back with a fine bunch of grapes and a handful of cakes.

"That's not a poor man's alms, Miss Clare," said Francis. "I recognize you—you used to come and buy silk with your mother in our store."

She looked at him with surprise and respect, and when she put the food in his hands, she acted as if it were all a dream.

"God bless you," he said, and he bowed to her. When he was in the street again, he said to himself: "Now I have enough for more than a week."

He intended to go outside the town to eat his lunch, but he realised that this would be an act of pride, and so he overcame the impulse. He went and sat down by the fountain on the market square. Setting the grapes and cakes aside, he murmured: "They're for the little priest, the good old man."

Then he took a look in his pail. He felt nauseated when he saw its mess of leftovers. With thumb and forefinger he gingerly fished out a little piece of meat and tasted it. It wasn't too bad. Next he took some of the red cabbage—and let it drop. Raising his eyes to heaven, he implored: "Jesus—!"

He saw a woman with her little boy leaning out of a window, watching him, and doubt began to attack him. Was this really necessary? Did Jesus require this of him? Suddenly he laughed: "Does this affect the soul? Brother Ass, young fellow, you're still letting yourself be led around by the Devil. Away with him!" And he began to put the food into his mouth. He closed his eyes, smacked his lips, chewed thoroughly, and swallowed it down.

"It must taste good!" he muttered. "It must!" and kept on eating, with his eyes shut. "Look at it too, Brother Ass!" he exclaimed, and he opened his eyes as he ate up the leftovers from rich and poor kitchens. He ate his fill, while the sweat ran into his beard. "The rest

72

is for tonight and tomorrow," he said. Then, cupping his hands, he took two mouthfuls of the clear fountain water to wash it down. "It's better than I thought," he murmured. In that moment pearls of joy filled his soul, and he smiled toward heaven in a friendly and very grateful way as he said: "Thank You, Lord, for having made me like Your little birds!"

There was one big thorn in this begging: he was always afraid of meeting his mother. He could face anything—but not that! It would hurt her too much. He must not make her suffer that way. Of course she knew about it. But that she should see him with her own eyes —please, Lord, spare her that! Therefore he never went along the street where she lived.

But one day when he was making his rounds with his pail, suddenly he heard an uproar in an inn, and his father rushed out. Before Francis could do or say anything, the father snatched his pail and dashed it onto the ground, shouting: "You swine! You louse! I curse you! I curse you!"

The curse pierced Francis' heart like a bolt of lightning. He had not expected anything like that.

"No! No! Don't curse me," he begged, twisting his hands.

"I curse you!" the father repeated several times more.

A crowd had formed. Women were crossing themselves. Francis turned deathly pale. "And every time you begin again, I curse you again—you cur!" shouted the father again, before he went back into the inn.

Francis fled from the town along a short cut and then sat down sadly and pensively, holding his head in his hands. He had been cursed! That suddenly extinguished all the light in his heart. But what could he do about it?

The next day he knew what to do about it. When he got to the market place with his little pail, he went to the fountain and spoke to a beggar who looked exactly like statues of St. Peter: he had the same kind of circular white beard and wisp of hair on his bald head. Beggars willingly help one another, so Berto went along with him as he began to beg. Francis' father appeared, bursting with anger. But when he was about to utter the curse, Francis kneeled down, and Berto blessed him.

Then Francis exclaimed: "While you curse me, another father blesses me—and that cancels out your curse!"

All day long, dark clouds blew across the sky. The wise little priest said: "There'll be snow tomorrow." That evening already, the snow began to fall heavily, and the next day the mountains and the valley were completely white. The chapel was snowed under and that put an end to Francis' work on it. So the two of them just sat around a small log fire and prayed as they waited for spring.

Francis now worked entirely on his soul. He spent hours kneeling in the cold before the holy crucifix, praying. He visited the lepers and the sick and went begging. Hardly anyone still considered him a lunatic or a fool. They had become used to him, and they had forgotten the rich young son of Bernardone, which gave Francis a spiritual satisfaction.

People gave him alms because he was shivering from the cold and because his bony knees stuck out of holes in his robe. They gave because they pitied him and especially because he was always friendly. With his long hair, his beard, and his nice brown eyes in that thin, pale face, at first sight he made one feel like crying. But soon one felt a strange and beautiful joy streaming from his whole being. It was wonderful how he could console people and put them in a good mood with just a simple word. Really, it seemed as though he were rich and they were poor.

The snow made everything in the distance very clear. Little houses that he had not seen before were now seemingly transparent. And now he could also make out the sloping little steeple of Our Lady's Chapel of the Portiuncula among the trees in the oak forest down in the valley. It too needed a stonemason. And then there was also the Chapel of St. Peter up in the mountains. Yes, there certainly was enough work ahead—all right, let it come, he could take it!

But masonry work—was that all he could do? "Lord," he asked, "is there not more to be done in Your garden? Am I not too young to lead such an easy life here? I'm getting moss-covered! And You came and died for us! Send me off among the savages—take my blood!"

He stood with open hands raised toward heaven as he begged for harder work. Those hands which used to sparkle with jewels had become rough and tanned, like the hands of men who eat from wooden bowls. But as long as no sign came, he had to keep at his masonry work. He waited for the coming of spring—and for a meeting with his mother . . .

It was a hard winter up there in the hills, yet every morning while it was still dark Francis was standing before the door of the church in Assisi, waiting for it to open. And one day on the porch of the church he met his mother. He was coming out and she was going in. They stopped and faced one another. He recognised her easily, with her pale features under her shawl.

They looked at each other. Francis' legs felt weak, then a white hand came out from her shawl and rested on his. "Child, I am proud of you!" his mother whispered, and she went quickly into the church, for she was afraid.

But those few words of hers made Francis so happy that he danced as he ran back to St. Damian's. What a joy it was for him to know that his mother was with him heart and soul when he was begging, when he was hungry—to know that in spirit she tucked him in and caressed him and encouraged him in his striving to live as much as possible like Jesus Christ!

With great joy he told the little priest what had happened.

"Now your poverty has been blessed," said the old man.

At Candlemas the snow fell on warm stones. Spring was creeping over the country, despite hail and dark rainstorms. And one quiet evening the sunset was like a fiery oven. "That means good weather," said the little priest. "Don't you hear my bees announcing it?"

The next morning the sun was shining fiercely in the sky. "Do you hear the springs gurgling and the pigeons and blackbirds calling?" said the priest. "Look at the rabbits hopping around and the daisies blinking in the light!"

"Back to work!" exclaimed Francis. "I can go begging again for stones and mortar." So many wheelbarrows began to arrive at St. Damian's—sent by Bernard, of course—that Francis soon had a great surplus of stones, and so he built a small rectory for the little priest. Toward Pentecost he fixed the cross on the roof, though first he blessed the whole world with it in all four directions of the compass, crying out: "Peace! Peace!"

Peace in a world of Christians, yet a world torn by so many conflicts and wars . . . On the Feast of Pentecost the old priest said Mass in the restored Chapel. There was quite a crowd present. And with tears in his eyes he gave a fine short sermon in which he thanked the Holy Spirit and his young stonemason.

That same week Francis began to work on St. Peter's Chapel. And within about a month he was through. But then came the big job: the Chapel of Our Lady of the Angels, down in the oak grove at the Portiuncula.

It was an hour's walk away, in the valley. First he went and looked it over carefully, like a good builder who goes on Sunday to survey the job he will have to do during the following week.

Yes, there really was a lot to be done there. He could not finish it by the end of the year. What of it? Wasn't it a pleasure to be able to work for the glory of the Blessed Virgin? Such work was fun. And the chapel was so lovely there in the glade in the woods, where everything was so peaceful and mystical, with the singing and chirping of the birds, so far from the world . . . "Oh, if only I could always live here!" thought Francis.

Then he began to transport his materials down to the forest. He carried the ladders and buckets and scaffolding and mortar and the rest of the stones—and he did it all during a heat wave that made the air so hot he thought he was breathing fire. But Francis endured it.

And he found his construction work in that solitude a marvelous experience. He was all alone in the silence of the dark green trees, without ever being disturbed by anyone. Sometimes while he was working, he was so overcome with an indescribable feeling of beauty and love that he got down from the scaffolding and knelt on the grass and worshipped God with tears in his eyes —occasionally for hours at a time. Some evenings he did not go back to St. Damian's but remained in the woods, praying in the moonlight. Then he used to lie down and sleep on the ground, in the chapel or outdoors, depending on the weather.

It was a fine summer, and a fine autumn too. All the time the fire in his soul burned more fiercely—and so did the question whether he could not do more for God than to build. He was ashamed to be living such an easy life. As he prayed, he slowly realised that the words of the crucifix might well have another meaning . . .

Something was happening within him, something

77

profound and potent. What would come of it? What must he do? He waited and listened. God had only to say the word—Francis was ready to obey, with his tears and with his blood.

Winter came early, and once more at St. Damian's the two friends sat around their little log fire, praying.

When spring returned, Francis went back to work. To save time, he stayed down in the valley. He lived in a small hut that he had put together himself with some rushes and straw. He spent only his Sundays with the little priest, when he served as altar boy at Mass and Benediction.

How beautiful life was in the woods! The birds came to know him, and so did the rabbits and the squirrels. They no longer ran away when they saw him. They even came and listened to his singing.

Although Francis sang, the unrest in his heart slowly increased. It was not dread or fear, but rather a premonition of great happiness. He still did not know what it was, but it prevented him from sleeping.

One day the little priest said to him: "I don't think you are going to build churches much more. I believe God has other plans for you."

"We'll just wait," replied Francis.

"That's right," the little priest agreed, "we'll just wait. When will your chapel be ready?"

"I'd like you to come and celebrate the first Mass there on the Feast of St. Matthias."

"I'll come," said the little priest.

And Francis served the Mass. One other person was present: a very old and quite deformed shepherd who with his own ears had heard angels sing there many years ago. Francis was nervous and troubled.

The little priest came to the Gospel and turned to

face the congregation—that is, the shepherd. But he looked at Francis as he read the Gospel.

Francis listened reverently. It was the word of God. A great light came over him. The little priest was looking at him in a sharp and piercing way that he had never used before. And Francis was rapt in a holy ecstasy when he heard the words with which Jesus Christ had sent His Apostles into the world: "And as you go, preach the message: 'The kingdom of Heaven is at hand!' Cure the sick, raise the dead, cleanse the lepers, cast out devils. Do not keep gold, or silver, or money in your belts, no wallet for your journey, nor two tunics, nor sandals, nor staff; for the laborer deserves his living. And whatever town or village you enter, inquire who in it is worthy, and stay there until you leave. As you enter the house, greet it. If then that house be worthy, your peace will come upon it. But if it be not worthy, let your peace return to you."

Francis felt streams of light pouring over him. God had spoken! To be an apostle—to spread peace and love, to rebuild broken-down souls—and to be poor, utterly poor, like a sparrow! That was the life for him!

Peace. Love. Poverty. His lean body thrilled with spiritual joy. He served the rest of the Mass as well as he could, and when it was over, he shouted his happiness into the little priest's ear.

The old man said: "I don't know why I had to look at you that way. Some strange power gripped me. You see —you won't always remain a stonemason. You're going to preach fine sermons—you'll see!"

Francis ran to his hut, took his most tattered robe and put it on—he did not have to bother about a shirt because he didn't have one—and he replaced his leather belt with a rope. He took off his shoes and stood in his bare feet, and without shirt or shoes, wearing only a robe, he was happy, ecstatically happy. "These are my feathers!" he exclaimed.

"You are a lark of Our Lord!" said the little priest, and he was crying as he embraced Francis.

Francis was standing barefooted in the market place, preaching, and the people were listening intently to every word he said. He was speaking in a very plain and simple way, and they listened less to his words than to the melody of his heart.

"Good people," he said. "No, let me rather call you: 'Brothers.' For God is the Father of all of us. Let's live in peace and sincere brotherhood and joy, like children. We're all made of the same dough—we're just baked into different moulds. Everyone has his faults, but luckily everyone has a good side too. Let's look right through our faults for God, who dwells in our hearts through grace, and then we'll love one another in spite of our faults. So let your inner life govern your outer life. Love God in one another.

"God is great and infinite. He made the stars and the sun—and us too. We live in His breath. We move in His light. He is in Heaven and on earth and everywhere. He is in us through His Holy Spirit. And in the Holy Eucharist He gives Himself to us as the Flesh and Blood of His Son, Our Lord Jesus Christ. Oh, how wonderful it is to have the gift of life, for we live in Him and through Him! When you sleep, when you cook a soup, when you make shoes, God is always in your heart—don't forget it. And if you don't forget it, then you will be like children.

"Just look at children: they are happy and they don't worry about tomorrow. When they catch sight of some flowers, they shout for joy. When it snows, they sing. They hold their hands out toward the sun. And they laugh when it rains. That's the way you must be! Be happy, and be filled with wonder.

"And as they love their parents, we too must love our Father in Heaven and have confidence in Him day and night! Let's not get angry if our Father sometimes boxes our ears. He knows why—and what is a little pain compared to eternity? Love Him day and night. Love Him in His creation, in the rain and snow and stars—and in adversity. Above all love Him in His bitter Suffering that is going to last as long as sin rules men. Make His Cross and His Suffering lighter by taking over a bit of it yourselves. Do penance! Penance is a bitter medicine that heals and purifies the soul. Don't you willingly take the worst-tasting herbs to cure your stomach-aches? God wants pure souls. Only a pure soul can see the purity of the work of His hands. Then you will be able to praise and to admire it. Love Him. Live in peace with Him, with one another, and with yourselves. Peace in little things brings peace in big things. We lost the earthly Paradise through sin. Up yonder there's another Paradise a thousand times more beautiful—Heaven. Holy Church shows you the way to it. It is the way of Love. Our Blessed Lady and the Angels are waiting for you and will go with you.

"Live like brothers and like children!

"Peace be with you! Amen."

Had he spoken well? Was that the right way? He was worried. Had a seed fallen into their hearts?

Sometimes not much is needed to enkindle love for God in a person. Someone may wake up with it one morning. Another after long years may hear just a word or two, and then a thin shell, that had already been cracked, breaks open, and he is stirred to the heart. Still others seem to be encased in walls, and the mightiest hammer blows have no effect. The workings of grace are strange.

Had he spoken well? At any rate he noticed that Bernard, who was in the crowd, had listened with devout attention, and that Peter of Catane, the vicar at St. Nicholas' Church, had repeatedly sighed with emotion.

81

And one poor woman had covered her face with her apron. But how about the others? Hadn't it gone in one ear and out the other?

He went into the church to pray that his words may have fallen into good soil, and his heart told him: "Don't look backward. A farmer doesn't look back when he sows. Sow! And just let God provide the rain and good weather." All his anxiety left him, and he went out.

A beggar was passing by, cursing because he had been given nothing at a rich mansion. Francis said to him: "Brother, our dear Lord also begged, but was He angry when they gave Him nothing? No. He said: 'Peace be to you!' Say it too—say it all the time, to those who give and to those who don't give. And you'll see: you'll have bread and peace!"

"Our Lord didn't have six children," grumbled the beggar.

"That's right. He didn't have six—He had a hundred thousand and more. He had the whole world, with the good and the bad. Yet He let Himself be nailed to the Cross for everybody, and then He even prayed for His executioners. Spread love, and you will receive love."

"How can a fellow argue with you?" said the beggar. "You look sick from hunger yourself!" and in his embarrassment he went off in the opposite direction.

Francis spoke to everyone who gave him a friendly nod. He met a farmer and talked with him about cattle and about God. He stood and talked with a charwoman about her children and about the Sorrows of the Blessed Virgin. The woman listened, with the duster in her hand, as though he were telling her some sad but important news. A little later he was sitting on some alley steps telling a swarm of dirty urchins about the Stable of Bethlehem. When he got back to the Portiuncula that evening, his hunger reminded him that he had forgotten to beg.

"Brother Ass," he said to his body, "just keep quiet a while, little fellow. Tomorrow I'll make the rounds and get you something to eat!"

And Brother Ass kept quiet.

Francis went around the country with his sermons, like a street singer with his ballads. He spoke to the peasants in the fields, to the woodcutters in the forests. He spoke in farmyards, in little village squares, among the lepers, in alleyways, and on market places and church porches. He was as busy as a bee, always speaking about the same thing: about Christ, poverty, and living the good life. But each time he spoke differently. It was a pleasure to listen to him.

Some people wanted to give him food or offered him money. But he did not want money, and he took only enough food for one meal: a bowl of porridge, sometimes a couple of slices of bread and butter with a bit of cheese, which he ate as he walked along, washing it down with some water from a stream. He slept wherever night overtook him, in a barn, under a cliff, or beneath the open sky.

People were talking about him everywhere. They often recalled his former life—what a playboy he had been. And now he spent his nights praying in the woods, holding his arms outstretched. Some thought he was ridiculous, while others admired him. And both sides supplied a wealth of details with their imagination. Some said that he ate grass with worms and ants in it. Others said that he was a saint and that in the evening a halo of light glowed around his head . . .

Late one day he returned tired out to the Chapel of Our Lady at the Portiuncula, and found a young man waiting there for him. He handed Francis a note, with Bernard's greetings: the latter was inviting Francis to spend an evening with him and have a talk together.

"I'll be there tonight," said Francis. He sensed that Bernard's soul was troubled.

They took a light meal together. What a striking contrast they made: Francis in his mud-stained robe and his bricklayer's hands, sitting at the richly laden table in that fine dining-room, and Bernard dressed in silk and velvet! He was a tall pale man with light blue eyes. He said little, for he was shy and gentle-mannered. In a discreet way he asked Francis how he had actually happened to take up this life of poverty. It was obvious that his soul was troubled.

Francis sensed that Bernard was approaching the climax of some spiritual crisis, and so he gladly told him the story of his life. To Francis, it was as if he were reliving it all. And he spoke with such fervor and sincerity that tears kept flowing down Bernard's cheeks.

It took Francis over an hour, and it was late when he was through. He intended to go back to the woods, but Bernard insisted so strongly on his staying overnight that Francis yielded. They went to bed in Bernard's room, which contained a bed in each corner. A small lamp was burning before a skillfully designed triptych. Soon they both began to snore, and each seemed to be trying to snore louder than the other.

But both of them were pretending.

Bernard was planning to watch and see what Francis did. He too had heard that Francis got up at night to pray, and he wondered whether he would do so now. Bernard's motive was not ordinary curiosity but a profound respect and desire for his own spiritual good. For he had long been wanting to lead a life like that of Francis, but he was extremely cautious by nature. So now he pretended to sleep while watching Francis through half-closed eyelids.

Francis too was only pretending to snore. He waited until he thought Bernard was sleeping soundly, and then he got up very quietly and kneeled in front of the bed. And holding out his arms, he whispered very softly: "My God and my All! My God and my All!" That was all he said, just: "My God and my All!" Each time he said it, he paused for a moment. "My God and my All!"

Sometimes it sounded like a sigh, other times like a joyful exclamation, or a prayer, or an expression of fear. Occasionally as he said it, he covered his face with his hands. Then he would hold his arms out, or he would bow down reverently. It was a beautiful and a holy sight.

Bernard watched him carefully by the light of the lamp. He was so moved that he forgot to snore. Finally, as the heartfelt prayer—"My God and my All!"—went on and on, he repeated it each time very quietly to himself.

When dawn came, Francis quickly got back into his bed. A little later the church bells began to ring, and Francis and Bernard pretended that they were waking up. As soon as Bernard had dressed, he went to Francis and said: "Francis, I would like to live like you. What must I do?"

Francis was surprised and overjoyed. He exclaimed: "Oh, Bernard, God be praised! God be praised!" And he embraced his friend, adding: "You want me to decide that for you? No, no! I am too insignificant for that —and the question is too important! Oh, how wonderful! Our Lord will help us. Let's go to church—that's where He gives His Light. Oh, how wonderful, how marvelous!"

They both hastened to church, each hurrying faster than the other, and finally they ran. As they entered the Church of St. Nicholas, Father Peter, the vicar, was just beginning his Mass at a side-altar. They heard it through, in a spirit of deep recollection. When the Mass was over, Francis went right to the priest in the sacristy and explained Bernard's problem to him, and asked him to consult the Gospels for Bernard.

85

"What a lucky man!" sighed the vicar, and he went with Francis to the altar, where the Missal was. Then Francis motioned to Bernard to approach and said to the priest: "Open the Holy Book three times in honor of the Blessed Trinity, and each time read a verse!"

The vicar did so. The first time he read: "If thou wilt be perfect, go, sell what thou hast, and give to the poor. And come, follow Me." The second time: "Take nothing for your journey, neither staff, nor wallet, nor bread, nor money." And the third time—with a sigh: "If anyone wishes to come after Me, let him deny himself, and take up his cross, and follow Me."

The priest's tears were dropping onto the page, and he was trembling like a reed. Bernard showed his acceptance by kneeling down. And then Father Peter also fell on his knees, and holding out his hands toward Francis, he begged: "Me too—me too!"

This incident naturally made quite a stir in the town and in the whole district: two respectable citizens, a gentleman of independent means and a priest, had suddenly taken up Francis' way of life! But what everyone wanted to know most of all was: what was Bernard going to do with all his money? That was what mattered most—the money! Was he going to give it to his family or to the city or to the Church?

He sold all his property, his houses and estates and furniture—everything. And it amounted to a very fine sum. What was he going to do with it now?

All Assisi was in an uproar when it heard that Bernard was going to distribute his money personally to the poor the next day on St. George's Square! The poor were so excited they could not sleep, and some of them spent the night waiting in the little square. The sick were brought from their beds and from the hospital. Everyone of them had to be there, young and old, and those who could not walk were carried. People in the lower middle-class were envious. The upper middle-class and the nobility thought that the whole thing was an outrage! The money ought rather to be spent on good works: a paved street, a church, or the hospital. But just to give it to the poor, who would merely waste it—why, that was too shocking for words!

Rich and poor, young and old, thronged to St. George's Square. The city guards were obliged to maintain order. The poor were placed in two rows in the center of the square, and the crowd surged around them. Francis and Bernard and Father Peter arrived at about three o'clock. And the poor immediately began to shout: "My husband hasn't had a job for three years!" . . . "Mine is blind!" . . . "Mine is crippled!" . . . "I have more children at home!" . . .

They exaggerated and they lied. The noise and confusion defied description. The guards were busy keeping everyone in place.

Each of the three friends was carrying two heavy purses filled with money. Bernard began to hand it out, with a guard at his side, and he distributed the coins just as he picked them out of the purse.

Greed was flickering in the eyes of rich and poor. A man could count on his fingers those who looked on with unselfish happiness and approval. The poor pushed and pressed toward the spot where the money was being given out, and the guards had to keep them back with their lances. In order to prevent them from getting two shares, everyone had to stay in his place until the distribution ended. The money seemed to be burning their hands, and those who had received theirs kept counting the silver coins over and over. To get through quicker, Francis and the priest also gave out the money.

Francis had hardly begun when Father Silvester, the pastor, elbowed his way through the crowd and said:

"Here! You haven't paid me back for the sack of mortar!" and he thrust out his hand.

Francis looked at him sadly. He looked right into his soul. Then he quickly took up two handfuls of coins and gave them to him. "Is that enough?" he asked.

It had the effect of a dagger blow. Father Silvester started, became angry, grunted, felt ashamed, and wondered whether to throw the money back in Francis' face. But he just laughed scornfully and sneaked away, while the crowd muttered that he was a glutton and a greedy fellow. Bernard and Francis continued to distribute the coins.

But five minutes after they were through, there was no one left in the square—because there was no money left. And the three friends stood there without a penny to their names. Francis took them to an old second-hand clothes dealer, and the two exchanged their suits for brown robes with a cowl, like those of the shepherds in the mountains.

"I have some more in stock," said the old dealer, "all sizes—the best in town!"

Then the three friends went down to Our Lady of the Angels together, and their six bare feet were all in step.

That day, business in the inns and taverns was as good as during the biggest fair of the year.

Poets by the Dozen

That same evening the little priest of St. Damian came hobbling down to wish them luck. He loaned them a tin chalice and a Missal, and they obtained some oil and wine and hosts for Mass.

He embraced Francis like a child and said: "You will grow in numbers. If I was a bit younger, I would join you. But I can't leave my goat and my bees."

They slept on the ground in the little hut. The next morning, Peter said Mass—and what a beautiful Mass it was, with the fragrance of spring in the woods coming in through the open door up to the altar! Then each of them went off by himself to earn his bread and to speak to the people about God.

In the evening when they came back, they told their adventures. Peter related with sighs—he was always sighing with longing for God—that he had been able to take a meal with a peasant and that at a crossroad he had talked about poverty to at least twenty people.

Francis had begged a bit at first and then visited a sick man named Morico who used to take care of the lepers. "Brother Peter—for now we are going to call one another 'Brother'," said Francis, "tomorrow I'll dip a piece of bread into the oil of the altar lamp, and you'll take it to him and tell him to eat it without delay."

Brother Bernard showed them his delicate hands: his palms were covered with blisters. He had helped a farmer to load a wagon with manure, and so he earned a bowl of soup and a small loaf of bread. He had eaten the soup and brought the bread along.

"Let's rejoice," said Francis, "that our hands are getting rough and coarse, because don't forget that Our Lord will look at our hands as well as our souls. Let's ask God to give us a lot of work!"

Eight days later, as Francis came out of the forest, a young peasant, dressed up in his Sunday best, was praying on his knees beside a big loaf of white bread. He ran up to Francis, knelt down, and asked: "For the love of God, will you let me stay with you?"

"What is your trade, son?"

"I'm a woodcutter, Sir Monk."

"I'm little Brother Francis. What is your name?"

"Giles, Sir Little Brother Francis."

"Drop the 'Sir'," laughed Francis.

"I brought along a loaf of bread for you," said the young man.

"You'll eat it with us, Brother Giles. When the Emperor selects someone to join his inner circle, everyone wants to be chosen. Rejoice and be proud now that it is God Himself who has chosen you to join the Knights of Lady Poverty!"

Hand in hand they went into the woods. First they prayed for a little while in the small Chapel. Then Giles explained somewhat bashfully that he came from the forests on Mount Subasio. One day up there he had heard a shepherd talk about Francis. He had thought it over day and night, until finally he had felt irresistibly drawn to go and live the same kind of life. So that morning he had said goodbye to his father, who had given him the bread, which he had baked himself. And with good luck he had found his way to the Portiuncula.

"You've got a good nose," said Francis. "I believe you're going to make a fine Brother. How happy the others will be this evening when they hear about it! Who would ever have thought that little Brothers were going

90

to come and join me? But now let's see about your feathers!"

Every day the Brothers went out preaching, begging, and working. They spent the night wherever it overtook them—under the stars, on the bare earth. That was nothing for such men. And they themselves became like a piece of earth, a product of Nature, filled with fresh vigor, like the spring.

People listened to them as if a new era was beginning. The Brothers did not need a crowd to start a sermon. If they caught sight of a lonesome shepherd sitting on a mountainside, they climbed up there to preach the Gospel to him. They went right up to a farmer's wife while she was milking her cow. And a peasant ploughing with his oxen need not lose any time in order to listen to them: while he walked behind his plow, a Brother strode along beside him, talking about sowing seeds for Heaven. They left no one alone. Everywhere they seized souls: women at the village fountain or tramps on the road. They stopped a wedding procession and talked about God. There was no holding them back.

And people found it very fine of them that they would not accept any money or even a piece of bread and butter if they were not hungry. And those who willingly listened to them were made so happy that they began to sigh from sheer joy.

The Brothers went as far as some of the neighboring cities and even into other provinces. But in the cities the people were no longer so simple. Their faith was weaker. And sometimes when one of the Brothers was preaching, men and women would begin to sing vulgar songs and urge the children to throw mud at him. But was it not a blessing to have an opportunity to suffer for Jesus? The Brothers were always joyful, and nothing could dampen their fervor, neither hunger nor scorn nor any kind of bad weather.

"The weather is always good, but in different ways," said Francis, and the others used to repeat that saying of his.

Many days later, when Francis returned from the region of Ancona with that fine fellow, Brother Giles, three men were sitting in front of the Chapel, waiting for him—with their habits.

They were: Morico, small and broad-shouldered, who had been cured by the piece of bread dipped in oil; a man named Sabatino who looked devout and very scholarly; and the third a heavy-set lad called John, with a stubborn chin and a pointed nose. He was the son of the greedy grocer who had not been willing to give Francis even half a stone—and now his own son was giving himself to Francis. This John wore a big hat. The other two were also from Assisi. When they saw Francis, they fell on their knees and asked him to let them become Brothers too.

"God be praised!" cried Francis. "Three flies with one swat!"

Behind some bushes they took off their city clothes and put on their habits.

"You have no cowl on your cloak, like us," Francis said to the grocer's son.

"I tore it off," replied John, "because I can't stand it. I wear a hat, and it's as good as a cowl."

"That won't do," said Francis. "We are birds from the same nest, and we must all have the same feathers."

"But I can't stand a cowl," John objected. "It's much too stuffy."

There ensued a long discussion over the hat. But John refused to yield either his point or his hat. After all, can someone who wants to lead a life of poverty like Christ be sent home—just on account of a mere hat?

"All right," said Francis with a smile. "As knights are named after the countries they conquer, and as your hat is so dear to you, we'll call you Brother Hat. I bless you, Brother Hat!"

Now they were seven. It was getting to be a family. All seven were laughing the next day as they sat in a circle, sharing the food they had begged. Francis assigned the job of distributing the supplies to Brother Hat, since he was a grocer. And he went about it like a greedy grocer, taking after his father. He weighed the bread in both hands, and no one got any more than his share. They really enjoyed their meal. And soon whole coveys of little birds came to get something too . . .

But a dark cloud came over them and disturbed their peace. It seemed that His Excellency the Bishop of Assisi was displeased and did not approve of their doings! And the people's attitude also began to change. They were saying that the Brothers were crazy: first they gave all their money away, and then they went around begging!

The Brothers were afraid, but Francis wanted to drive away their fears, so he went to see the Bishop. It was true: His Excellency did not approve of them. He said that their complete poverty could not last, that they should have a monastery and live simply, but still with some supplies, and so on.

Yet it was the Bishop himself who had encouraged Francis to take up a life of poverty. Francis could read his heart, and so he was bold enough to say to him: "Your Excellency, if we own property, we will also have to arm ourselves with weapons in order to protect our property, and we will have to engage lawyers to settle lawsuits and conflicts—and then we won't be able to serve God freely any more . . ."

His Excellency was thinking it over. Francis wiped the sweat from his face, he was so anxious to know what the Bishop would say.

And His Excellency said: "I admire you. Get up and go in peace!"

They spent the summer working, preaching, praying, and begging—most of all praying. How wonderful it was to pray in the little oak grove without being disturbed by anyone, with the wind rustling in the leaves, in the green light and quiet of the twilight, amid all the holiness of Nature and the silent animals! One could spend hours kneeling there, immersing oneself in God's infinity. When they went off to work, or when they gathered at meals, and one of them was missing, they knew that he was praying somewhere in the woods, and they did not disturb him. If someone was missing in the evening, they did not call him, but just went to sleep in their hut. The next morning the Brother would come back, wet with dew and sighing with happiness.

The Holy Spirit was working in those seven men.

Francis was like a morning star. His fiery soul seemed to glow through his body and shed its light on the others too. Sometimes one of them would go to him, kiss his hands reverently, and tell him his troubles. And Francis would console him, but in doing so he opened the wounds in his own heart. For just as the Brothers felt small before him, so he felt himself a thousand times smaller and more despicable in the eyes of God. He was conscious of his own nothingness and of all the weakness of his flesh, which he mastered with penances and fasts yet which still longed continually for things that his heart scorned. But he also had the will to conquer himself, a fresh young will. And then too he had his powerful love for Jesus Christ.

Toward the end of the summer a new Brother joined them: Philip, whom they called Tall Philip because he was over six feet tall. Naturally his habit was too short, so Brother Morico had to cut a strip off his own, which trailed on the ground. And Brother Hat, who knew how to sew, sewed the strip on with a borrowed needle, which was carefully returned to its owner with the rest of the thread, because they did not want to possess anything, not even a needle.

Then autumn came with its dark days, its mud, and its rain. The rain dripped through their dilapidated thatched roof, and their bare feet floundered in the mud. They were soaked to the skin. The wind howled through the trees. It was dark and cold, and they were so cold that they trembled and shook. As soon as they lit a fire, the rain put it out. And the nights were becoming terribly long. At times some of them sat there thinking and day-dreaming, with discouragement in their eyes. Were they thinking of home, where it was warm, and bacon was sizzling in the pan?

Francis did not like to see them dreaming like that. One of those days he said: "Come with me. Twenty minutes from here, over at Rivo Torto, there's a well covered shed, not far from the lepers' place. It's a bit small, but with good will there'll be room enough for all of us."

That very moment they set off, without taking anything along, because they had nothing to take. On reaching Rivo Torto the first thing they did was to plant a big Cross in front of the shed.

But winter was coming on. Francis was afraid that their courage might collapse. What were they to do during the winter, with its long nights, short days, bad roads, no work on farms, bad times, and closed doors? He asked God for advice. And he got it. When they were all together, Francis announced: "Brothers, Sir Brother Winter is coming, and we cannot sit here with nothing to do. God wants us to work. So tomorrow we're going off, two by two—there are eight of us—to

preach the Gospel in foreign lands. In memory of the
Holy Cross of Jesus, we'll go in four directions: Bernard and Giles will go west, another pair will go north
and another east, and I'll go south with Morico. And
we'll come back in the spring."

"Yes, that's fine!"

"A wonderful idea!"

One after another agreed enthusiastically. They were
happy to be able to go and do some good work for God,
and to set off as free as birds. They went to bed early.
The next morning it was snowing—that was a good beginning! They went to pray together in the Chapel once
more, and Francis gave them another inspiring talk:
"Be gentle on your trip. Preach. Work. And beg. And
know that God is with you!" And he gave them more
beautiful instructions, which they drank in like milk.
Then he blessed each one separately, and they embraced one another, and went off in the four directions
of the compass with fresh manly courage.

Snow was falling on their cowls and on Brother Hat's
inseparable hat. Snow was falling on the little Chapel
and over the whole countryside. And four happy songs
could be heard moving farther and farther apart.

Francis went south with Morico, that stocky fellow
with a simple heart. The little nest was empty. The
birds had flown away to distant unknown lands. Francis
wondered whether he had not asked too much of them.
They needed him so much. They were still only begin-
ners. Where were the poor little lambs now?

"God will take good care of them!" he told himself,
yet he could not stop worrying. And then his conviction of his own unworthiness began to oppress him
more than ever.

They preached in the villages and towns of the valley
of Rieti and in the villages that lie at the foot of the
Abruzzi mountains. And the more he told the people

to put their souls before their senses, the more he felt that he himself was nothing but a lump of sinful flesh weighed down by all the sins of his former life. It is true that he was not actually committing sins. But desires were stirring in him as in a worm's nest. Besides, people did not listen to him. They laughed at him and drove him away as though he were a heretic. "I deserve it," he reproached himself. "A sinner like myself has no right to teach others."

Everything went wrong. They suffered from hunger and cold. People were afraid to give them shelter. They slept on the porches of churches, under a wagon, or in the cleft of a rock. The wind blew, and it rained and it snowed. It was cold enough to make the stones split in two.

Everything was hard—the weather and men, and there was not a grain of consolation in Francis' heart. Nevertheless he refused to be sad, and he sang. And finally the sour-faced Morico sang with him.

In Poggio Bustone the pastor of the church drove them away from his door and said: "Go into a monastery—otherwise you'll end up as criminals!"

Morico wept.

"Let's hunt for a cave," said Francis. "A soul seeking consolation will always find it in a cave."

They climbed up over snow-covered rocks that rose into the sky behind the village to an altitude of at least two thousand feet. The mountains were a terrifying sight. When Francis and Morico were fifteen hundred feet high, they found a cave, a big dark hole like a dragon's mouth. It was full of hanging bats. They spent the night there, and the next morning Morico went to beg in the village.

As soon as he had left, Francis threw himself onto the ground and cried so loud that the cave echoed like a church: "Who are You, my God—and what am I? A little earthworm. Oh, Lord, let me love nothing but You!"

Like a dying dog he crawled around the cave, crushed under the weight of his doubts, his distrust of himself, his fears, and his grief. Suddenly he noticed that a bright light was shining on his hands. He looked up. The whole cave was filled with light, and he heard a melodious Voice that seemed to resound throughout the cave from within his own heart. It said: *"Be strong. All your sins are forgiven!"*

And while the Voice was speaking, he saw a beautiful supernatural vision: from all directions thousands and thousands of Brothers—whole armies of them—were running toward him, and they were all radiant with joy!

The vision vanished. Francis sprang up and staggered out of the cave. A violent snowstorm was raging. The wind rushed at him and whipped through his clothes, blew his cloak around, and drove his long hair into his face, but he shouted into the wind and the dark clouds and the snow: "Little Brothers! Dear little lambs! Come back from your trip. God has given us His blessing! Come—let's dance with joy!"

And as he called and shouted into the hurricane, the wind and the gusts of snow carried his words away like seed.

And from all four directions, just as they had set out, they came back. How happy they were to see one another again, and how fervently they thanked God! Then, in the shed at Rivo Torto, sitting around the fire, they told about their adventures.

They wept when Francis described his vision, saying: "I can hear and see them coming, those new little Brothers of ours! No, don't be afraid and discouraged by our small number and by the simplicity of my life and your life. They are coming from all countries. Their footsteps are echoing along the roads!"

When he said that, they all embraced one another.

Then it was the others' turn to tell their stories—and what stories!

Brother Bernard and Brother Giles had been driven away from the gates of a house in Florence, and then they had been welcomed by a man from whom they refused to accept any money. And he had been so impressed by their stay in his home that he had then and there given away a large part of his wealth to the poor. Brother Giles was without a cowl. He had given it to a man whose ears were nearly frozen, and consequently he almost lost his own ears.

Peter and Tall Philip had been stoned once, and each had tried to protect the other by getting in front of him.

Brother Sabatino's sleeves had been torn off, and he had been dragged along a street by his cowl, lying on his back like a sack of flour.

They had tried to force Brother Hat to drink wine and throw dice. When he refused, they had beaten him up and stripped him—but he still had his hat, which made the Brothers laugh heartily.

Unfortunately there was a great deal to tell about the evil that men did and very little about the good. The Brothers had suffered a lot, and often their courage had dwindled almost to the vanishing point. But now that Francis had told them about his vision, they faced the future with joy, and they felt that it was a pleasure to be the bridegrooms of Lady Poverty! Now let it rain cats and dogs. Let the snow fall until it was knee-deep. Let their stomachs feel so empty they would have to tighten their cords to make the emptiness smaller. All that would not make any difference as long as they had the holy fire of love within them.

They were so filled with high hopes that they began to sing together.

But now they went through hard times. Eight big fellows who were used to eating themselves full at least twice a day—and they had barely enough for two. Brother Hat weighed their food in his hands as if it were gold. Sometimes they had to go to other towns through rain and hail to earn something. And very often they came back without a mouthful to eat.

Brother Morico chewed on a piece of wood to ease his hunger.

One of those days, when their stomachs were aching and they had all gone out to hunt for work and food, a purse containing some gold coins was left in the shed. "Dirt and filth!" said Francis, and Peter had to take it away that same evening and throw it onto a garbage pile in town.

One day Sabatino came home and said that a farmer had given him a big loaf of raisin bread, but on the way back he had presented it to a poor old woman.

Something was in the air again. For several days Francis had been praying long and hard, and when the others noticed it, they left him alone. One evening when they had all come home and were sitting around the fire—the snow had begun to melt, and everything was dripping, the trees and the roof and their soaking clothes—Francis stood up and said: "Little Brothers, from now on we are going to call ourselves the Minor Brothers, because they are the smallest people of all. And I have something to tell you."

He was standing in the light of the fire. His eyes were bright, and his voice was as sweet as honey. "I am very glad that you believe firmly in our future, even though no one else has joined us yet. But they are coming—I can hear them coming! And since so many are going to come from all countries, and there will be little bridegrooms of Lady Poverty in all countries, we will also have to have a Rule, a fixed Rule—otherwise one Brother will do one thing and another will do something different, isn't that so, Brother Hat?"

"That's right," said Morico.

"Right!" agreed Peter.

"This Rule must be approved by Our dear Lord, but it is not so easy to meet Him, and you can't say to Him: 'Please come in here a moment and put Your signature here.' So there is someone on earth who does that in His place."

"The Pope in Rome," said Giles.

"Yes! Yes!" exclaimed the others.

"That's right," cried Francis. "We're going to Rome, to the Pope, as soon as the weather turns good! Tomorrow with God's help I'll write the Rule. And when the Pope approves it, then they will have to stop calling us heretics like those beggars from France."

"Fine! Fine!" they all shouted.

"So let's start a strict fast right now," said Francis. "Let's put our supper aside and pray hard that God may enlighten me for the Rule."

Everyone agreed, except Brother Hat. "No!" he said. "I haven't prepared my stomach for that. And I've already divided up the food. I haven't had a bite to eat all day. I'll fast all day tomorrow—but not now. The food is here, and it must be eaten."

"And supposing there wasn't any?" asked Francis.

"There is some."

"But supposing there wasn't any?"

"Then I wouldn't have been counting on it. But that's not the case," and he began to eat his share.

"Brother Hat, my friend," said Francis, "go ahead and eat. But eat our shares too. And then we who are also hungry will fast twice as much by watching you eat."

Brother Hat felt ashamed of himself, and he said: "No. I'll fast with you."

And he kneeled in front of Francis . . .

The next day two of them went to Assisi to borrow some parchment and an inkpot and a goose quill. An hour later Francis was kneeling and writing on a log under the cross which Giles had painted red. The others were praying in the woods or in the Chapel.

There happened to be a little sunlight from a pale yellow February sun which was not warm enough to dissolve the mist. Francis was writing the Rule of Poverty. He was singing it. Now and then, while writing, he sang out the sentences as he gazed lovingly up at the big red cross:

"Most Holy Trinity, we love You and we adore You —and we submit like children to Your Vicar, the Pope in Rome—We little Minor Brothers of Poverty have come together to live in obedience, in chastity, and without property, and to try to follow Jesus in His humility and His poverty. We will welcome among us as a friend anyone who has given his money away to the poor—And with God's blessing we Brothers will always go around dressed in clothes that we can patch with sackcloth and other patches—and there is to be no distinction among us—and we are going to work, because a man who does not work has not earned what he eats, and in return for our work we will accept whatever we need, except money, and we may beg—And we will be content with our food and with something to cover us, and we will find happiness in the company of common and despised people, the poor, the weak, the sick, the lepers and beggars—We will have no arguments or quarrels, either among ourselves or with others—and we will take nothing along with us, no wallet, nor bread sack, no money, no staff—and we will wish God's peace to everyone everywhere—and if someone strikes us in the face, we will turn the other cheek, and if someone takes our habit, we will give him our underwear too—And if they take everything away from us, we will not try to get it back. We will be Catholics and live and talk as Catholics. We will honor the high and low clergy, considering them our masters and revering their ministry in the Lord—Little Brothers of now and later, rid yourselves of all that is bad, and persevere in the good until the end. Fear and honor and praise and bless, thank and worship the Lord God Almighty in the Trinity and Unity, Father, Son, and Holy Ghost, Creator of all things! Amen!"

He was laughing and crying, alternately.

Then he jumped up, put his hand to his mouth, and shouted: "Come, little Brothers! Come and listen— it's finished!"

The seven others came running out as fast as they could from behind the trees. Francis stood under the Cross and they stood around him while in a singing voice he read their contract with Lady Poverty. As they listened, tears flowed down their faces. One Brother let them flow unheeded, but another lowered his head and held his hands before his face. Another kept wiping his cheeks. One was sobbing. And Brother Hat pulled his hat down over his face to hide the tears . . .

Francis' heart was so overflowing with joy that he had to go and take a long walk up in the hills. When he came back that evening, he met a knight riding on a horse. Francis raised his arm and called to the Brothers who were praying under the Cross: "Here is a new Brother! He heard me preaching in the valley of Rieti, and now he has come to us of his own free will, inspired by God. In the world he was a knight, but now I'm going to make him a knight in the Army of Christ! His name is Angelo. This is a good beginning for the spring!"

103

Before the buds on the trees opened, three more young men joined them: John, Barbaro, and another whose name was also Bernard. Three more—and the shed was already so small that they were packed in like sardines.

"Make room!" said Francis. "You must all make yourselves thinner."

But then each of them wanted to give the others a good place and went outdoors, even to sleep, so the rest could be more comfortable. That is the way they were now. Francis, however, wanted them all to be inside. And to avoid conflicts, he made a mark with a piece of chalk above each Brother's sleeping place: for himself a cross with the form of a T; for Peter the priest a chalice; for Giles a flower; for the cautious Bernard a dove; for Brother Hat a hat, of course; and for the others something that suited their name or their character.

"We are twelve now," Francis exclaimed joyfully. "Twelve apostles! Don't forget that our dear Lord is among us. Let's take care that none of us betrays Him."

Good weather was coming, and the sun was beginning to warm everything up. So when it had reached high in the sky and carpeted the earth with flowers, the Brothers, under the leadership of cautious Bernard, set out for Rome with their little roll of parchment, singing and praying as they went.

Looking as white and awesome as a thundercloud, the Pope was sitting on his throne, surrounded by purple-clad Cardinals. At his feet knelt Francis, barefooted, with dishevelled long hair, wearing a torn and dust-covered habit. He pressed his hands to his heart to keep it from beating too violently. Behind him kneeled the Brothers, perspiring, praying, and trembling. Soon they would hear whether their Rule was approved or rejected.

The suspense was terrific. The great Princes of the Church seemed like Egyptian idols, powerful, cold, and learned, wearing golden crucifixes and holding thick books. Tapers were burning in silver candlesticks, making mysterious reflections on the gold mosaics in the dome. And then the Pope! Who would not tremble if he had to obtain a favor from such a Pope? Although not yet fifty, and his sallow face seemed still younger, he was as forceful as the sea. He had a lofty conception of the Papacy, and he wanted above all to be an effective ruler. He did not know what fear was, and his plans were those of an empire builder. He was a Pope whose pronouncements were heard with awe, like thunderclaps. A Pope who, when he stamped his foot in Rome, made things shake across the water in England, who drove out heretics like wasps, who maintained order among his spiritual subjects with an iron hand, who organised crusades and never retreated before a war, who crowned emperors, and at whose feet princes and kings knelt with beating hearts.

Now, in the presence of this giant, this great ruler of men, Francis was waiting for a decision on his Rule of Poverty. Just one word—and his ideal would either lie in the gutter or shine with dazzling brilliance . . .

This was the third time that he had come before the Pope. The first time, upon meeting him by chance in a hall of the palace, Francis had greeted him in a friendly and joyful way. But the Pope had been curt and displeased. He had had enough of these groups of poor men. Like those who were known as the Poor Men of Lyon, they always ended up as heretics. How could such a ragged little fellow talk of renewing and rejuvenating the Church? A different type of man would be required for that task! So he had merely exclaimed: "Leave me alone!" And then he had forgotten all about the incident.

But the flame in Francis' heart continued to burn

fiercely. He managed to obtain an interview with a certain Cardinal, John of St. Paul. And the prelate, after listening to Francis, had struck the table and said: "You are the one man who can save the Church! I will use all my influence for you!" And he did so, enthusiastically, like someone who has discovered a new world. And so the beggars from Assisi were granted permission to go and read their Rule to the Pope.

The reaction of the Cardinals after they heard the Rule was definitely hostile: it would not work—human weakness could not stand it—and so on and so forth. They fired all the lightning bolts of their scholarship against the simple little Rule as if it were a heresy.

Then Cardinal John of St. Paul sprang up and said indignantly: "If you think that it is impossible for men to live the life of the Gospel, and if you prevent those who want to try it from doing so, then what on earth are we doing here? That is blasphemy against Jesus Christ Himself!"

The Cardinals were speechless in their humiliation, but the great Pope was so stirred by these burning words and so touched by Francis' little Rule that he said to him: "My son, go and pray that Jesus may make His will known to Us."

And then Francis and the Brothers had prayed and prayed, with all their heart and soul. And now here he was for the third time. Now the matter was going to be settled once and for all.

The night before, both the Pope and Francis had had strange dreams. The Pope dreamed that he saw the Church splitting apart, and when it was about to fall into pieces, a little bit of a man came up and put his shoulder against the building, and with one shove he set the Church back onto its foundations like new. And Francis had dreamt that he was standing in front of a big tree. He held his arms out toward the top, and as he stretched them out he grew taller and taller. And all of a sudden, of its own accord the top of the tree bent down toward him.

Francis fervently hoped that the tree represented the Pope, and the Pope was utterly convinced that the poor little fellow who had set the Church straight must be Francis.

Now the Pope was staring at him as if he wanted to read the innermost secrets of Francis' heart. The scholarly arguments over the impracticability of the Rule had begun again. But the Pope was not listening. And suddenly he asked Francis: "Are you perfectly sure that God and men will continue to help you?"

"Of course, Holy Father!" exclaimed Francis. "I'm going to tell you a little story—listen. Once upon a time there was a beautiful young girl, but she was poor and she lived in a desert. A rich king saw her and married her, and they had some handsome children, who resembled them both. Then the king went back to his country, and left the mother to bring up the children. When they grew up, she could no longer support them, and so that they should not suffer from hunger, she sent them to their father. He at once recognised them as his children, embraced them, and gave them the best place at his banquet table in the presence of strangers!"

"And what does this story mean?" asked the Pope, who had been listening to it as if it were a troubadour's song.

"That I am the poor woman whom God loved, that these little Brothers are my children, and that the King of Kings, who gives material goods even to sinners, will certainly not forsake us, His own children . . ."

The Pope was deeply moved. And to everyone's amazement he came down from his golden throne, went over to Francis, and embraced him! The tall tree bent down toward little Francis, and then in a strong voice, to impress his words on the minds of the Cardinals, the Pope declared: "Go now with God, and preach penance

107

to all men as God shall inspire you. And when the Lord shall have made you increase in numbers and in grace, come back to me with joy in your hearts. And then I will grant you more favors and safely endow you with still greater power. I give my blessing to you and to your children. Lead them well!"

And the great Pope blessed them, while the Cardinals exchanged cautious looks.

Later Francis and his Brothers received the tonsure, as a sign that they belonged to the clergy.

The large Church of St. Rufinus could not hold all the crowd. People were even standing outside on the porch. Francis was going to preach; the Pope had given him his approval, and so the Bishop had asked him to come and preach.

Everybody was there: the ecclesiastical and civil authorities, the nobility, the rich, the middle-classes, the workers, the beggars, and the peasants. Even Francis' mother and brother—and his father!—were there too. Although Peter Bernardone had aged as a result of what he had gone through with Francis, still he was glad now that it was his son whom the Pope had embraced, that it was his son whom the whole country was talking about, and that it was his son who was going to preach!

"He's the most famous man in Assisi," the father said to himself. "Oh, if only he dressed better—he, the son of the biggest cloth merchant in town!" He had come to hear Francis, even though he was a bit ashamed of himself. But he was also too proud to stay home.

During the first part of the Mass, Francis was praying on his knees before the altar. After the reading of the Gospel, he went to the pulpit. Everyone stared at him in silence. He certainly was a skinny little fellow! His chest hardly reached the edge of the pulpit. So this was the man who had made such a great impression on the

Pope! Yet there was something heavenly in his features.

And then he began to preach. His clear voice rang out under the vaulted arches. It was not a sermon. It was a poem! His theme was always the same, but the way he said it made it sound so wonderful, so full of beauty, so new and so fresh. It was like surging waves of love, explosions of godlike charity! "Love one another, and forget that you are rich or poor. For a man is worth no more than what he is worth in the eyes of God. I am a worm and not a man. And we must never want to be above others, but humble and submissive toward one another. God is in you—in the beggar just as in the rich. So you are brothers. But God is not in you when you are in mortal sin. Then darkness is in you, and your heart is a den of the devil. You can know only one treasure, and that is the Light of God in you. Pass it from one to another like torches in the night. By living virtuous lives, you are not only the children of Jesus Christ but also His brothers, His spouse and His Mother—"

Just then Francis caught sight of his own mother. She was gazing at him. And his father was standing beside her, leaning forward slightly. As he wondered how it was that they were there, a thrill of joy ran through him. Oh, to be able to preach before his own parents, especially before his mother! His words soared aloft like skyrockets.

"Oh, life is so simple! The essence of life is Love!"

How easy it seemed to live that way when one heard him speaking of it! Everyone caught some of the holy enthusiasm of his soul. Hearts softened. Souls opened up. And healing tears flowed softly. For a whole hour the church echoed to his love song. He seemed to be dancing in the pulpit.

And when he came down, the crowd, under the spell of his personality, surged forward like a wave, shouting, crying, sobbing, and stretching out their hands to touch him or to kiss his habit. All of a sudden it was as if there was a riot, as if the church were falling down. And above the noise Francis cried out in alarm: "Not me, but God!—not me!"

A bright moon was climbing up through the trees, from branch to branch. The Brothers were sleeping. Between the trees stood the dark figure of a man, who silently came nearer and nearer. You could hear his sighs and repressed sobs. He stopped, and from behind a tree he gazed at the Brothers, who were lying asleep in the moonshine as peacefully as plants. For a long while he stayed there, and from time to time he sighed: "Oh, to be able to rest like that . . . Peace!—Peace!— Peace! Lord, help me to confess . . . Give me enough courage!"

One of the Brothers stirred, got to his knees, and began to pray, bending over. Then the man retreated cautiously into the woods. The next day at sunset he was back.

The Brothers were sitting with their bare feet dangling in a dry ditch, talking over how they had spent the day. Giles was just telling about the trees he had cut down, when Brother Hat, who was always on the alert, whispered: "There's a spy over there!"

They looked where he pointed. The man's figure stood still, though he wanted to run away. As quick as a squirrel, Francis jumped out of the ditch and ran toward him. He spoke to him for a moment, and the Brothers saw the stranger suddenly kneel down and kiss Francis' feet. Francis called out: "Another little lamb! Come and see!"

They all ran up together. Who was it? Father Silvester, who had taken so much money for the bag of mortar. The strong and ruddy-complexioned man seemed to be broken and defeated. He was no longer recognisable. "I couldn't rest any more, my conscience hurt me so much," he sobbed. "Day and night remorse has been driving me mad. Among you I will be able to rest, do penance, and find peace! Thank you! Thank you for accepting me!"

Francis embraced him, and the Brothers sang a psalm. "But there's no more room in the hut," said Brother Hat with a touch of irritation. "We can't make ourselves any thinner."

"Then I'll take you on my lap, Brother Hat," said Francis. "Is that all right?"

Brother Hat became as silent as a fish.

Life went along in a simple and happy rhythm. One of the Brothers would cut wood, tie it into bundles, and go to town to exchange it for bread. Sturdy Morico usually did that job. Giles had become a basketmaker again. He was a fine fellow, and his hands were skilled at all kinds of work. He would go up and down the streets and roads shouting: "Do you want some good strong baskets?" And on the way he would give a little sermon to the people he met. Sabatino was working in the olive orchards. Tall Philip was helping with the harvest somewhere, and every day he brought back a bag of corn, which Brother Hat ground into flour and baked into little loaves of bread. Angelo went fishing and caught a lot of fish, which he then bartered from door to door for oil or bread. Thus they all had something to do now. And Francis too. He was working in the vineyards. They kept busy with visits and care for the lepers and the sick, besides their sermons. But when they had a few minutes to spare, they would creep into a grove or a cave to pour out their hearts in prayer and to talk with God.

They were always gay and cheerful in words and gestures, and whenever they met one another they exchanged a modest embrace. Francis was their model in

111

everything. He embodied their will to persevere. He was their father and their mother, to whom they opened their hearts, who looked right through them, and who guessed immediately what was wrong when they had something on their minds. He gave in to their little whims as far as he could without harm to their souls. They depended on him. When he was away, they were awkward and shy.

Their greatest delight was to listen to him speak about the soul's longing for Heaven or about the sufferings of Jesus. In such moments he relived what he was describing so intensely and so irresistibly, and he spoke so beautifully and so fervently, that they sobbed and wept as if they were watching it happen right before their eyes.

Winter came early. It rained without ceasing—more, ever more rain. The rivers overflowed their banks and flooded the valley. There was water in front of the Brothers' hut. When they wanted to go out, they had to pull up their habits and wade through a pool. The cross began to lean over, and they had to prop it up. But they were not able to stop up all the holes in the roof. They were cold and wet all the time. They had to stop work. Now they just sat around with their thirty-two bare feet next to one another. For three more Brothers had joined them: Barbaro, Juniper, and William. Now there was not an inch of space left in the hut. Life seemed to be nothing but rain and dire poverty . . .

It had been raining all morning, and the weather gave no sign of clearing up. The sky remained overcast. The Brothers were sitting around daydreaming. Their faces showed their dejection. For days they had been aching with hunger. Now it was noon, and still there was nothing to eat. One Brother after another came back with empty sacks.

Francis tried to cheer them up by singing. Bernard sang with him, to please him, but the others just sat silently, shivering from cold or praying. They kept their cowls over their heads on account of the holes in the roof.

Francis stopped singing and said: "Look, little Brothers. This really is true poverty now. And if you endure it with patience and joy, it will lead you straight to Heaven. So let us rejoice that God has given us this opportunity to suffer destitution. Because we must always have joy in our hearts. And sour faces don't get to Heaven!"

"Then let's fill our stomachs with something," sighed Peter, cheering up a bit. He was in charge of the household, its work and organisation, and so Francis called him "our mother."

"No," said Brother Hat. "First let's see if someone will bring back some food." And he pulled his hat farther down on his head and went out into the rain to see if anyone was coming along the road.

"He's always the same," said Sabatino. "He can never agree to anything."

"Don't say that when he is absent, Brother," said Francis. "Now you must tell him that you spoke against him."

Brother Hat came back into the hut. "Nothing but rain," he announced.

Sabatino went to him, took his hand, and said: "Brother Hat, I've just spoken badly about you. I said that you can never agree to anything. And I ask you to forgive me."

Brother Hat was flattered that Sabatino had humiliated himself before all the others. Brother Hat certainly was a strange fellow. But after all he was one of the Brothers too, in fact one of the first five. Now he said: "I forgive you from the bottom of my heart, Brother Sabatino." And after embracing him, he added:

113

"If anyone should ever say something against me, I would prefer that he should not ask me to forgive him, because I am not worthy to do so."

"That's fine of you!" cried Francis, and he put both arms around Brother Hat and hugged him.

This incident pleased them all and put them in a better mood. Then they prepared to eat what they had in their emergency supply of wild roots: one gray-looking root which tasted so bad and so disgustingly bitter that it nearly made them vomit. Still, they had to stick something into their empty stomachs. Brother Hat cut the wild root into slices. And after saying grace, they began to gnaw at it.

They looked at one another. But then they were desperately hungry and feeling cheerful, and it didn't taste too bad after all, so they all made jokes about their wonderful banquet. And Francis exclaimed: "Now the devils in hell are raging with anger!"

Soon after they finished eating, they heard voices singing in the distance. Two of the new Brothers, William and Juniper, were coming back from their begging trip, singing! Big Brother Juniper yelled: "We've got bread for at least twelve men!"

"And a quarter pound of pears!" shouted William.

And they went on with their song.

"Splendid!" exclaimed Francis. "Blessed is the Brother who has a light step, begs humbly, and comes home with good cheer!" He ran to them and gave each an affectionate kiss.

The bread disappeared quickly, but Francis did not take any. Instead he said: "A minute ago I took a vow to fast for three days, so that joy in poverty may always dwell among you."

Silent Brother Angelo said nothing, but he quietly hid his share. He wanted to fast too, but he did not say so, simply because he was too modest.

After the meal the Brothers went off. Francis, Silvester, and Peter remained in the hut, as if they were expecting someone. And suddenly, without their having heard a sound, they saw standing in the doorway a poor woman holding one child in her arm and another by the hand.

"Please give me something," she said. "My children haven't had a bite to eat since yesterday."

"I'm sorry, my poor woman. You know we would gladly give you something," said Peter. "But this time we can't help you. We haven't anything ourselves. Isn't that so, Father?"

"No," said Francis. "We do have something. We have a tin chalice, a missal, and two copper candlesticks. Go get them, Silvester, and give them to her."

"But then there won't be any more Mass!" exclaimed Peter in dismay.

"Then we'll go to Mass in Assisi," said Francis. "But it is not right that there should be people who are poorer than we are. Our only boast is that we are the poorest of the poor!"

And Silvester meekly went and fetched the chalice, the missal, and the copper candlesticks.

That evening when the others came back, a light rain began to fall. Through the roof the raindrops pattered down like rosary beads onto their cowls, their bare feet, and into the smoking little fire of wet wood. At times the smoke filled the hut so densely that it was better to go and stand outdoors in the rain. Then Brother Juniper would wave his cloak and drive the smoke out.

Francis gave them a beautiful meditation on the poverty of the Mother of Christ, and they recited and sang some psalms. Then they all simply reclined on their backs—that was all they had to do in order to go to bed.

The acrid smoke of the little fire hung motionless in the hut. Through the holes in the roof the drops thudded dully on their habits. Night crept slowly over the world. Suddenly there was a piercing scream. They all awoke with a start. It was gentle Brother Angelo, writhing with pain.

One of them lit a lamp. Francis was already holding Angelo in his arms like a little lamb. "What's the matter, little Brother? Come on, tell me what it is."

"I can't, Father. I don't dare tell it."

"You must. I want you to."

"I've fasted too much, Father. I wanted to imitate you, and I can't stand it . . ."

"So you didn't eat anything today?"

"No, Father. I hid my share. Here it is—" and he pointed under the straw, where he had hidden it.

"Eat!" said Francis. "Eat it right now! And I'm going to eat with you—even though I've just begun a fast—so as to do away with your scruples!"

And they ate together. Each had half a slice of bread and half a small pear, with some water that had just dropped from the sky.

"Bring the lamp nearer. Otherwise we can't find our mouths," said Francis. Giles held the earthen lamp close to their faces. "Wasn't that good?" asked Francis.

Angelo nodded.

"Now roll up your sleeves and show us your knees, Brother Angelo, because when I held you in my arms I felt something made of iron. Let's see."

They came near, and all of them seemed frightened —all except Brother Hat. As Angelo was slow in obeying, Francis himself raised his sleeves and habit. In the crook of his elbows and knees Angelo had fastened heavy iron bands that cut into his flesh so sharply that at the slightest movement he had to moan from pain. Francis exclaimed heatedly: "Are there any others doing this? Then let them come here and take off such things at once!"

All of them stepped forward—all except Brother Hat.

"How about you, Brother Hat?"

"I never do such things—look!"

116

And he pushed back his sleeves and showed his long hairy arms. "I do only what you say."

The others stood there, looking sheepish, shuffling, and helping one another get loose from their instruments of self-torture. "This is disgraceful!" cried Francis. "Everyone must fast and do penance according to his own capacity and strength. It's just as bad to take and to do too little as too much. God wants mercy and not a victim. And from now on there's going to be no more fasting or penance without my knowing it."

When they had all fallen asleep again, Francis was still praying on his knees.

Toward Candlemas, when the weather was becoming milder, the little old priest of St. Damian died. He was found lying dead beside his goat. All the Brothers went to his funeral. "He was our godfather," said Francis. "We must pray a great deal for him."

One morning Francis came dancing joyfully along with a small primrose in his hand. "Rejoice, little Brothers!" he cried. "Spring is coming! The sun's kisses have made this tiny golden flower come out of the earth. Let's praise the Lord for the sun and for the primroses!"

But what was happening in the hut? All the Brothers were standing outside, peering in. They seemed embarrassed. And who was making all that noise in there?

Francis came running, while Bernard and two others went to meet him, complaining loudly: "A donkey driver has thrown us out, and he won't leave!"

Francis went into the hut. A rowdy muleteer was squatting there drinking wine, and his lean donkey was shivering on its aged legs. Before Francis could say a word, the fellow shouted at him: "Another loafer! Go where you belong! I'm staying here with my donkey!"

So the sixteen of them were to be driven out of their home by this scoundrel! Juniper was tempted to beat the fellow up—but then they were trying to live their religion. "Come, little Brothers," said Francis. "God did not call us to be stable boys. Let's go back to Our Lady of the Angels." And thus, driven away by a donkey, they left Rivo Torto, where life had been so beautiful and so hard . . .

"Go and pray," said Francis, "while I ask the Benedictine Fathers whether we can live there."

The Abbot of the Benedictine monastery on Mount Subasio was pleased with Francis' request, and said to him: "The Portiuncula is yours!"

"That is not what we want," replied Francis. "We do not want to own any property. So let us rent it in return for our work."

"But I don't want anything for it," said the Abbot.

Francis would not change his offer. And after a long discussion the Abbot declared: "All right then, since you insist, bring me each year a basketful of fish from the river."

"I accept," said Francis.

"But also," added the Abbot, "on condition that that place shall ever remain the center from which your Order will spread."

"I agree to that too," said Francis, and they shook hands as cordially as two peasants making a deal in the market.

On the way back Francis said enthusiastically to Bernard: "We'll build little huts made of earth and wood —one hut for each Brother to pray and sleep in! Oh, it will be beautiful there in the shade of the little chapel! Really, God is much too good to us! And we'll put up a hedge, and then no lay person can ever come and disturb us. Everything we say inside that hedge must be about God or our souls. It will be beautiful!"

The Brothers felt like dancing in a circle when they heard the good news. "Let's get right to work!" shouted Giles. And they began.

They broke off branches and stamped out clay. Each one could locate his hut wherever he wanted within the space to be inclosed by the hedge. One wanted his near the church, another under the trees, another facing east, another behind the hazelnut bushes. They all helped one another, shouting gaily. They worked all through the night, with the moon as a lamp. To put up such plain little huts with clay did not require much time, especially when Giles, that jack-of-all-trades, lent a hand.

That morning the sun rose over their little huts. "Tomorrow the hedge," exclaimed Francis. "And I want the good monks to be paid their fish in advance!"

They all went down to the river—all except Brother Hat. "I can't stand fish," he said. "They're too slippery."

He always had some excuse. But when a child acts a bit peevish, his father does not love him any less—on the contrary. And that's the way Francis felt about Brother Hat, though he worried about him, and sometimes he would say with a sigh: "If only that little lamb doesn't go astray . . ."

He had often overlooked Brother Hat's faults, and now he did so again. Brother Hat was allowed to stay home and measure how many stakes would be needed for the hedge. Brother Hat proceeded to pace out a big square, taking long steps. At every other step there would have to be a stake, so he would stop and make a small hole with his heel.

Meanwhile the others were fishing in the swift river, which was full of pebbles. Some of them waded in, with water up to their knees. They fished with sacks and little baskets. And they caught some perch, smelt, and pikes —a whole big basketful of sparkling, floundering fish that was a pleasure to look at! The two youngest Brothers went off with the basket, while the others set to beg. And the two Brothers came back with a large jug of oil which they had been given as a receipt.

Now that the huts were built, and tomorrow the hedge would be up, and they had paid their rent and received such a fine receipt, they had a feeling they had never known before: they had a home! "Let's celebrate!" they cried. So Francis blessed each hut, and then they had a feast. They dunked their begged bread into the good clear oil, which they then licked off their fingers. And as at every feast, everybody had to sing a song. Giles sang the "Laudate," Brother Hat the "Miserere," Sabatino a hymn to Mary, and so on.

And Francis sang a song in praise of Lady Poverty. And out of reverence, he sang it standing up.

A year later there were over forty huts. The midsummer sun was boiling hot, and the mountain stood out in blue outline in the bright light. Heat waves shimmered over the roads and houses. But at the Portiuncula, under the ancient oak trees and their thick foliage, it was cool and pleasant.

Everything was as peaceful as a scene in the Gospels. Francis was in the little Chapel, praying. And Brother Jack was behind him. Whenever Francis bent over, Jack bent over too. When Francis sighed, Jack sighed also. When Francis coughed, Jack coughed after him. That was simply Jack's way of following Francis.

One day Francis had gone into a church somewhere up in the mountains, and he had found it so dirty and neglected that he immediately ran out, made a broom from some branches, and began to sweep the place clean. While he was doing so, a deformed peasant came in to say his beads. It was Jack, and he saw what Francis was doing. But before he realised that it was Francis, whom he had once heard preach, he was filled with awe and wanted to help him. So he went right out and made himself a broom. And then he helped Francis sweep out the church. And when he asked Francis whether he could join him, Francis consented. So Jack immediately drove his oxen and wagon home, put on his Sunday clothes, said goodbye to his brothers and sisters, and left with Francis.

Thereafter he imitated Francis in everything he did—except speaking. At first the others laughed a lot about it. But Jack, like the simple dove that he was, merely said: "Francis is a saint. So if I imitate him, the devil will have no hold on me."

When Francis had to go away for a while, then Jack would not say a word or make a move. He just sat praying in a corner like a timid mouse . . .

Of the other Brothers, Sabatino and Rufino were walking through the woods, saying some prayers together. Rufino came from the aristocratic Scifi family. He was a profoundly devout man, but when he had to go out and preach, he was so scared he got gooseflesh!

Morico and Silvester, with some others, were building four huts. Brother Masseo, who had joined them in the spring of the past year, was talking to a group of young Brothers about the Holy Spirit. He had the dignity of a king. And he spoke with such fervor and deep understanding that some of the Brothers were kneeling as they listened to him, as if they were rapt in an ecstasy. Tall Philip and Barbaro were cutting wood, and Bernard Vigili was carving wooden cups.

Brother Leo, whom Francis called "Little Lamb of God" because he was so holy and humble and perfect, was in his hut, writing. He was Francis' secretary and confessor. People called him "the Angel." Occasionally when he looked up from his parchment, his blue eyes seemed to be gazing at some vision of unseen beauty.

Brother Hat was mending habits with a thick needle. Before each stroke he stuck the needle into his long hair under his hat, to make it pass more easily through the tough material. Francis was having a hard time getting him to have his hair cut in a tonsure like the others.

One of the Brothers was praying behind a bush, others were doing the same in their little huts. The whole atmosphere was filled with peace, bright sunlight, and a spirit of friendly good will. Birds were singing in the trees, and rabbits were running around quite freely and boldly among the huts and around the Brother's bare feet.

But there was also a Brother who was sick, very sick. He was a youth named John, and he was lying, pale and panting, on his straw bed. Even outside the hut they could hear his breathing. By his side was Juniper, that big fellow with an unkempt beard, deep-sunken eyes, and broad heavy hands. He was watching over John and praying with his eyes closed. From time to time he opened them and gazed compassionately at the sick boy. "Do you want to drink something?" asked Juniper.

"No," panted John, "but I certainly would like to have a boiled pig's foot—it would cure me."

"A boiled pig's foot?"

"Yes."

Juniper frowned, and his forehead became creased with furrows as he tried to think. Suddenly he said: "Wait. I'll get you one!"

Just like that, as though all he had to do was to pick one up.

He went right to Bernard Vigili. "Give me a sharp knife," he said.

He got a sharp knife—yes, it was sharp, for he tested it with his big thumb—and off he went. He saw Francis praying in the Chapel with upraised arms. Jack was doing likewise. Juniper wanted to get his permission, but wouldn't it be a sin to interrupt him when he was deep in prayer, just for a mere pig's foot? He strode on, taking long steps, like a farmer sowing, holding the brightly polished knife in front of him. As he went out of the woods, the hot sun burned down on his bare head. He made his way over rocks and bushes. He knew exactly where he was going.

He laughed as he caught sight of the swine and heard the swineherd playing his flute in the hollow tree where he usually sat.

Juniper went to the fattest pig, which happened to be sleeping. And as the swineherd began a new tune, Juniper suddenly threw his heavy body onto the pig, skillfully seized a hind leg, and then—the knife cut through the leg, the pig squealed, the blood spurted—and Juniper had his pig's foot!

He ran off, laughing. But the swineherd ran after him, cursing long and loud. And all the peace and quiet of the Portiuncula was suddenly destroyed. The Brothers had to hold back the swineherd, otherwise he would have beaten Juniper. He roared and cursed and shouted: "You thief! You jailbird!"

Francis sprang up. So did Jack. "Leave this man alone," exclaimed Francis, and he asked what was the matter.

The peasant was so angry he couldn't say a word. So Juniper spoke for him, making broad gestures with his blood-covered hands: "Well, that poor lamb John, who is so sick, wanted to have a boiled pig's foot to cure him. You can't pluck pig's feet from trees—you find them on pigs. We haven't any money to go and buy one in Assisi. So I took one from a pig. Now what is a pig's foot compared to one of the Brothers' health? If the pig knew what we need his foot for, he would gladly give his three other feet too."

"Why didn't you first come and see me about it?" asked Francis.

"Because you were praying so hard," Juniper replied.

When the swine-keeper heard that, his anger subsided.

"Listen," he said, "now that I know how it happened, I have nothing more to say. I guess I should have done something for you Brothers long ago, because at times

I forget about Our Lord, you see. So I want to do something for Him, and I'm giving you the whole pig!"

Brother Juniper danced with joy. He went to kill the pig with the swineherd. And he was singing when he returned, carrying it on his back.

"Half of it is for the sick!" exclaimed Francis.

While the others carved the pig, Juniper cooked the foot over a little fire of twigs and brought it on a cabbage leaf to John, who ate it with relish.

Francis laughed happily and said: "If only I had a whole forest of such Junipers!"

And he looked Brother Hat straight in the eyes.

Francis had gone out with Brother Masseo to preach and to found some small hermitages in which three or four Brothers would live and form little nests of the real Gospel life. They had been on the road for three days. Masseo was walking ahead, while Francis followed behind, rapt in prayer. They came to a crossroad where people and wagons were constantly passing by, because it was vintage time. One road led to Siena, another to Arezzo, and a third to Florence.

Masseo asked: "Father, which road shall we take?"

"Which road? Why, the one that Our Lord will indicate to us!"

"But how shall we know which it is, Father?"

"This way: in the name of holy obedience I command you to go and stand in the middle of the crossroad and then to spin around on the same place as fast as you can, like a child's top, and to keep on spinning around until I say stop."

Brother Masseo gazed at Francis in amazement, yet he did not hesitate to obey. He began to spin around. The handsome fellow with the dignity of a king began to spin around like a lunatic, holding his arms out, first on one leg, then on the other.

While the people passing by laughed and the women

giggled, Francis, with his eyes closed, was praying to know the will of God. Suddenly he shouted: "Stop!"

"Which way are you facing?" asked Francis.

"Toward Siena," panted Masseo, who was dizzy.

"So we're going to Siena. It's the will of God."

Rufino came out of one of the caves on Mount Subasio. He had been there a whole week. And he seemed to be suffused with the light of the Holy Spirit. When Francis noticed that he was so filled with divine inspiration, he said to him: "Brother, tomorrow I have to preach at the ten o'clock Mass at St. Nicholas Church. But since I see that you are so inspired with the love of God, you will preach in my place."

"Oh, Father, please don't—you know I can't preach!" Sweat was running down his face.

"Just trust in God, and you'll be all right," said Francis.

Rufino was unable to sleep all night, for he was trembling like a reed. The next morning he tearfully begged to be dispensed from the sermon. But Francis was displeased by his lack of confidence, and he said: "I command you to go. I even command you, in the name of holy obedience, to go without your habit, wearing only your breeches, as a penalty for your lack of trust in Our Lord!"

Rufino turned white and then red. The others thought the penalty was too severe, but they said nothing. Rufino took off his habit and left, clad only in his breeches. He felt ashamed and humiliated, but he went.

When they saw him, the people of Assisi acted as if they were possessed. Gangs of urchins walked along with him, making fun of him, while grownups jeered and hooted. The Mass had begun when Rufino came in. The pastor was so astounded that he almost fell over backward. "Francis wants it this way," said Rufino humbly as he climbed into the pulpit.

125

When the congregation saw his lean hairy chest above the pulpit railing, they simply did not know what to think. And then the sermon! He tried to say something about hypocrisy, but the words stuck in his throat. He stuttered, and repeated the same words four times. Then he paused too long and could not get out another word. His whole body was covered with perspiration. The people felt ashamed for him, and they did not dare to look at him . . .

Rufino had hardly left the Portiuncula when Francis realised his mistake. "Oh, how wrong of me to let people ridicule such a holy man just because he has an inborn defect!" he said to himself, adding: "You despicable creature, you worm, you have enough trouble with yourself, aren't you ashamed to humiliate someone that way? Go and punish yourself by taking your own medicine!"

He got up, quickly took off his habit, and ran off. "Aha! Another lunatic!" shouted the people of Assisi. "The whole bunch has gone crazy! Soon they'll be running around without breeches. They should be locked up!"

Francis was glad to undergo this humiliation. He entered the church with a crowd following him, ran right up into the pulpit, and ordered Rufino to step down. Now the people were even more astonished—but not for long. Francis explained why he was there. He humiliated himself before everyone. And then he gave a sermon on the nakedness and poverty of Christ that was so beautiful, so profound, and so charged with emotion that it was the most moving sermon that anyone had ever heard him give. And after the Mass was over, they fought to be able to touch him as he left.

Then Francis became somewhat sick. So Juniper caught a blackbird for him, and fried it perfectly in olive oil. Francis took such pleasure in this delicious

126

blackbird meat and ate it with such relish that he licked his thumbs and fingers—but not all of them. When he reached the eighth finger, he cried: "Stop!"

His conscience began to bother him. And he said to himself: "You glutton! You luxury lover! I, Francis, am always preaching to people that they ought to live a life of penance and poverty. I drove Brother Fly out of the Order because he liked good food more than work. I refused to accept another man because he gave his wealth to his family rather than to the poor. And meanwhile I secretly eat delicious bird meat! Brother Ass, you're going to pay dearly for this!"

He called Jack and told him that they were going to Assisi and that he should bring along a rope. When they reached the city gate, Francis made a halter with the rope and put it around his neck and then told Jack what he was to say and do. "All right," said Jack. Without questioning, he always did exactly whatever Francis said—and gladly too—because Francis was a saint.

So they went through the streets of the town. Jack was holding the rope that was tied around Francis' neck. Francis followed him meekly. And Jack shouted as loudly as he could: "Look, everybody! Here is the man who comes and tells you to fast and do penance, while in secret, just because of a little stomach-ache, he eats delicate bird meat! He is a glutton—a lover of good food—a hypocrite!"

And thus they went through the town, with a mob following them.

Francis' message spread over the country like a new dawn. Whereas formerly he had had to run after the peasants, even when they were working in the fields, now they left their plows in order to come and hear him. Wherever he preached, the churches were packed. Something was happening in the hearts of the people.

His words and his appearance were enkindling faith and love in them. Those who heard him began to long for simplicity and kindness. They began to repent, to forgive one another, and to become reconciled.

The number of men who wanted to become Brothers grew so great that Francis was kept busy founding little hermitages of the Gospel life here and there in the woods and mountains. People who had formerly ridiculed and insulted him now became his defenders. For instance, Marietta's father, who had given him the spoiled red cabbage on his first begging trip, was now willing to do anything for Francis. He had become devout and calm, and when he was carving his crucifixes, he tried to give them that expression of intense love and suffering which Francis often described. Through the power of his example, men and women who had been bitter, indifferent, and mean, became gentle and Christian in their conduct.

Among the many who eagerly drank in his words was a lovely blonde girl named Clare Scifi who had given him the raisins and cake when he first went begging. He noticed how she listened without blinking her eyes and how at times a glow of sweet religious emotion suffused her pale aristocratic features. And stirred by the heavenly beauty that animated her, he directed his words toward her like the light of a lantern.

"She's an angel," he thought, "an angel among human beings." And he said to Masseo: "There is an angel living in Assisi. Let's pray that this beautiful soul may not be devoured by the world."

One day Francis was coming back from Perugia with Brother Leo. They had been on a preaching tour. Snow lay deep on the ground, and still more snow was falling as they struggled along, Leo leading the way. They had tied sacks around their feet. Their cowls were pulled down tight over their heads, and they kept their hands in their sleeves. The wind was blowing through their habits. But they fought their way ahead, praying and shivering.

Suddenly Francis shouted: "Little Lamb of God, even if all the Minor Brothers gave the finest examples of holiness and virtue, and healed cripples and could make the blind see, drive out devils, and even bring the dead back to life—remember and note that perfect joy does not lie therein!"

Brother Leo did not answer, but kept on walking.

A moment later Francis exclaimed again: "Even if we knew all there is to know and could predict the future and read the secrets of men's consciences and hearts, note that neither is that perfect joy."

Again Brother Leo did not reply as he walked on. Out of respect for Francis, he did not want to disturb him in his meditation.

A little farther on, Francis cried out: "Even if a Minor Brother could speak the language of the angels, describe the course of the stars, know the qualities of plants and the strength of birds and men and fish and every creature on earth, note that neither in this is perfect joy."

Brother Leo leaned still more into the wind, which was blowing gusts of snow into his face. He was listening more and more intently, because he knew that something wonderful was coming.

A moment later Francis again shouted: "Little Lamb of God named after the lion, even if the Minor Brothers could preach so well that they succeeded in converting all the heathen to the religion of Christ, note that perfect joy does not lie in that."

Meditating thus, they walked another mile through the snow. But finally Brother Leo could no longer restrain his holy curiosity. And he asked what perfect joy really was.

Then Francis cried out with great joy, like an organ pouring forth music from all its stops: "When we arrive at the Portiuncula in a little while, wet to the skin by the snow and freezing with cold, plastered with mud and tortured by a gnawing hunger, and then, when we knock at the door and the Brother Porter asks: 'Who are you?' and we answer: 'Two of your Brothers,' and he says: 'You are lying. You are two tramps who go around deceiving the people and robbing the poor! Get out of here!', and he leaves us standing outside in the cold and the snow until late at night, and we humbly and meekly realise how well he knows us, and we knock again, and he angrily strikes us down and beats us with a club, and we endure it all willingly, without complaining and lamenting, out of love for our Lord Jesus Christ —O Little Brother Lamb, note that that is perfect joy! For above all the gifts of the Holy Spirit which Christ gives to His friends is the grace of conquering oneself and of suffering pain, injustice, and mistreatment willingly, for love of Christ! We cannot take pride in any of the other gifts, because God grants them to us. Why should we glory in something that is not ours? But we can glory in the tribulations of the Cross, because we take it upon ourselves of our own free will, and it is ours. I want to glory in nothing but the Cross of our Lord Jesus Christ!"

Deeply moved, inspired, and inflamed by the beauty and power of Francis' soul, Brother Leo embraced him, weeping with joy.

A Holy Love Song

The half-moon was shining right above Francis' hut. Brother Jack saw it just as he was going to call Francis. For Brother Jack, it was a good omen and a blessing, something like the Star of Bethlehem. When he saw that Francis was kneeling, he kneeled too, and then he said: "Father, I've come to tell you that it is six o'clock, as you asked me to."

Francis did not answer. He raised his arms and crossed them on his chest, as if he were taking something out of the air and hiding it in his heart. Brother Jack did likewise. Francis then stood up and greeted him, and Jack returned his greeting in exactly the same way.

Going through the little gate, Francis walked into the woods until he came to a spot where a small spring bubbled out of the ground. There he stopped. It was so quiet in the dim light that the only sound was the chattering of the brook. Spring was in the air. Francis looked around, but he saw no one. He had become very thin from his fasting and penances. His features showed that he had been sharing the sufferings of Christ in His fast. Still, now and then a flash of joy flickered in his eyes.

He bent down and took up some water in his cupped hands, and he said to the water: "Clear Sister Water, chaste and innocent creature, how beautiful and how good God has made you, for the welfare of men, for their holy baptism and for their thirst. O Lord, keep the young Lady Clare thus in all her clarity of soul, for the welfare of mankind!"

In his mind he saw the young Lady Clare again as he had so often seen her in church or when he was begging or singing or preaching on the market place, but especially as he had seen her during the lenten sermons that he was giving in St. Rufino's Church this Lent. He had almost been preaching for her alone. He had silently called to her with his whole soul to give herself to God. And he had seen in her flashing eyes that she understood and was detaching herself from the world.

She was an angel! How often he had wished to talk with her! But out of chastity he had mastered this longing. Then this noon, as he was coming from a visit to a sick person, her aunt had spoken to him and asked him whether Lady Clare might have a talk with him without her family knowing about it. And he had chosen this spring for the meeting . . .

The water had run out of his hands. "Sister Water! Brother Tree!" he exclaimed. "Rejoice with me! An angel is coming!" As he let the drops roll off his fingers, he heard some twigs crack, and he quickly wiped his wet hands on his habit. There she was, with her aunt.

The aunt stopped, and Clare came forward alone. She was wearing a long cloak over a green silk dress. Francis took a step toward her and said respectfully: "God's peace be with you."

There she stood, like a dream—a dream of youth and beauty. She was a slight girl of eighteen. And with her pale face, her big blue eyes, her straight nose and small red mouth and light golden hair, she seemed like a spring morning in human form. As they looked at each other, they were so moved that the world around them vanished like mist. They saw God in each other—God who had brought them together as someone joins his hands in prayer.

"Sister," he said, motioning her to come nearer.

She was honored. He whom she admired so much had called her 'Sister.' She took his outstretched moist hand and sighed: "Brother . . ."

Hand in hand they stood silently by the spring. They had had so much to say to each other, but now that they were together, they were too filled with joy to think of it.

"I would like to share your life of poverty for the love of Jesus," she whispered.

"God be praised!" he exclaimed with calm and holy rejoicing. "God be praised for the first Sister of Poverty!"

"Bless me, Brother," she asked.

She bowed her head and kneeled down. Her hair fell over her cheeks as with her hands crossed on her breast she awaited his blessing. But he too was kneeling before her. Then with a hand that trembled, he slowly made a great Sign of the Cross over her. Raising her up, he said: "Come back tomorrow, Sister."

"I will come, Brother," she replied, and walked silently away over the thick moss.

He stood there watching her go, and when he was again alone in the forest, he covered his face with his hands.

The secret meetings of Clare and Francis were known to no one but the Brothers and her aunt, who always accompanied her. Each time Francis and Clare spoke about the same things in different words. The theme of their conversations was: Jesus—Heaven—Poverty. He listened to her, and she listened to him.

He told her about his life, and she told him that ever since her childhood she had been waiting for a miracle that would transform her ordinary life into a burning flame and light. And now this miracle had been wrought by him, by his poverty and his preaching . . . They decided that she would become a Sister of the Order on the night of Palm Sunday. But the figure of her father loomed over their mystic joy like a shadow, for he was capable of murdering all the Minor Brothers if they took his daughter away from him.

Francis worried greatly about this, but he would not give Clare up for a thousand such fathers. Frail little Francis' only weapon was prayer.

One evening he called the Brothers together and explained the situation to them. "Brothers, help me now with your prayers!" he said. "Next week Jesus will begin His Passion. Let us make His suffering a bit lighter by placing our first Sister on His Heart like balsam. And now let us thank God in advance!"

He fell on his knees, and they all knelt too. The moon broke through the clouds and shed its light among the trees and over the men lying prostrate with their heads on the ground. But one of them was standing up. He wore a hat. He went into his hut, saying to himself out loud: "No—no women here," and he shut the door.

The whole world seemed to Clare as if it were absorbed into eternity. Still clad in her white silk dress, she was kneeling in her dark room. She was not praying. She could do nothing but yearn and listen. She listened to the night outside, but there was not a sound to be heard. Then she tiptoed to the small window. She had never before seen so many stars. "God!" she murmured, and lowered her head, and in an ecstasy of happiness, filled with a joyful longing for God, she looked up and beyond the stars . . .

After a long interval the half-moon rose above the valley. She tried to make out the woods in the soft darkness, but she could see nothing. Then a tiny light began to move way down there—it was in the forest! Her heart began to beat violently. She listened: someone was tapping very lightly on the door. She felt the draft as the door opened. Making her way toward it, she clasped the outstretched hand of her aunt, who was trying to find her in the dark. Her aunt's hand was trembling.

They went down the stone stairs and reached the garden, where the aunt put a cloak around Clare's shoulders and led her far across the lawn to a little gate that had not been used for years. In the dim starlight some wood and mossy stones and a broken statue could be seen lying among the weeds and ivy. Carefully yet hurriedly the aunt cleared a way for them.

"If only the gate opens!" whispered Clare. "Otherwise I'll climb over the wall!" She felt a sudden surge of anxiety, as though everyone in her home and everyone in Assisi were coming after her to hold her back.

"Don't worry," said the aunt proudly. "It was unbolted yesterday." She pushed some more stones away with her foot, and then with one quick effort pulled the gate open. The valley lay at their feet in the weak moonlight. "Come!" said the aunt.

They went down a narrow path strewn with large rocks until they reached the level ground and followed a small stream. Then a light appeared in the distance—and another—and another, until there were about ten.

"The Brothers!" exclaimed Clare.

As they came nearer, she recognised the little man in their midst: Francis! She stopped and bowed her head. "God be praised that you have come," he said in his melodious voice, and in silence, surrounded by the Brothers with their torches, they went through the woods together to the Portiuncula.

They knelt before the altar and with intense emotion gazed up at the dark image of the Madonna. Then Francis stood in front of Clare, with a habit on his arm. Some of the Brothers were standing around her, holding torches and looking like bronze statues, while others were outside, because the little Chapel was much too small to hold them all. And in the sacred silence Francis said: "Sister, here is the heavenly garment of Poverty."

"Thank you," said Clare.

Her aunt helped her to take off her jewels and her white silk gown. Then Francis handed her the habit, a coarse brown habit with patches here and there, and a thick cord to go around the waist.

"Your shoes, Sister," he said.

She took off her red silk slippers and her white stockings, and put her white feet into wooden sandals.

"And—" He did not utter the word. But a Brother gave him the shears.

She looked at him with keen joy, because he was about to take so much from her. For the more hair he cut off, the greater would be her merit. She shook her hair loose, and it fell down over her shoulders and her back like a cloak of gold. Then she leaned forward.

His long, thin, sunburned hand grasped her beautiful blonde hair. He opened the shears—and made three or four quick cuts. As he released his grasp, the hair fell to the ground in disorder beside her silk gown, her silver belt, her pearl headdress, her jewels, and her slippers, which lay there like a mass of faded flowers.

Then he gave her his blessing. "Sister," he said, "now you are the Bride of the King of Light!"

She looked at him gratefully, with tears rolling down her cheeks, and the Brothers began to sing: "With palm branches the children of Israel went forth to meet Him . . ." Their voices echoed through the forest.

"Come, Sister," said Francis, and they went out through the chanting friars into the woods, accompanied by two Brothers with torches. They went to hide their precious treasure from the anger of her father in the Convent of St. Paul, which was located in the marshes.

The light of the moon showed them the way.

A Crown of Roses and Thorns

The great news was spreading everywhere: the Moors had been driven out of Europe and had fled across the sea, back to their forests and deserts—"those dirty heathens who worship Mahomet and desecrate the Holy Sepulcher of Our Lord!"

"All right," said Francis, "but Our Lord came and died for all of us, for those who have dark skins too! Who is going to tell it to them? Who is going to bring them a little Light?"

He constantly thought about the poor Moors. And in prayer he begged: "Let me go to them, O Lord—if I am worthy . . ."

Yes, he was willing to let them beat him to death, nail him to a door, or saw his body in two—oh, if only they would! For was there any greater happiness than to be able to shed one's blood for their conversion?

Finally nothing could hold him back, and he set out for Rome to ask for the Pope's permission to preach to the heathen.

He obtained the Pope's consent. The Holy Father was happy over the growth and splendid perseverance of the Friars Minor and over the foundation of the Poor Sisters.

For Clare had not remained alone for long. Her young sister Agnes had also run away from home and let Francis cut off her hair too. Soon some other young women had joined them. And Francis obtained permission of the Benedictine Fathers for the Sisters to lead their life of poverty in the little house attached to St.

Damian's Church. And the Scifi parents, who in their first fury had attempted to take Agnes back by force, were now completely resigned to the situation. As Clare's father put it: "Only people with noble blood can act with such will power."

Meanwhile Francis stayed in Rome and filled the churches by his beautiful sermons. People were running after him all the time, trying to get him to visit them. "It will be a blessing and an honor for us," they said. But he visited none of them. He stayed in the monastery of the Order of the Cross.

Among those who invited him was a young woman with two children, whose name was Lady Jacopa Frangipani. "Go and visit her," said the Prior of the monastery. "She lives like a saint." So Francis went.

Why to that particular family and not to another? That was Providence.

She was a handsome and stately woman of twenty-five, with big black eyes. She did not receive him in one of the rich halls of her palace. She took him to the room in which she lived. It was like a monk's cell: white stone walls, a white wooden table, two wooden chairs, and a sack filled with straw on a board. On the walls there was nothing but a crucifix.

She offered him some bread and water.

He clasped his hands and exclaimed joyfully: "This is it! This is it!"

"Now you too must taste the little cakes I have baked for my children!"

She brought him a tray with yellow cakes made of honey, ground almonds, and wheat flour. "Marvelous! Perfect!" cried Francis. "I'll never forget this taste!"

He took three more, then a fourth, then more and more. He who begged for his meals and was satisfied with leftovers, he who had let himself be dragged around Assisi by a rope tied to his neck because he had once eaten some blackbird's meat—he was greedy

138

for these cakes without being in the least ashamed of it.

As long as he stayed in Rome, he went to visit Lady Jacopa every day. And he talked with her about God. And he ate her delicious cakes. "Lady Jacopa," he said to her, "your great devotion and your love of poverty make you one of us Brothers. You are Brother Jacopa!"

Francis left for Africa with Brother Bernard. But after a few days a mighty storm arose, and the ship was driven aground with broken masts and torn sails somewhere on the coast of Slavonia. That meant the end of his trip to the Moors, as to go any farther before the next spring was out of the question. "It must be that I am not worthy of being killed and eaten by them," Francis sighed.

They traveled back to Italy on another ship. After landing at Ancona, they made their way home on foot, preaching as they went. Many new Brothers joined them on the way—at least thirty of them left their parents and relatives for Francis' ideal of love and poverty. Among them were laborers and peasants with big hands and dull minds, clever lawyers, innkeepers and soldiers. All of them were transformed into new men by good will and the burning flame of faith.

One day Francis preached in a convent. The famous poet and troubadour Divini also happened to be there, visiting his sister who was one of the nuns. Divini had been crowned king of the poets in Rome. In the course of his wanderings he had attended all sorts of parties in royal courts and castles. And yet in spite of his fame and his skill, he was far from happy. He was a dissatisfied man who felt tired of living, nervous, and worried, though he was only forty. He had a hunch that he would soon die in debauchery or suicide.

When he first heard Francis preaching, he thought: "What nonsense!" But as he continued to listen, his eyes were opened, and his heart too. Divini was won over. He clasped his hands over his heart and exclaimed: "So that is really what I have been longing for all my life—and I never knew it!"

All day he was deeply troubled, but that evening his new vision of life was burning so intensely within him that he rode after the Brothers. They were singing as they walked through the fields. Divini fell on his knees before Francis and begged: "Peace! Give me Peace!"

"Get up and come with us, Brother Pacifico—Brother Peace," said Francis. And he blessed him.

Francis was amazed when he heard that this was Divini, the great Divini whom he had so much admired when he too had intended to become a troubadour. And now the King of the Troubadours had come to him!

Francis kissed his lean face. And they all sang a song of thanksgiving. Then Divini gave his horse to a poor farmer and left his mandolin in a small country chapel at the Madonna's feet. And he put on a patched habit and went up into the mountains with the Brothers.

Their trip home became a regular triumphal march. People came running out of their villages shouting: "Here comes the saint!" and everywhere they rang the church bells to welcome him.

Francis was embarrassed, and he cried: "Please stop. Don't say that! Don't forget that I am a human being like you, and that I am still capable of having sons and daughters. A sinner can do all that I do. Fasting, praying, weeping, mortifying the body—a sinner can do all that too. But to remain faithful to God—that is something that a sinner cannot do . . ."

Everybody in Assisi came out to meet him with banners and music, while the Brothers chanted psalms. If only they knew how he had to battle against Brother Ass every day, he thought, then they would not acclaim him that way. But just try to make them understand that!

Amid all the honor and praise Francis seemed lonely and lost. His heart was yearning for God. He was sad, and no one could cheer him up. He tried to drive away his depression by singing, but that only made it worse. There was only one person who could give him a little light, and that was Clare. The next day he went to see her.

The convent at St. Damian was snowed in. He made his way to it through two walls of snow. Inside it was dark and cold, as in a cellar. The dripping moisture on the walls was frozen like crystal.

When Clare heard that Francis had come, she quickly ran to him and led him into the bare refectory. How he had aged! His cheeks were so emaciated, and his lips so white! She immediately had a little fire started to warm his feet.

He could not take his eyes from her. How she had changed in these few months. What strength and beauty and spiritual power streamed from her being! She seemed to breathe peace. In her eyes shone pure joy and love.

He felt the infinite distance between them. She possessed that true clarity of soul which he had to struggle to attain even slightly every day. In her light he felt his own darkness.

And yet she admired him. She drank in his words, his simple words describing the failure of his trip. His advice sounded insipid to him. How could someone like him give advice to her? It was absurd. He felt ashamed of himself and said: "I will come back soon . . ."

When he was outside he felt his own nothingness more keenly than ever. As he tramped through the deep snow, he was depressed by his unworthiness. "I should never have begun this work," he said to himself. "I'm good for nothing and a burden on others. Wouldn't Clare and Leo and all those fine souls have achieved as much without me? I've thought too much of myself. I would have done better to have remained an ordinary man, like that peasant there. He is good for something at least: he has children."

A peasant was passing by, carrying a child on his shoulders and holding an older one by the hand. He gave Francis a cheerful greeting.

Francis gazed at him. "He has children."

It is strange how an idea or a desire can develop. This thought of having a family, of being a useful person, remained suspended in his mind all day. No one dared to speak to him, and then the voice of despair whispered to him: "Everybody can be happy except someone like you who drives himself too hard."

That night he could not sleep. The next day he went off alone. He had to be alone. His head seemed to be about to split. He went far up into the mountains, to be utterly alone. He wanted to cry out loud. The snow-covered mountains re-echoed with his voice. But it did not help.

That evening he came to a mountaintop above the Lake of Trasimene, which lay like a black spot amid the snow down in the valley. In the distance, while the dark red sun was setting, night fell on Assisi. He staggered on to one of the little hermitages that he had founded in the hills. The Brothers were overjoyed to see him, for they were snowed in during the winter. But he could not give them any inspiration. He just sat there without saying a word.

They persuaded him to drink some warm milk. One of the four Brothers asked: "Are you feeling sick, Father?"

"Yes. In here," he replied, pointing to his heart. "I need air," and he went out and wandered on.

A Brother followed him from a distance, for fear that something might happen to him. The wind was blowing stronger and sweeping the moonlit snow into long clouds of snowdust.

Nothing could calm the storm in Francis' heart. He crept into a hole in the rocks, fell onto his knees, and tried to pray with his head touching the ground. But he kept thinking of having a wife and children, and then sensual images filtered into his mind twice as strongly.

"No! Not that!" Francis revolted. "Not that! Away from here, Satan!" he shouted. "I'll drive the Devil away!"

Taking off his habit, he began to whip his lean body with his cord. He whipped himself as if he were beating a mad wolf. His cries cut into the silence of the mountains. The pain became so intense that he put his hand to his ribs: it was wet with blood! And yet the sensual images did not cease.

He ran out into the clear moonlight, dug his hands into the snow, and packed whole armfuls into a pile, shaping it into a rough snow figure of a human being. As soon as he had finished, he feverishly got more snow and quickly made six smaller figures. His body was drenched with sweat, and he was panting and gasping like a dying man.

Then he looked at the seven snow men standing there in the eery light of the moon amid the endless silence of the mountains, and he said: "There is my family! The big one is my wife, and the others are my daughters and sons, with the servant boy and the maid. And I have got to work for them and support them. They are dying from cold, and I have to get them clothes. They are hungry, and I have to feed them. But I cannot do it. I have not enough for myself. So if I find it too hard to take care of them, then I should be glad that I have no one else to serve but God!"

And he broke into a loud laugh. It was the laugh of someone who has been inwardly liberated.

A little later from a cleft in the rocks there came a sweet and pure song that was as full toned as a viola: "My Lord and my God, I love You more than all living creatures! I love You more than anything!"

During the night of Ash Wednesday a small boat was being rowed toward the little island in the middle of Lake Trasimene. Francis was sitting in its stern, holding two small loaves of bread on his knees. The boatman would willingly have joined the Minor Brothers if he had not had a family to support. Nothing could be heard but the strokes of the oars and the water that dripped from them. There was not a ripple on the surface of the lake. The stars were shining as clearly on the water as in the sky.

When the boat slid into the reeds on the island, the boatman exclaimed: "Here we are!"

Francis sprang ashore and said: "So, as we agreed: not a word to anyone! And you won't come for me until the morning of Holy Thursday. God bless you!"

The boat disappeared in the dark. Francis was alone on an island where no human being ever went. He sat down on a stone to wait for dawn, and he gazed at the stars and longed for God and Heaven.

Later Mount Subasio became rose-tinted, as the light of day sprang from one mountaintop to another. When Francis could see well enough, he explored the wild little island for a good place to pray. Everything was still bare as in winter. Birds flew up before him, and rabbits hopped away. Now great beams of light were stabbing into the sky from behind the distant mountains, and the lake was shimmering with golden scales. Suddenly Francis stopped before a hollow thornbush. "That's it!" he exclaimed jubilantly. "A hut like a crown of thorns. Thank you, O Lord. Could I find anything better?"

Pulling aside a few branches, he crept in, fell on his knees, and cried: "God, give me the strength to spend the forty days of Lent fasting here with Your Divine Son!" And then, without again looking at the sun or the moon, he began to pray aloud and to sing to God.

The days slipped by. Each evening he walked around the little island, which was hardly as big as a village, and then returned to sleep in his thorny hut.

One morning when he awoke, a rabbit was sitting near him. Its lips kept quivering as it stared at him, but it did not run away. He stroked it, and it let him caress it. When he took a walk, it hopped along beside him. It stayed near him when he prayed and accompanied him on his evening trips around the island. He searched for food to give it, and the rabbit ate out of his hand, while his own stomach was aching and gnawing with hunger. Every day he was visibly growing weaker and losing weight.

But he did not touch the loaves of bread. Only now and then did he swallow a mouthful of water to quench the fire in his throat and chest.

Hunger and self-denial made his soul sparkle with spiritual joy. Now there was room for God. He filled himself with the love of God. And at times his heart was so overflowing with heavenly bliss that he just stood still, weeping and singing and holding up his arms toward God. The solitude, the lake, the mountains, and the sense of infinite peace were so filled with beauty that it seemed like paradise. Had he been there long or not? He did not care. The weaker he became, the purer was his happiness. He scorned the little loaves.

One morning when he dragged himself out of his hut of thorns—for he could no longer stand on his legs —he saw the boat approaching. So it was Holy Thursday! He jumped into the air for joy. Like Christ, he had fasted for forty days. Suddenly he shuddered with sorrow: now he had to go back among human beings, where one's soul becomes dull and depressed. How he wished that he could stay on the island amid all its beauty!

Then, to his great surprise, he noticed how the spring had come: everything had turned green, and there were plants and daisies and violets everywhere. His crown-of-thorns hut was all covered with white flowers. All around him the birds were singing. He had been so utterly absorbed in his inner life and in God that he had not paid any attention to his environment.

The boat had nearly reached the shore. He glanced at the loaves of bread. He had fasted for forty days, like Christ! Suddenly he turned red with shame and amazement. "No, Lord!" he cried. "I don't want to compare myself to You!"

Taking a stone, he hastily broke off a bit of one of the forty-day-old loaves. Then he dipped the bread into the water and ate half the loaf, out of respect for Christ's fast. As the boat slid into the reeds, Francis shook hands with the rabbit. "Goodbye, Brother Quiver-lips!" he said, then with the other half loaf in his hand, he stepped into the boat. The boatman kneeled down when he saw Francis, for there was a heavenly light in his eyes.

At Pentecost, all the Brothers from far and near assembled at the Portiuncula to hold a Chapter meeting and to hear Francis' instructions. They had now increased so much in numbers, and they lived so far apart that it was impossible for him to visit all the hermitages and monasteries. So they were having this Chapter meeting on the Feast of the Holy Spirit, in order to fill their hearts with new inspiration through good spiritual fellowship and brotherhood.

They made themselves huts with branches. People contributed food, and the birds ate it with them.

All the Brothers had an opportunity to speak freely, and each of them gave a frank, informal talk filled with true charity. Francis made a fine sermon. Then they all went home feeling renewed and refreshed and inspired with new courage.

After they left, Francis went out preaching with Angelo. One day they came to the little town of Montefeltro. A great festival was being celebrated in the castle: one of the noblemen was being made a knight. All the nobility of the district were strutting around in their finest costumes and watching the jousts and tourneys from platforms.

"We're going to have some good fishing here!" said Francis. "Come on."

One tournament was ending, and another was about to begin. The trumpeters were just going to blow a flourish when all of a sudden a little barefooted monk was standing in the middle of the grounds, uninvited and unexpected! Everybody was amazed. But before anyone could cry out either for or against him, Francis began to sing a troubadour's ballad. And then he preached about the great reward of a life of penance, which is Jesus Christ. He stood there, dishevelled and emaciated with prayer and fasting, in his patched and tattery habit, talking and shouting to all the noblemen and aristocrats of the region. His gestures were vivid, and his voice was stirring. At times he was so carried away by his fervor that he seemed to dance.

They all listened to him as people listen to thunder or distant music. It was so quiet that the flags and banners could be heard flapping in the air. Some of his listeners were crying. Others lowered their eyes. Many felt their hearts beating unusually fast. Some of them sighed with longing. And when Francis left the field, they gave him a deafening ovation!

147

Before he had gone far from the castle, a Count named Orlando came running after him. He wanted to talk about the salvation of his soul. "All right," said Francis, "but first go and enjoy your meal."

They met later in an orchard. Francis spoke so beautifully to him that the Count wept. And as a token of his veneration he gave him a mountain to pray on: Mount Alverna, which reaches up into the clouds, in the Province of Casentini.

Francis accepted the gift, but on the way home it seemed to him as if he were carrying the whole weight of the mountain on his shoulders. An entire mountain to go and pray on! Ever since the forty days on the little island his longing to live a solitary life had been growing more and more intense. Now he yearned to go high up on a mountain and converse with God. But was not such a desire selfish? Was not the world calling him to preach to it? He was trying to follow the way of life of Jesus Christ—and Christ had certainly mingled with men!

He became so confused that he was not capable of making a decision. He turned to Holy Scripture. First it said: "Serve the Lord in solitude." But then again it said: "Go and teach all nations." In prayer he begged for God's help. But God did not reply.

At the Portiuncula Francis just sat around, bent over, gazing with empty eyes at the calm assurance of the other Brothers—until suddenly he thought of Clare, whose very name denoted clarity.

At first he intended to go and see her himself, but he changed his mind: she would again honor him and serve him as if he were a master, and he could not bear that, because such a weak and irresolute person as himself did not deserve it. He called the worthy Brother Masseo, explained his problem to him, and said: "Go to Sister Clare, that bright light, and ask her what I should do, and go see Silvester too in his cave up on Mount Subasio—and I'll do what they say!"

He spent that night on his knees, stubbornly rejecting all his longings for solitude. He wanted to let God speak clearly through those two crystal-clear souls. And the next morning when he saw Masseo appear out of the fog, he reverently went to meet him. "Don't say it yet!" he begged. "Later, in the woods. First I will wash your feet and give you something to eat, because you are bearing the word of God in your mouth, like an angel."

He washed Masseo's feet and gave him some bread and milk. Then they went into the woods. There in the silence and the dew of the spring morning Francis knelt before Masseo, and crossing his arms on his chest he listened with utter self-surrender and humility, like Mary when the angel brought her the good tidings.

"Preach," said Masseo.

"Preach!" cried Francis, and his whole being thrilled with the Spirit of God.

Freed from all his doubts, he joyfully set out with Masseo and Angelo, but they could not keep up with him. He was so eager to start preaching that he would run on ahead of them, and he would burst into song. He had become intensely aware of the beauty of life. The clouds, the grass, the animals, the human beings, the earth, the sun, the stars—they had all sprung from the hand of God. All creation was filled with His divine Spirit. He was everywhere. And all creatures lived and moved in Him.

"Brothers, Brothers!" he cried, opening his arms to everything he could see and to everything that he could not see. "We are all brothers! Let us all serve our Father together!"

As they were entering the valley on the road to Bevagna, they noticed something strange going on near some solitary trees. Hundreds, even thousands of different kinds of birds were sitting there or hopping or flying around, whole droves and swarms of them, like armfuls of grain tossed into the air. The atmosphere was vibrating with their singing and chirping and twittering. As Francis approached, the birds chirped and whistled louder, and they swarmed and teemed all over the trees and in the grass and in the air.

The two Brothers had stopped and clasped their hands in amazement. When they saw the birds suddenly begin to fly around Francis' head, they said to each other: "They are honoring him!" and they remained respectfully at a distance.

Francis was astounded at finding so many different birds there together: familiar ones like storks, nightingales, starlings, wrens, crows, robbin-redbreasts, and his friends the larks, and pigeons and sparrows, and so on. But there were also unfamiliar birds, some of which were so beautiful that he did not recognise them. They were of all colors: pink and blue and speckled and scaly, with golden and red and green hues. Their colors were like a sunrise, like mother-of-pearl shells, like brocade and flames and silk and snow and silver-thread. They were strange and beautiful in shape and form, with crinkly and frizzled necks and hoods and tufts, with tails like sunsets or frost designs on windows. They were a dream-like vision of colors and tints, with the sunlight shining on them all, making the whole scene gleam and sparkle. Each bird was uttering its own cry or song. And they were all flying and flapping their wings around Francis.

He was so filled with joy that he was trembling. "This is not for me," he thought, "but for my love of God!"

His heart was throbbing, and he felt an urge to speak. He wanted to say a few words to all these birds.

He raised his hands. And suddenly all the thousands of birds became still and sat around him in a circle. The smaller ones crept forward under the big ones. The trees were packed with them. Not a leaf could be seen. Every branch was crowded with the finest feathers and silks and downs. Some of the birds even came and perched on his shoulders and on his outstretched arms.

"Listen!" whispered Brother Masseo. "He is speaking to them!" Masseo's eyes filled with tears as he listened.

"Dear little Brothers," said Francis, "praise and thank God, who is your Father as well as mine. For we all come from His hands. His love enfolds us and sustains us. Just look how He has taken care of you. He preserved you in Noah's Ark. He has given you the joy of flying wherever and whenever you please. The whole sky is yours. He has given you warm feathers and thick little cloaks against the rain and snow, and your children have them too. And you do not have to sew or spin your covering—you just get it free. And how beautiful your plumage is—as lovely as flowers and rainbows! God provides your food, which you find ready for you on trees, in the fields, in the streams and fountains and on the roads. He gives you clefts in the rocks to dwell in—and tree holes and poplar trees and roofs. He has given each of you a song and a language by which you call to one another and converse and praise and thank Him. Do you see now how God loves you? So do not be ungrateful. But remain simple and poor, as a good example to men and to the Minor Brothers. And do your best to praise and thank our Father every day with zeal. Your song is your prayer. Sing! Sing!"

All the birds began to chirp and to whistle, each in its own way. And they bowed their heads to show that they had enjoyed his sermon. And when Francis saw and heard them do so, he raised his arms and joined in the singing with intense happiness and gratitude.

The two Brothers, who were kneeling at a distance and marveling over this wonderful sight, saw Francis then make the Sign of the Cross over the birds. And suddenly the swarm of birds seemed to burst open and gush up, way, way up into the air, like a fountain of water. And then they all flew off toward the four points of the compass in the form of a Cross.

"Thank You, O Lord! Thank You!" cried Francis. And running to the Brothers, he shouted: "Come, come! Let's preach! If the birds listen, why shouldn't men?"

They began to preach with fervent enthusiasm. Francis would even greet the flowers now. He said "Good day" to a dog. And when he saw a pig, he called out: "Hello, little pig!"

He preached to a poor family right at their door, and to a peasant woman who was carrying a basket of eggs to market. And he sang some songs for a child who was playing in the mud. And he preached in full churches and to crowds of farmers in the fields.

But whether he was speaking to one person or to a hundred, he always spoke with equal sincerity and fervor and conviction. Sometimes his sermon seemed like a bouquet of violets. And at other times, when he spoke about Hell, his words were awe-inspiring and terrible. He was like a divine blacksmith, throwing out sparks right and left, from one heart to another.

People were irresistibly drawn to him. His sermons seemed to be like a beautiful melody running through the countryside, and so everybody went to see him and hear him. People ran after him and came out to meet him in processions, with candles and banners. And they brought along the sick and the crippled. Bells were set ringing in the church towers. People kissed his habit and snipped off pieces of it whenever they could. A bowl or anything that he had touched was considered a holy relic that would ensure salvation and protection from all illness.

Popular enthusiasm for his Order went so far that he had to restrain married couples who wanted to separate in order to follow him and Clare. So he would say to them: "No! No! Wait a bit longer. With Our Lord's help, I'll arrange it so that you will not have to separate."

He was almost frightened by the great number of Brothers who joined the Order.

Wherever he had passed, miracles and cures sprang up like flowers in spring. But he was no longer troubled as before by all his fame and honors. Then it had made him suffer. Now he realised very well that the glory was not meant for himself.

"I am just the violin on which God plays His tunes. They come to listen to His music."

Still, Masseo was astounded at all this success. And he said to Francis: "And yet you're not such a handsome young fellow—you're not a scholar—you're not . . ."

"That's just it!" exclaimed Francis joyfully. "That's just how you can see that it is God who does it. And in order to show clearly that it is His work, He chooses for it the ugliest and the most unworthy and the greatest of sinners. So whom could He choose better than myself? Without God I am a mere nothing, just a simpleton incapable of doing anything. So let us thank Him and love Him because He makes use of the most miserable sinner . . ."

And then he added: "Love—love is everything! Anybody can carry a candle in a procession or give money to the collection—that is nothing. The only thing that counts is to be joyful at all times with what we receive from God's hands. That is love!"

They spent the whole summer preaching in towns and villages. And when the grapes were being gathered, Francis said: "Let's go home now, little Brothers, because this month I want to go to the Moors again!"

They set out for home, singing and preaching on the way. One evening as they were going through a rockbound pass in the pale light of a new moon, a man who had been waiting for them jumped from a cleft in the rocks and stood before them on the lonely path. He was an impressive kind of person, with a heavy figure and a big black beard. And he was holding a habit on his arm.

He knelt solemnly before Francis and with well-chosen words requested that he might join them, because he had not been able to find peace in books and now he wanted to live in poverty for Jesus' sake. "Get up," said Francis. "Who are you?"

"Elias, a notary from Bologna."

For a long time they looked at each other. Elias had large black eyes, and his hard cold stare pierced right through a man's heart. Sometimes when he smiled it was hard to tell whether he felt scornful or happy. He was the kind who attracts and crushes others. Neither of the two lowered his eyes.

"Come with us," murmured Francis, yielding, as if he had been forced to say it. Then he had a pang of uneasy foreboding, and he regretted having given his consent. But Francis was a man of his word. With him, yes was yes. So he quickly repeated twice: "Come with us, Brother Elias. Come with us."

Elias joined them as they walked on. The other two Brothers were no longer at ease. Their good spirits had vanished. They no longer sang. And they looked at one another as if to say: what sort of fellow has he accepted now?

Elias told them in scholarly language that he had known Francis before, when he had been just a mattress maker in Assisi, which he had left as a youth, and that after a great deal of studying he had become a notary, due to his will power, efficiency, and intelligence.

They spent the night in a barn. The three Brothers lay down in the straw, but Elias sat on a box and leaned his head against the wall: that way he would not get dirty. When they awoke, he had already put on his habit. He wore it neatly and fastidiously, as if it were made of silk.

The others did not care where they stepped, whether on rocks or in the dust or in mud puddles. What did they care about tattered clothes and dirty feet, as long as their souls stayed pure!

Elias said: "Nevertheless, a soiled habit does not make a clean soul!"

He always scraped off the tiniest spot on his habit, and he took good care of his hands, his large well-formed hands. From the beginning he was very respectful toward Francis. He would wash his feet in the evening and see that he had some soft straw to sleep on. And while Francis slept, he would watch over him reverently, with that strange smile on his lips.

He also preached, but just as if he were reading a formal legal document: firstly . . . , secondly . . . , and so on.

After a few days Francis realised what sort of a man he was dealing with: someone with two personalities. On the one hand Elias had a lust for power, yet on the other hand he could be very devout. Francis said to him: "If you can do away with your pride, you will become a good Brother."

"That's why I came to you," replied Elias, but he had turned red and was obviously repressing his anger.

Francis kept thinking: either he will become a great saint—or he will die outside the Order. And strange to say, he felt great respect for Elias. Why? It was one of those things you cannot explain. And he said to Angelo: "No black thoughts, little Brother. We must

155

accept everyone. The fact that they ask to join shows their good will. So we must start with that. Many whom we accept may in the beginning seem to us like agents of the devil, but later they will become true followers of the Gospel. Was it not that way with me?"

Angelo sighed.

When they arrived at the Portiuncula, Elias was acting like a lord with three mud-spattered servant boys. The Brothers were glad to see their spiritual father. But with Elias around, they no longer felt at ease. He seemed to be a regular professor.

Brother Juniper, the big bear, began to avoid him right away. And Brother Jack looked at him fearfully, as if he expected Elias to give him a slap. But Brother Hat found him very much to his taste, a real gentleman!

The following week Francis sent Elias to Florence, to defend the Minor Brothers against the scholars, lawyers, and theologians. That was just the thing for Elias: firstly . . . , secondly . . . !

And Francis announced: "Now, children, let's pray and prepare my spiritual baggage, because day after tomorrow I am leaving for Africa, to give the Moors a white soul!"

He seemed to be intoxicated with the Holy Spirit. This time he would surely succeed! He kept singing all the time . . .

Six months later Francis was sitting in the sunlight at the door of his little hut at the Portiuncula. He was sick. His trip to the Moors had failed again. He had fallen very ill in Spain and had to stay in bed all winter. And in the spring they took him home. Yet he had planned to accomplish so much . . . After having spent some days in prayer on the wild Mount Alverna, here he was back in Assisi with a sick liver and stomach ulcers.

The rose bush near his hut gave forth a delightful

fragrance. Birds were singing in the trees, while rabbits were playing on the grass near him. Some white pigeons were walking on the roof of the Chapel. They were the children of a couple which he had one day begged from a boy who was taking them to a dealer to be broiled. And now they had a big family. Clare had also received some, and each Brother coming for a visit from a hermitage could take along a couple.

The weather was wonderfully mild, and Francis sat there enjoying it like a child. He looked at everything and admired everything and was grateful to God. Now and then a cricket hopped onto his hand and kept turning around until Francis said: "Brother Cricket, praise the Lord!"

Then the cricket began to chirp so strongly that one wondered how such a tiny creature could make so much noise. And it would not stop until Francis had sung with it. But after a while he said: "Now that's enough, Brother Cricket, because I must not get tired, as I am nothing but a sick little man." Then the cricket would fly away—and later come back and start the same game all over again.

Everything was peaceful at the Portiuncula: the Brothers were working and praying; in the woods two young Brothers were singing a hymn. Francis said to himself: "So many Brothers living together for nothing but God—may they stay that way, just like joyful and innocent children!"

And he thought of the trouble that some of the scholars were stirring up in the Order. They were beginning to undermine bit by bit the Rule of Poverty, in order to amend it so that they could have books and libraries and study theology and other sciences. They wanted to restrict the Brothers' liberty to go around praying and working and preaching.

"No—never!" Francis had declared when they first approached him with their suggestions. And his whole

157

heart and soul continued to insist: "No—never!" He had a strong feeling that Brother Elias was behind the troublemakers. "When you don't stay plain and simple, evil comes rushing right in!"

Just look at what had happened when he went to Spain: during his absence Brother Peter built a house next to the little Chapel, yes, a regular stone house, a sort of mansion with decorations! And it was for the Minor Brothers! It was a disgrace! When Francis saw it, he flared up: "Tear it down!" he shouted. And even though he was sick, he climbed up onto the roof as nimbly as a cat—and the tiles came raining down! Only when they promised him that the house would be for pilgrims did he let it remain. But no—he did not want to think about those sad things. The weather was fine. And God was holding His protecting hand over the Brotherhood.

Francis whistled once, and the Brothers immediately came running to him. "Sit around me, close up," he said. "I'm feeling well enough now to tell you about Mount Alverna."

"Ah, at last!" exclaimed the Brothers, who had been longing to hear about it for some time.

And as they sat close together on the grass around him, he began: "God found me still unworthy of going to the Moors. And then He called me to Mount Alverna, up among the high mountaintops. When we had built a hut under a beautiful beech tree, where I could pray all alone, suddenly a robber came out of the forest! He had many knives on him, and he was carrying a heavy club.

" 'I'm the Wolf of these mountains,' he said. 'I'm the master and ruler here. And if you don't disappear before I count two, I'll beat you to a pulp with this club. Go on—get out!'

"He had already raised the club over me, when through the grace of the Holy Spirit such good words

158

came from my mouth that before I was through telling him how good was Our Lord, who died for him too, he was on his knees asking to become a Brother also. With joy in the Lord I gave him my blessing and named him Brother Lamb, and as I saw that he seemed to have grown up on the mountain, I made him the guardian of Alverna. And now he is helping to build a little stone chapel which Sir Orlando is having his laborers set up there.

"So, children, you see how good is Our Lord, who changes wolves into lambs. And if you ever have the happiness of going to pray on that holy mountain, where the rocks split apart when Our Lord died on the Cross, treat Brother Lamb with all the respect and affection that a holy man deserves.

"And now let's all thank God together for everything, and let's also pray for Brother Lamb, because even the holiest men still need prayers."

Brother Leo led the prayers, and they recited half a dozen Our Fathers for Brother Lamb.

Tall Philip was appointed to be the spiritual director of Clare and her Sisters. And every time he came back from their convent, he reported that they very much wanted Francis to visit them a bit more often and to bring them light and consolation.

Unwillingly he let them persuade him to do so. In his eyes, Clare was holy, and his soul glowed in her presence. He would gladly have gone to see them every day. But Clare and her Sisters treated him like a saint—and he could not stand that! It made him feel like sinking under the earth, such a sinner and a worm as he was! But this time he decided to teach them not to treat him like that.

They acted just like before. They kissed his habit, and they wept. Clare had some water brought in, and she washed his feet as a mark of submission. She looked at him with veneration shining in her eyes. He neither could nor wished to see it, so he kept his eyes shut. All that attention, those flowers, the food and fuss and trouble and admiration—why, they were almost capable of throwing feathers under his steps! No—this must not go on!

First he went to pray a while in the little chapel before the crucifix, and there he got a good idea. He stood up and asked the Sister Sacristan for a bowl of ashes. When she came back, he took it in his hands and turned to the nuns, who were standing as still as statues, ready to drink in every word he said.

Then, instead of preaching to them, he took up a handful of ashes and let them fall onto his head, over his pale face, in his beard, and on his shoulders. He did the same with another handful, and he dropped the rest around his feet. Then with hands outstretched he began to sing, as he walked out: "Have pity on a sinner like me!"

Francis stayed away from St. Damian, and Clare did not dare to invite him again. But she requested the honor of having a meal with him some day at the Portiuncula. Francis refused. She repeated her request six times, and he refused six times.

Leo and the others thought it was a pity, and they said to him: "It was due to you that she took up the life of poverty. She is so shut in. And it would be such a consolation to her . . ." So he let them persuade him to see her again.

One morning some Brothers went to get her, while Francis waited in a little cypress grove. Now that he had consented, he was glad. Now for once he could welcome her as a saint. He bowed to her, kissed her habit, took her small hand which had become hard and dark from work, and led her past the huts. All the

Brothers bowed respectfully—all except Brother Hat, who walked away as she approached.

After saying a prayer in the little Chapel, they went to eat in the pilgrims' house. There the feast was spread out on the bare ground: it consisted of cheese, bread, and milk. Clare and the Sister who accompanied her and all the Brothers sat down—all except Brother Hat, who refused to sit and eat with women. His place remained unoccupied.

After the broth had been poured into their wooden bowls, and after Francis had said grace, suddenly, as though inspired by the purity of Clare's soul, he began to talk about God so wonderfully and so beautifully that they all became inflamed with a godlike love. All that was of the earth and of the senses lost its hold on them. Their souls glowed and shone with a mystic fire. Its supernatural brilliance blazed out through the roof and the walls of the building, shedding a vivid red glare over the Chapel and the forest, like a great crimson flower.

Brother Hat left the Order. It had been in the air for some time. Yet when it happened it was nevertheless quite a shock. He had been grumbling against Francis and the Brothers, saying: "I've had enough—I'm fed up! I'm not allowed to teach the lepers in my own way, but your little favorites can do it their way. They can do anything—and I have to work myself to death serving them. You've had it in for me from the beginning because I wear a hat. Why don't you make a set Rule, as Elias and the others wish? Then everybody would know exactly what he can do and what he cannot do. You don't dare! What is the Rule now? It's you. Your whims are the Rule. I'm tired of it. I'm going to found a new Order, one with a Rule. And even if I haven't got enough brains to do it, still it will be done. And

161

everyone who is not as crazy as you are will join. Why, you don't even know how many are on my side, because your little lambs don't tell you. Your Order is breaking up! What a pity I wasted so many years in it! Goodbye!"

He pulled his hat farther down over his ears and left. The Brothers were deeply troubled. After all, Brother Hat had been one of the very first who joined the Order.

Francis said: "Don't be depressed, little ones. It's just a test. Let's pray for the lost sheep and also for those who might do the same, because . . ." He stopped. Like a bird, somehow he felt that dark clouds were blowing their way.

He spent most of the next winter in a cave on Mount Subasio, up above a thundering waterfall, praying for the conversion of sinners and for the souls of the dead. When he was almost fainting with hunger, he staggered out to beg in the villages. To avoid being recognised, he pulled his hood way down over his head and changed his walk and his voice. For as soon as people recognised him, they immediately filled his arms with supplies. That was not begging. There was no merit in that, either for him or for those who gave. He wanted to be given alms just like a real beggar. Did not a piece of bread given out of compassion make Jesus happier than a feast like that of Cana where He was the guest of honor? To be poor, and even to be driven away with a dog after you—that was good for the soul, Francis felt.

The birds had a hard time that winter. Half of what he got on his begging trips was for them. First he would stamp the snow down firmly, and then he would break the bread into tiny pieces and spread it out for them. It was as though the little feathered Brothers smelled it. They came at once in droves. And if some kind person happened to give him some honey or some sweet wine, he would take it and put it in a hollow tree for the bees.

162

Yet he did not forget his human Brothers. For hours at a time he would struggle through the snow to visit the little hermitages where a few Brothers were snowed in. And how glad they were to see him! He brought a ray of light into the gloom of their long winter. He would stay with them for two or three days and then go on over the mountains.

One day he arrived at the monastery of Monte Casale. The Brother Porter opened the door and exclaimed: "Didn't the robbers attack you?"

"I haven't seen any robbers," said Francis.

"There were three bandits who came and asked for alms. But I slammed the door in their faces!"

The four other Brothers came running to meet Francis. But before he greeted them, he cried out: "Oh, those poor robbers! Those poor fellows!"

"What do you mean: poor fellows? They have been terrorising the district!"

"Oh, those poor robbers!" Francis repeated. Then he ordered: "Quick! Hurry! Take them some bread and wine! Is this your Christian charity? Are they not of the same flesh and blood that Our Lord took in order to come and die for sinners? Hurry! Hurry! Run after them and beg their pardon on your knees! I command you to do so in the name of Holy Obedience. And invite them to come in and eat and drink every time they knock on the door. And tell them about Our Lord, about what He has done for them. Quick! Hurry!"

So the Brother Porter ran out with some bread and a flask of Mass-wine, for that was all they had. No matter how hard a man's heart may be, it cannot resist such charity.

Of course the robbers did not show up immediately. They went at it by degrees, for they were ashamed. Several times they left some fuel wood at the door. And once a pheasant. Then they would stop by and chat a bit with the Brother Porter. And finally they came in—three big fellows who looked like bears and had hands like coconuts. They sat down and ate some eggs and cheese and bread with their faces close to their plates, as shy as little children.

Francis waited on them. And he spoke to them about religion in such a beautiful, clear, and simple way that the three robbers began to sob. Grace touched their hearts. One after another they knelt down and asked him to let them stay in the monastery.

Francis was praying in the little Chapel of Our Lady of the Angels one night while a violent storm was approaching. The atmosphere was heavy, almost suffocating, like an oven. Not a leaf was stirring. The Brothers were tossing restlessly in their huts. They could not fall asleep. Flashes of lightning kept flickering in the dark sky behind the mountains. Though his face was running with sweat, Francis was absorbed in prayer. He was begging for the forgiveness of humanity's sins.

As the storm came nearer and nearer, suddenly a mighty wind arose and made the trees whistle and crack. The sky seemed to open and shut, breathing forth fire and flames. But it did not rain. There were only gusts of hot sand that rushed by, while thunderclaps shook the earth. Francis gazed beseechingly up at the image of the Madonna as flashes of lightning illuminated it every few seconds. "Forgive them! Forgive them!" he begged hoarsely.

And suddenly, as in the midst of a thousand bolts of lightning, he saw a marvelous vision above the altar. Jesus and His Mother appeared to him in a cloud of translucent angels that were like millions of suns. And the melodious voice of God rang in his ears and in his soul: *"What do you wish Me to do to help poor sinners?"*

164

Francis was so happy that he wept.

But what should he request, when God suddenly asked him such a question? Still, he managed to murmur: "Lord God, grant a pardon to all who, after a good confession, come and visit this Chapel!" And he held his hands out toward Jesus and Mary.

Jesus looked inquiringly at His Mother.

She nodded.

And then Francis heard that it was all right, but first he must talk it over with the Pope. He ran outdoors and shouted into the burning wind and flashing lightning: "Brothers! Brothers!" And in the wild storm that still had not turned into rain, he told them in a loud voice what he had seen and heard. He could not restrain himself. He embraced Juniper and Jack and Masseo.

"Come! Come! We're going right to the Pope—he's staying in Perugia now—what luck! And I won't come back until I get the Indulgence!"

He hurried into the forest with Masseo, as the thunderstorm retreated. Daylight gradually spread across the sky, yet the air remained as hot as an oven.

A great crowd was massed in front of the Pope's palace, for the Pope was dying. He had contracted a sweating fever from having eaten a poisonous apple. The sickness was said to be contagious. Tomorrow the whole town might catch it! The two Brothers looked at each other in dismay. What now? "Whether the Pope is sick or not," said Francis, "we are going to see him!"

They pushed through the crowd, and suddenly a cry went up on all sides: "It's Francis! The holy beggar!" Instinctively the crowd made way for him.

Inside the palace, cardinals, bishops, and prelates were coming and going through the courts and halls, whispering and conversing secretively. The Pope was not yet dead, but they were already intriguing over the election of his successor. Several Monsignori were standing before the door of the Pope's room, while another was peering through the keyhole.

"Is this where our Holy Father is suffering?" asked Francis.

"Don't go in, my son," said the prelate who had looked through the keyhole. "It is a contagious disease, and the doctors in there have forbidden us to enter."

"If there is no danger for the doctors of the body, there is still less for those of the soul. Our Lord the Pope needs our medicine more than their bottles." And Francis went in.

The Pope was lying on a high bed between two thick candles. There were moist towels on his livid perspiring forehead. He had a high fever. On his chest he clasped a crucifix as if it were a sword. Three doctors were searching for better remedies in some books and bottles on a side-table. Francis kneeled down for a moment. Then he went to the bed and kissed the Pope's warm hand.

The Pope opened his eyes. For quite a while he stared incredulously at the lean dust-covered little friar —for he was used to seeing around him men dressed in brocade. He blinked his eyes. And then he recognized Francis. The Pope smiled. He wanted to say something, but he could not.

"I've come to pray for you," said Francis.

The Pope smiled again. And a tear slipped from each of his eyes as he closed them again. This great Pope who had won so many battles and before whom everybody had trembled, lay dying alone, abandoned by those who owed their rank to him. They were afraid. Only this little friar in his tattered clothes, smelling of straw and caves, had come and sat by his bedside and held his hand . . .

Francis prayed, holding the Pope's hand, which throbbed like a hammer from the fever. The room was quiet. The half-drawn curtains and the rugs absorbed all sound of footsteps. Now and then the door cracked, and in the opening appeared the head of a cardinal holding his hand before his nose and inquiring how the Pope was feeling. Otherwise nothing stirred.

Thus some time passed. Francis was praying that the Pope's sins be forgiven—after all he was also a mere human being. Suddenly Francis shuddered: he became aware that the hand which he was holding was as cold as a piece of ice. He jumped to his feet. The Pope had died—with a smile on his lips.

That evening the corpse, which gave forth a nauseating odor, was carried in a solemn procession amid torches and singing through the hot streets to the church. The people had to hold their noses as it passed near them. The stifling heat remained suspended in the air, like a curse.

The next morning a sudden alarm was sounded: during the night thieves had robbed the Pope's body of robes and jewels, the golden crucifix in his hands, the ring on his finger, the red leather slippers on his feet, his embroidered cloak—everything! Now the body was lying almost naked and in a state of advanced decomposition.

At the first report Francis ran into the church and covered the nakedness of the Pope with his cloak.

Then, for fear of an epidemic which in such a heat wave might wipe out all the inhabitants of the province, they hastily buried, in the cloak of a poor Minor Brother, the Pope who only yesterday had been as brilliant as the sun. At the grave Francis prayed: "God, have mercy on our latest Minor Brother!"

The burning heat which was enough to drive men mad, the sudden death of the Pope, the fear of an epidemic, the sacrilegious robbery, the mutual recriminations, and above all the political intriguing over the choice of a new Pope, for schemes were being hatched throughout the city as well as in the palaces—all this together had aroused the populace to the point where a revolution was imminent. And that only hastened the election of another Pope.

The very next day, when the former Pontiff's tomb was hardly closed, a new Pope had already been elected: Honorius, a simple and devout man. No one had expected the choice to fall on this quiet and just man who had given his great fortune to the poor.

"He has the soul of a Friar Minor!" exclaimed Francis with joy, and he resolved to submit his petition without delay.

The next day he knelt before the Pope. And with all the fire and spirit and song in his soul he described—as only he could describe—his vision in the Portiuncula and what Jesus had said to him.

The Pope reacted very favorably. But the Cardinals thrust out their chins. The Pope was enthusiastic. With his simple soul, he found it all sublime. But he was the Pope, and that meant that he would often have to set aside his own feelings.

Francis held out his arms and cried: "What I am asking of you, Holy Father, does not come from me but from Our Lord, who has sent me to you!"

And the Pope exclaimed fervently: "Then—in the name of Jesus Christ—yes! Yes! Yes!"

Now the Cardinals exploded with indignation. That was going too far! The Indulgence for the Crusade would lose its popularity—and then the Crusade itself would fail. Who would now undertake a Crusade if he could obtain the same privilege merely by visiting a church? That way anyone could have his sins forgiven! They urged the Pope to retract his words.

The Pope refused to do so. However, he was not a stubborn man. The Cardinals were also theologians, and so on their advice he declared that the Indulgence could be gained on only one day in the year, the day on which it was granted.

Francis bowed gratefully and began to run off.

"You simple fellow," cried the Pope, "you have no certificate!"

"Your word is enough," cried Francis gayly. "I need no other guarantee. Our Lady is the document. Christ is the notary. And the Angels are the witnesses!"

And he danced out of the hall.

"I want to make you all go to Heaven!" he had announced to the crowd when the little Chapel of Our Lady of the Angels was dedicated by seven Bishops on the second of August.

How he wished he could shout the news of the great Indulgence everywhere from the rooftops! But he had to give up the idea because of the sharp conflict on the subject which divided the prelates. Still, it certainly was wonderful to see all the thousands of people who stood in line from dawn to nightfall, advancing step by step, in order to have their sins pardoned in the little Chapel. The nobility, the rich and the poor, the clergy —all of them thus admitted that they were sinners. The sight of such beautiful self-humiliation kept filling Francis' eyes with tears of joy.

Among the visitors there was also a Cardinal named Hugolin, who was a nephew of the late Pope. He was famous for the power of his intellect, and he was also rather a martinet for discipline and order. Cardinal Hugolin was deeply impressed when at last he saw the great poverty of the Brothers, about which he had already heard people talk so much. Shaking his lean head, he went to Francis and clasped his hand, saying with emotion: "What place in Heaven will God give to us who live in comfort and pleasure! If I can do anything for your Order, you can count on me!"

When the evening star was twinkling brightly in the

western sky, Francis was the last of all to go and kneel in the Chapel and beg for the forgiveness of his sins. Heavenly voices were singing above his head. And as he listened, he wept over the beauty and love which God was giving to him and to mankind.

"O Lord," he murmured, "I am ashamed that You use a worm like me as a channel through which You pour forth Your Love over humanity!"

Twilight

His heart began to beat faster when he thought of the coming Chapter. And he said to Leo: "You'll see: they will consider me too simple, too little. They will not want to have anything more to do with me. And they will put me out."

"Yes," sighed Leo, "there has been a great change since so many scholars joined the Order."

At the Chapter about three thousand Brothers sat in a circle to hear Francis preach. Listlessly he climbed into the wooden pulpit. His feet seemed heavy. He was as white as plaster. And he felt deeply troubled. Day and night in his hut he had thought over what he should say to keep them all united in peace and charity. Yet now as he stood there before them he still did not know what to say.

He was trembling, and he raised his eyes imploringly toward the sky. There was silence. Everyone felt that it was a historic moment. The silence could not have been more complete if no one had been there. Only the birds could be heard singing in the trees. And while his tortured heart was groping for the right words, Francis listened to the birds. High above their singing, like many little musical fountains, he recognized the warbling of the larks—his friends, the larks!

A smile appeared on his features, and with enthusiasm he began to speak to the thousands of Brothers about the lark: "Brothers, listen to him—the lark, our bird! The bird of the Friars Minor! He has a little cowl like us. And he lives so humbly that he hunts for his food along the roadside and even on manure piles. But when he flies, he soars way up in the sky, full of fervent longing. And he sings the praise of God very sweetly and gayly, like devout Friars Minor who are more concerned with Heaven than with the world and who love nothing more than to praise God. The lark's feathers are the same color as the earth, and that teaches us not to wear costly or colorful clothes, but simple and natural ones. Brothers, he teaches us holy simplicity and poverty. Poverty is such a lofty and sublime and godlike treasure that we are not worthy to bear it in our bodies! For it is the heavenly virtue which scorns all earthly and passing things and which removes all obstacles from the soul's path, so that it may freely and nakedly unite itself with God for eternity. Poverty is the virtue that makes the soul converse with the angels in Heaven while still here on earth!"

As Francis' spirit soared into the infinite, his words cast sparks of heavenly light into the hearts of the thousands of Brothers. And his critics felt defeated, crushed, and once again filled with supernatural love, which after all had been the primary impulse in their souls when they had joined the Order.

After his sermon, a fine spirit of fellowship reigned again among them, as in the early days when they had been only a few. Still, since there were now so many of them, Francis had to yield a bit.

He had always been the kind of shepherd who tried to keep his little flock together, apart from the world. But now that was no longer possible. There were too many Brothers. He could no longer look after all of them personally. Now they were spread out over great distances, in forests and on mountains. And the scholars were causing confusion.

So there was nothing for him to do but appoint other shepherds: a leader for each Province, a sort of

Minister who would take Francis' place and keep up the right spirit among the dispersed Brothers. Such a step was risky, because one Superior might act one way and another in a different way. No doubt it was a pity, for then some of the early simplicity, some of the youthful spontaneity of the springtime of the Order would disappear. When he told them his plan, some of them wept.

He made his idea of a Superior perfectly clear to them: "To be a Superior is not to act like a lord and master," he said, "but to be the Good Shepherd of the Gospel! It means to be like a mother who takes care of her children, like Our Lord who did not come to be served but to serve. Whoever lets one sheep go astray through his fault"—and his eyes flashed—"will give an account to God! And let him who has a complaint come to me. For not a letter of the Rule is to be changed!"

Nevertheless fear clutched at his heart and filled his soul with sorrow. A crack had appeared in his work. Yet he did not lose courage. "God knows why it happened!" he said.

No. He did not lose courage. On the contrary he became inspired with a great ideal. His ideal, his dream was that all men might come to know and to love God!

He himself had twice set out for the land of the Moors. Now he exclaimed enthusiastically to the assembled Brothers that the Light of Christ must shine on men everywhere. So there would also be Provinces of the Order in other lands! The Brothers applauded the idea vehemently.

"Who will bring joy to Spain?" he cried.

Hundreds raised their hands.

"Who will go to Germany?"

Again there were well over a hundred.

"Who will go to the Moors in Syria?"

Then not one of them raised his hand—out of respect for Francis. They all knew of his longing to go there

173

and his setbacks. So they expected him to raise his hand.

He did not do so. He felt that God did not want him there. "Who will go to the Moors?"

No one moved.

"Who will go to the Moors?" he asked a third time.

Then Elias stood up and raised his hand!

Who would ever have expected that of Elias? He was known to be one of the most convinced members of the group that wanted to transform the Order the way the scholars wished. Yet now he was standing there calmly with his hand in the air and with that mysterious smile half hidden in his beard.

Francis did not know whether to be glad or sorry. He both admired and feared Elias. With difficulty he murmured: "Elias is going to the Moors."

Then hundreds of others raised their hands too. Francis was touched by so much courage and generosity on their part. And he shouted: "I am going to France, the country where Our Lord is most honored in the Holy Eucharist!"

Again many hands were raised. Joy and enthusiasm were spreading among the Brothers. Adventure, new experiences, the will to go and do great things, the attraction of the unknown—it all blew a fresh breeze into their hearts and minds.

"Brothers," cried Francis, "when you are on the road, two by two, going to your far-off hermitages or to your distant lands, keep silence as you walk, and pray as if you were in your cells. For no matter where we are, we always take our cells along with us. Brother Body is our cell. And our soul is the hermit who dwells in it, praying and thinking of God!"

Before leaving for France, he first went to Rome with Masseo, in order to pray for strength and a blessing at the Tomb of the Apostles there.

One day while they were on the road, after having begged for their food in a small town, they were sitting by a spring in an isolated spot in the country. The spring water was as clear as crystal and as cool as night air. It bubbled out of the ground and ran down among the flowers and pebbles with a little song. The food which they had begged lay on a large white stone. Each had gone begging by himself. And because human nature is that way, since Masseo was a tall handsome fellow, he had received a lot: big slices of bread, freshly cut and nicely buttered. But with Francis, who really looked like a poor tramp or yokel, they had just thrust into his hands what they would otherwise have thrown to the chickens. The two shares lay beside each other like a servant beside a king.

Francis laughed.

Masseo looked depressed. He was having a bad day—which can happen to anyone. "Why are you laughing?" he asked.

"Because we are so lucky!" said Francis gayly.

"Lucky? You call us lucky?"

"Of course! Look at the sun, the water, the food!"

"Yes, look at the food . . ."

"Why, we are not worthy to have such wealth!"

"But Father," said Masseo incredulously, "how can you call this wealth when we are in dire poverty and have to do without everything. We have no tablecloth, no knife, no plates, no pitchers, no house, no servant . . ."

"That's just it!" exclaimed Francis. "It is just because we have to do without all those things that this is great wealth! Because here nothing is arranged by human hands, but everything has been supplied by God's Providence—that's why! Just look, Masseo—look at this bread we begged for, this fine white stone that serves as a table, and then this cool clear water! Isn't it wonderful? Is there anything more beautiful? And

175

so let us pray God to make us love with all our hearts that Holy Poverty to which He subjected Himself from His Birth until His Death! In the name of the Father and of the Son and of the Holy Ghost . . ." And they prayed.

Francis' words had completely changed Masseo's outlook. He felt the power of the Holy Spirit in them. So as they ate heartily and drank out of their hands the cool water which dripped from their beards, they laughed and joked together.

Then, two by two, Francis and some of the Brothers set out for France. He went with Pacifico, the king of the poets. "Let us thank the Lord," said Francis.

"Yes, Herald," replied Pacifico. He always called Francis "Herald."

The two former troubadours, the two poets went together toward the land of the dreams of their youth, the land of troubadours and of poetry. And while they prayed silently on the way, their hearts were overflowing with joy. They were in such a hurry to reach France that they outdistanced the others.

When they arrived in Florence, Francis heard that the great Cardinal Hugolin was staying there, preaching the new Crusade. "Supposing I ask him to help us?" Francis reflected. For in Rome he had been told that several Cardinals were stirring up opposition to the Friars Minor, especially since the granting of the great Indulgence of the Portiuncula. "And suppose they convince the Pope, and one fine day he says: 'No more poverty.' Anything might happen . . ."

So he went to see Cardinal Hugolin. "Your Eminence," he said, "I have come to ask you to help us."

As they sat facing each other, Francis seemed like a hunk of earth, while the white-haired Cardinal was dressed in white lace and silk as red as a radish, and he was heavily scented with costly perfume. He listened with his pale blue eyes closed, stroking his lean chin. But when he spoke, he peered right into a man's heart. His thin lips hardly moved.

"I shall help you and protect you—I and my friends," he declared. "Your Order is of great value. If I were to begin all over, I too would be wearing the habit of your Order."

"Thank the Lord!" exclaimed Francis. "Now we can go ahead without worrying," and he joyfully told the Cardinal how he had sent the Brothers off to foreign lands and that he was on the way to France himself.

The Cardinal opened his pale eyes and said forcefully: "You are staying home, Brother Francis!"

"No indeed, Your Eminence!" Francis jumped up as if he had been stung by a wasp.

"Then we cannot help you!"

Francis wrung his hands and strode up and down the room.

"We cannot help you if you are so far away. You must stay here!"

Francis cried out as if he were burning alive: "Your Eminence, I am ashamed! I should send my Brothers away—and stay home myself? No! Never!"

"Why did you send them away to perish from hunger and want?"

Then Francis exclaimed heatedly: "Your Eminence, do you think that God called the Friars Minor only for this country? Truly I say to you that God has called them for the salvation of all men all over the world, even for the heathen and the Moors!"

"In any case you are staying home, Brother," said the Cardinal firmly and calmly, though he admired Francis' unquenchable fervor and thought of him as a "flaming pillar of the Church."

Francis was staring at the Cardinal just as strongly as the latter was staring at him. For a moment they stood there facing each other. Then a feeling of humility and submission came over Francis. He felt that there was a sign from Heaven in the Cardinal's words. And so he completely gave up his exciting, powerful, and tempting desire to go to France. He kneeled down and humbly crossed his hands on his chest. But there was a pang in his heart.

The next day he was on his way home through the wheat fields and vineyards, somewhat bowed under the weight on his heart. Seeing an ugly caterpillar creeping across the road, he took it up and placed it in the grass. "You must still become a lovely butterfly, Brother Caterpillar," he said. "Likewise one day our soul will leave its ugly and soiled body and fly to God like a butterfly." And he listened to the larks chirping over the countryside as they flew up out of the corn fields and vineyards into the clear morning air—the larks, his friends and models. And soon he too began to sing softly and fervently, turning his face up toward Heaven. He was smiling again.

One night in November, after a heavy snowfall, he was heard groaning and crying in his hut: "My Lord and my All, drive away these ugly thoughts—drive them away! I am not strong enough!" And again he sighed and sobbed and groaned and prayed and scourged his bare flesh with cords. Suddenly he shouted: "Brother Ass, you are going to pay for this!"

He flung the door open and came running out into the snow, stark naked. He ran to the rosebush near his hut, and thrusting out his arms like Christ on the Cross he threw himself onto its sharp thorns.

There was a crack. And there he hung, caught in the thorny branches like a fly in a spiderweb. As he sank deeper into the bush, the thorns tore into his skin and flesh.

"Thank God that the pain has driven away the ugly visions," he sobbed.

Although the pain was cutting through his body like a searing flame, he did not cry out. Then it hurt so keenly that he felt he could not bear it any longer. Whenever he made the slightest move, the thorns hacked and carved new wounds. His blood was dripping from the branches onto the snow. His moans and groans sounded like a melodious refrain under the silence of the stars.

The door of a hut opened, and Juniper stuck his head out, listening. Then the startled Brother held out his arms and shouted: "Father! Father!"

"It was necessary, Brother Juniper," murmured Francis. "Otherwise the temptations would not leave me."

Juniper saw that he could not pull Francis out of the bush by himself, so he called for help. Several Brothers came and got him out as carefully as they could, yet of course not without causing more wounds.

Francis' body was covered with bleeding wounds. It was a terrifying sight. They put a habit over him and wanted to carry him back to his hut. "No," he said. "To the Chapel—to thank God for the thorns that purify us."

Bad news came in from everywhere—except Syria, where Elias was. The Brothers were suffering one setback after another.

They were driven out of Germany, after having been punished in public and then imprisoned. In Hungary people had torn their habits off. And in France and Spain they were considered heretics. Neither bishops nor priests would allow them to preach. "Where are your papers?" they were asked. But they had none. So in one place or another they were stoned or insulted or humiliated.

"How wonderful to be able to suffer so much for one's faith!" cried Francis. "If only I could have been with you!" But when he saw so many Brothers coming back with sad faces, disappointed, bitter, and depressed, he was no longer so happy.

"Where is your love?" he exclaimed. "The first Christians rejoiced as they let themselves be eaten up by the wild animals!"

But now the discontented Brothers—as usual the scholars—had found a convincing argument to use against him. To one another and to the Cardinal they complained: "He does everything in a happy-go-lucky way. Why didn't he arrange for the papers? We would be twice as strong with them. Why doesn't he let us study, first theology and then the language and customs of the country he sends us to? Then all this trouble would not have happened. This way many Brothers had to suffer and endure a lot of things merely because they were not understood. He never takes precautions. He is going too far in his simplicity and poverty. He does not make allowances for the world and for human nature. He relies on God too much. What he does is to be admired but not imitated. He thinks we are all like him because it always succeeds with him. But then he is a saint . . ."

His Eminence merely said: "I will talk it over with him sometime."

Francis was upset. He felt that they no longer wanted him. He wandered sadly from one monastery to another, and then he decided to speak to the Cardinal about it himself. But on the way he dreamed about a little black hen who could no longer keep all her chicks under her wings, because there were so many of them. And when he awoke, he said: "I am that hen —so small and dark and no longer able to protect my little ones."

He hurried anxiously to meet the Cardinal, who was traveling to Rome, and he found him in a village along the road. "Help me protect my little Brothers," Francis pleaded.

"Willingly," replied His Eminence. "Come along with me. We will speak to the Pope about it."

"Yes, I will go with you. And let me have an opportunity to preach before the Holy Father, in order to make sure that he will protect us through you."

"All right," said the Cardinal somewhat apprehensively and cautiously. "But there must be no improvising! First write out your sermon and then learn it well by heart. Because they are going to weigh every word you say there. One word too much or too little is sometimes enough to ruin a man . . ."

So Francis joined the Cardinal's party.

His Eminence, having observed everywhere during his travels Francis' great fame and profound influence on the masses of the people, had conceived a far-reaching plan: he decided to co-ordinate Francis' ideal.

Francis wrote out his sermon in the home of Lady Brother Jacopa. When His Eminence read it, he found it satisfactory, though he struck out or added a word here and there.

At last the time came when Francis was to give his sermon before the Pope. On each side of the papal throne stood the Cardinals, including many who had already tried to transform or destroy the Order. But when Francis found himself standing there before the Pope, he could not remember a word of what he had written and learned by heart—not a single word. He wished he could sink into the ground. It seemed to him that the Cardinals in their purple robes were looming up like great rocks about to fall upon him and crush him.

Noticing Francis' embarrassment, Cardinal Hugolin began to tremble and to mutter prayer formulas, for he realised that the disgrace and humiliation would affect him as much as Francis. For a tense moment Francis' face turned alternately white and red, while he silently but with heartfelt fervor begged Christ to help him.

Then he made the Sign of the Cross, and with the Sign of the Cross inspiration came to him. And he preached—but not a word of the sermon that he had written. He preached what the Holy Spirit whispered to him. He preached about Poverty. And he became so carried away by the joy in his soul and by the music of his words that he began to dance and hop around, like King David before the Ark of the Covenant. At first everybody was puzzled. But soon they felt caught up in the whirlwind of his spirit and of his singing words. For his soul was aflame with the love of God. And everyone present, from the Pope to the guard with his pike, was deeply thrilled. The rocks turned into heaps of flowers.

"With such a man," thought the Cardinal, "I will conquer the whole world!"

The Pope appointed Cardinal Hugolin Protector of the Order.

As he went out, Francis suddenly noticed a tall young monk in a white habit standing beside him in the crowd. He had clear blue eyes and a broad pale forehead which seemed to shine with wisdom and intelligence. They looked at each other, and the divine fire lit up both souls. A holy smile appeared on their lips. Each felt a mystic attraction toward the other. Then with a sigh of joy, as if they had been searching for each other for years, they threw their arms around each other and exchanged a long and affectionate embrace.

"I am Francis!"

"I am Dominic. I had a dream about you. From now on, let's stand side by side—and no enemy shall ever be able to defeat us!"

"Yes!" exclaimed Francis.

Just then the Pope and his colorful entourage approached, and in the ensuing confusion the two friends became separated in the bustling crowd. Each sought the other, but without success. Cardinal Hugolin had seen them embrace. And he conceived a still greater plan. Dominic's Order, the Order of Preachers, had already been granted a written approbation. What could be better than to merge the two Orders into one —unite the Friars Minor and the Dominicans in one Order? Thus the mind and the heart would be united. And soon there would not be a single heretic left in Europe!

He summoned the two founders. When they were before him, he broached the subject very cautiously, because with Francis one had to be careful: he was so sensitive whenever his Order was involved. "Brothers," said the Cardinal, "Holy Church needs good, strong, saintly Bishops, real shepherds. Let me make a selection among your followers in order to fill the highest places in the Church!"

He had hardly finished speaking when Francis exclaimed: "Your Eminence, my Brothers are little, minor Friars. And God does not want them to become important personages."

Dominic agreed with him. Their Friars should be just busy little bees, nothing more. They should have no positions of honor, no opportunities to become proud. The Cardinal conceded that their attitude was fine, humble, sublime, and so forth and so on—but nevertheless it would mean a loss of strength for the Church and its glory!

The two Friars gazed with awe at each other. And then the one with the great intellect expressed to the one with the great heart the other great unspoken desire of the Cardinal: "Brother Francis, let us merge our Orders!"

Again Francis immediately resisted: "That cannot be, Brother. God wants us to remain separate, so that everyone may choose one Rule or the other, according to his preference."

Saddened by Francis' refusal yet rejoicing over his marvelous inner conviction, Dominic asked him: "Then give me as a souvenir the cord you are wearing."

Francis presented it to him, and when they left the Cardinal's residence, Dominic called to his waiting Brothers: "Francis is a holy man. Every Friar must imitate him—he is so perfect!"

Another Chapter: Assisi and its surroundings were teeming with Friars Minor, more than five thousand of them. A small town of hastily erected huts had grown up around the Portiuncula. The Cardinal arrived on horseback, accompanied by many noblemen. And when he got down from his horse, he took off his shoes and socks, set aside his robe, and stood there dressed in the habit of a Friar Minor. Brother Hugolin! After he had celebrated Mass, with Francis serving at the altar, the little founder gave a talk to the assembled Brothers. He explained what a blessing it was to beg for one's bread and to earn it with calloused hands. He spoke about the grace-filled water of Baptism, and about chastity and patience and obedience and the Church.

When noontime came, there was no food. "Do not be anxious about food and drink," Francis had said in his sermon, but now they were all famished—and nothing had been provided! Many of them wondered how Francis could be so careless as that—with five thousand hungry men to feed!

Francis did not make a move, but remained absorbed in prayer in the Chapel before the Blessed Sacrament. Then, soon after noon, they saw the food arriving along all the roads. People were bringing it on wagons, mules, wheelbarrows, and even on detached doors. There was enough food for ten thousand men. And not just bread and water, but fish, chicken, beef, fruit, wine, cheese, ham, and raisin cake—with plates, glasses, jugs, tablecloths, and knives. It was a banquet, and men who had lived for years in their mountain hermitages on nothing but onions, beans, and bread, now went at tender chicken legs with relish and gusto, while the noblemen and townsfolk took a holy pleasure in serving the food and drink to the Brothers.

Yet instead of rejoicing over this manifestation of Divine Providence, some of the Friars began to grumble: "This is all very fine. But can you base a Rule for everyone on miracles? That is risking too much! To be simple to that extent is going too far. Miracles will not happen all the time. We must become organised in a more practical way, with a definite Rule—otherwise the Order will fall apart."

Some of them went to the Cardinal and talked the problem over with him. He neither agreed nor disagreed, but he took Francis aside, and as tactfully as he could, he suggested to him that after all it would do no harm if he listened a bit to some of the educated and scholarly Brothers too, and if he accepted some points of the Rule of St. Augustine or of St. Benedict.

Francis flushed with indignation but said nothing. He simply took the Cardinal's white hand and led him to an open space in front of the Chapel where most of the Brothers were. When he raised his hand as a sign that he was about to give a talk, everyone near him sat down and prepared to listen, while the others came running up. And Francis cried out with burning fervor: "Brothers—my dearest Brothers. God called me to the path of humility and simplicity. And we are going to stay on that path—I and those who want to follow me. So don't talk to me about another Rule. I don't want to hear about any other Rule, neither St. Benedict's nor St. Augustine's nor St. Bernard's. Don't talk to me about any other path but the one which God in His mercy has revealed and shown to us. The Lord told me that here in this world I was to be another fool of Christ, and that He wishes to lead us only along the path of that science and that folly—and no other. For God will curse you with all your learning and with all your theology! I trust in God. And I foresee it all: He will send down on you His anger, which, to your sorrow and shame, will bring you back to your vocation."

The Cardinal was speechless. All the Brothers remained silent. The guilty ones did not raise their eyes. But the simple little Brothers who were like the larks gazed up at Francis with pride.

Then in the silence he announced new missions to distant lands. Hundreds of Brothers stood up and volunteered to go—without letters of recommendation. After all, did the Apostles have letters of recommendation? And with the Cardinal's consent, Francis declared that he was going to the colored people in Egypt.

The Promised Land

"Land ahoy! Land ahoy!" shouted the lookout on the Crusaders' ship one morning. At last! Francis made a great Sign of the Cross toward the East. And when he landed, he kissed the ground as if it were bread.

But he could not go farther inland. The armies were battling everywhere—Crusaders against Moslems. Before Damietta they were fighting so fiercely that blood ran into the sea. So he could preach only in the Crusaders' camp. Along with good Christians had come the riffraff of all nations, bent on plundering and stealing. In the camp there was continual carousing and quarreling, brawling and disputing. The atmosphere stank with sin, and soon the good also became depraved. The war had been dragging on too long.

Francis said to them: "It's not the Moors that have been holding you back for a whole year already. It is your own devil: your hate and your greed. You have forgotten that you bear a Cross on your weapons—bear it in your hearts too! If you came with love, then the tents of the Moors would fold up like magic. But now the Moors fear your hatred and your evil intentions. Swords win blood—love wins souls. That is why I lay down the sword, for I used to be a soldier too. And I pray that you will not reach the Holy Land of Christ until your souls are worthy of it! Cursed be those who fight for anything but justice and the liberation of the Holy Sepulcher! Purify your souls! Purify your hearts!"

Some of them took off their armor and asked for the habit of the Friars Minor. Francis sent them to Elias at Acre in Syria. Others kissed their swords as though they were crosses.

The war continued, with the Crusaders launching one attack after another. Once, after Francis had warned them not to attack, they lost more than six thousand men in one day. Fear, grief, and disaster opened the hearts of many, and then prayers rather than curses could be heard in the tents and around the watch fires. When there was an armistice, Francis hurried to the Papal Legate for permission to go and preach before the Sultan, in order to convert him and obtain peace.

The Legate laughed at him: "Tomorrow your head will be displayed on the end of a spear above the walls of Damietta."

"If only that were so!" said Francis, and with Brother Illuminato he set out for the tents of the Moors. "Sultan! Sultan!" he kept shouting.

Thinking they were peace envoys, the sentinels conducted them to the Sultan's pavilion. The Sultan's features were swarthy, and he was dressed in gold-colored silk robes. He sat cross-legged on a pile of cushions, holding a curved scimitar in his hand. Around his neck were numerous pearl necklaces, and delicate white plumes waved above his turban. The walls and the ground were covered with fine rugs, and a sweet-smelling perfume rose out of golden vessels.

Francis began to speak in French, which the Sultan understood. And he spoke about Jesus so clearly, so fervently, and so lovingly that the Sultan was moved to admiration for this preacher in rags. He held his hand before his face while listening. His officers were raising their scimitars to strike Francis down when the Sultan said: "Come back tomorrow."

So Francis stayed in the Moorish camp for several days. And every day he gave a fine sermon before the

Sultan. Yet the latter said not a word about conversion.

This could not go on, so Francis said to him: "Have a fire lit, and I will stand in it with your priests—and you will see who professes the true religion!"

The Sultan refused.

Then Francis cried out in desperation: "I will go into it alone! If I burn, blame it on my sins. If I come out unharmed, promise me that you and your people will then be converted."

This offer too was rejected.

Yet the Sultan said to him with a sigh—and it was obvious that something was troubling the heart of the powerful ruler: "Pray a great deal for me, that God may let me know which religion He prefers."

He gave Francis a seal with which he and his Brothers could travel freely through the Holy Land and visit the Holy Places. He also wished to give him jewels, pearls, and perfumes. But Francis firmly refused to accept them. "Then take this horn," said the Sultan. It was a cow horn decorated with silverwork. "Take it as a double proof that I have sent you." And Francis left the camp, grieving that he had not been able to win the Moor's soul—and that he still had his head on his shoulders . . .

During the peace negotiations, which lasted over two months, more Crusaders kept arriving. And in November the whole mighty army surged forward like a sea of iron. The air was black with arrows, and the earth red with blood. Damietta was taken. And then, all of a sudden, the Christians seemed to become possessed by the devil again. Hatred and cruelty quenched the light in their souls. They murdered, mutilated, raped, plundered, destroyed, quarreled, stole, and drank themselves drunk. Children, old men, women—all were slaughtered. It was as if hell had broken loose.

Francis was horrified. Holding his hands before his eyes, he cried: "Mercy! Mercy!" Then he fled far, far away—to the Holy Land.

The Holy Land! He walked carefully and reverently, as if every step he took might bring forth music from the earth. With four Brothers he went to the Crib in Bethlehem. He spent Christmas night in the grotto where Jesus was born. He experienced intense tenderness and radiant joy. He laughed and cried alternately. Tears dropped from his face and from his hands. He kissed the ground and the walls. He kissed the air. He crept around the grotto on his knees. He uttered cries of joy. He sang and he hummed. He lay flat on the ground as if to become one with it. Then he stood up and held out his arms and sobbed and sighed. The Brothers who were watching him by the light of a small torch did not know what was more beautiful, the holy Feast of Christmas or Francis' emotion.

His imagination became so vivid, under the stimulation of his fervent love, that he was obviously reliving the great event as if it were taking place before him. God became man there—God who slings planets through the universe like snowflakes. God, whom one would expect to be born in a gorgeous palace, became man in a damp hole in the rocks, in extreme poverty, poverty worse than that of the slums . . .

"Little Brothers," cried Francis, "here is the Crib with the tiny Child in it. He is just a ball of light, as though He were not yet quite a human being. And Mary, our poor sweet Mother, is kneeling there on some straw. And she is filled with heavenly joy now that she has brought into the world the Child from Heaven, formed with her flesh and blood. And Joseph is standing over there, trembling with happiness. Listen to the angels singing—look at them, up above that opening in the rock—the sky is full of them, of their light and beauty. There are rows and rows of them stretching right up to the stars—there is no longer any limit separating Heaven and earth! They are singing—and the whole world is echoing their song—every living creature, even the fish and the seashells are echoing it! Oh, what a marvelous mystery! And now the shepherds are kneeling here, clasping their rough hands and bending their worn faces forward . . ."

Then he suddenly exclaimed: "Dear little Babe! Look at us here. We are also little shepherds. But we have not brought You any eggs or milk or cake. Yet take our hearts, which we are trying to keep pure. We are beggars, for love of You, and we beg our bread from door to door. O little Babe, give us some of this music in our souls and some of Your light and Your love of poverty—some for us and some to take home for our little lambs. Dear little Jesus! Dear little Jesus!"

It was all too beautiful to comprehend at the time. His words were stifled in his throat, and he sank gently onto the cold ground and tried to dig his fingers into the earth. And he lay there weeping and sighing until the light of a winter dawn appeared.

Nazareth—a little white town on a green hill.

In one of those small white houses Mary had lived, in silence, praying. Humble as she was, she had gone down this narrow path with a pitcher in her hand, to fetch some water at the fountain.

It was at just such an hour as this, when everything was glistening with dewdrops, that it must have happened, perhaps under a palm tree: suddenly an angel had kneeled before her and had brought her the mighty tidings. And because she was so pure and so quiet, she had been able to say: "Be it done unto me according to thy word." And when she said those words, God began to flower in her womb. For He could become man only in someone who was pure and still.

Then, with a song in her heart, she had gone to visit her cousin Elisabeth. And John, in his mother's womb, had greeted Jesus in Mary . . .

Francis' eyes had become inflamed due to the stabbing light of the sun, and they were giving him much pain. Yet, holding his hands over his eyes, he sang the Magnificat under the palm tree.

The inhabitants of the village looked at the five foreigners with suspicion. What were these strangers doing there while the natives were being massacred elsewhere by invaders from overseas? Francis showed them the seal and the horn. That calmed them, and they even gave the Brothers some food: figs, cheese, and bread.

And now, on to the Holy City. Francis hastened ahead of the others. Once again he was the knight, the conqueror. Panting breathlessly he climbed up a hill, and when he reached the top, he held out his arms. There, bathed in the light of the setting sun, lay Jerusalem. He blew his horn, took off his sandals, kneeled down, and pressed his forehead onto the ground.

The gates of Jerusalem were open to these five men who were utterly poor and who came empty-handed, yet with love in their hearts, while others at a distance, armed with swords and pikes, were hacked to death by the thousands. For something was lacking in their hearts.

Good Friday! For weeks they had been waiting for this day. Holding out his arms, and with eyes as red as blood, Francis and his Brothers stood on the hill of Golgotha, where the Cross had been. He had spent the night in the little Garden of Gethsemani. He had wept for hours, and that had made his sore eyes still worse. Yet his tears kept flowing. It was as though they came from an underground spring. His face was haggard, pale, and lined; his cheeks fallen-in, and his lips quite white. Standing there like a cross, he opened his mouth and cried out mournfully and pitifully:

"Let me die for You! Let me suffer with You! Give me a drop of Your suffering! But one drop is perhaps too much for one human being—it might kill hundreds of us. So give me the suffering that I deserve!" And he saw the Passion of Christ unfold before him as in a vision. He heard Jesus' flesh tear, His muscles snap, His blood drip down. "Let me die for you!"

When night fell, he was still standing there with the Brothers at his feet. Then they went to the Holy Sepulcher, where they spent the whole night in prayer, as motionless as stone statues.

On Easter Sunday, as he smilingly embraced his Brothers, he wore a piece of cloth over his eyes, and he said: "I think that during these days I have cried the light out of my eyes. Now I have the opportunity to look within myself a great deal. That is where we find Him best of all!"

Into the Dark Night

From the promised land they led him to Elias in Acre. Francis seemed to be intoxicated with God's Light. But physically he was on the verge of a complete collapse. He was half blind, and his eyes were like cracked cherries. Attacks of fever had exhausted him, and his fasts, penances, and overwork made him look ten years older. He could no longer stand on his feet. He could no longer kneel.

The Brothers had a little hermitage in an abandoned Arab house that had been covered with whitewash as protection against the heat. Francis wished to lie outside in a thatched shed, facing the sea—a house was too good for him. Elias waited on him and took care of him, as a mother takes care of her child. One evening Elias and the Brothers came to him. Their features were grief-stricken. Elias looked reproachful as he said: "I bring you bad news. The five Brothers you sent to Morocco have been beheaded by the Miromolin!"

Francis jumped up with a start. He seemed half cured. "What good fortune!" he cried out. "What a grace! Now I can truly say that I have five Brothers. God be praised!"

While Francis sang hymns of joy, Elias walked away without saying a word.

The next morning a young Brother whom they had never seen before came running excitedly up to the little monastery and exclaimed anxiously: "Where is our Father Francis?"

"Here," said Elias, who was taking a handful of fresh fruit to Francis.

The Brother fell onto his knees before the straw bed, laughing and weeping. Then he exclaimed nervously: "Little Father! Little Father! So you are still alive! God be praised! They think that you have been killed by the Sultan. I have come from Assisi. Hurry back quickly! Come back as quickly as you can. Everything has been turned upside-down by conflicts and hatred. I ran away to find you and tell you all about it on behalf of many of the Brothers, and to call you back. The Ministers have made new regulations, something like the Benedictine Rule and altogether contrary to your ideas. They have added fast days. We have to keep silent all the time. There is no more freedom. Everything is bound by rules and regulations, like discipline in a monastery. Permission has been granted to build houses, big houses where many of us are sent to live a strict monastic life. So Brother Peter Stacia in Bologna made a fine large house into a monastery where they study and read books. No one mentions poverty any more. And the Brothers who go to other Provinces bear letters of recommendation, which you opposed so strongly! And . . ."

"That's enough!" moaned Francis. "All that is not the Gospel!" He sprang up and waved his arms. "Away with those letters and regulations and houses! May Peter Stacia be cursed! And they will have to get out of that house—I'll throw them out myself!" He leaned against the wall, consumed with anger.

Just then the other Brothers came running up to see what was going on. "Go away!" exclaimed Elias, who had been listening with his strange smile.

"No!" shouted Francis. "They must hear about it!"

And the messenger continued: "There is talk of not letting anyone join the Order without a year of probation, a novitiate. And no Brother can travel around any more without a letter from his Minister. The Reverend Mother Clare has also been put under constraint. Tall Philip, one of the first twelve Brothers, had a hand in it. But she bravely refused to yield. She said: 'You can deprive me of everything or impose anything on me—but you will never take poverty from me!' "

"How beautiful! How saintly! O holy dove, my true Sister!" Francis exclaimed.

"And whoever does not obey," said the Brother, "is persecuted and mistreated and then driven out of the Order like a mangy dog. There are revolts everywhere, but the bad ones are in control. And those who want to keep on living according to your ideal are being hunted down like game. They are fleeing from their hermitages and wandering around the woods and mountains, lamenting. Some have lost their minds from despair. Others have thrown away their habit. There are some who want to found a new Order. Brother Hat has assembled a group of lepers, and he is planning to establish a new Order. Oh, little Father, there is confusion, rebellion, and misery everywhere! Only you can set it all right again!"

"How about the Pope and the Cardinal, our Protector? Do they know about it? Do they let them do it?"

"So it seems."

Francis appeared to be swept off his feet by a whirlwind. He twirled around and beat the air with his arms. Then, with blood running from his eyes, he cried in a hoarse and trembling voice: "God, help me now! They have imprisoned Your little larks. Let me set them free! Come with me, Peter, Elias, Caesar. Help me! Oh, my poor, poor eyes!" And breaking down from the pain in his soul and in his eyes, he fell into Elias' arms and sobbed like a helpless and abandoned creature.

At last he had arrived in Rome to submit his complaints.

"You are a poet," the Cardinal said to Francis, who sat there all bent over, gasping and exhausted, his eyes covered with a cloth, his hand in Brother Peter's. The Cardinal continued: "What you have just said is true for yourself only, perhaps for seven or twelve, but not for thousands. So you have to go about it in a practical and cautious way. Your ideal has to be co-ordinated. Otherwise it will degenerate into heresies—and that is not going to happen!"

His Eminence rapped the table with his knuckles and peered intently at the cloth before Francis' eyes. "That is not going to happen! Your ideal is too beautiful. It is the finest ideal of all. But what can a swarm of wandering bees accomplish? They produce honey only in the hive. Yet they are the same bees. We must purify and sift the Brothers. The rascals and loafers must be expelled—hence the necessity for discipline and a novitiate. Once your ideal has been well organised, it will save the world—it will save humanity—it will save Holy Church. It is a beacon light in the gloom of our times. Is that not enough for you? Why, it is everything! Thank God that He sent you into this world to do that! Or do you want to save only yourself? Must not the individual sacrifice himself for the group? And your sacrifice is precisely the triumph of your ideal. But what must you give up? 'Winged liberty,' as you call it—yet it is physical liberty. That is hard for someone with a nature like yours. But that is where your greatness will lie."

"But it is not the Gospel life!" exclaimed Francis.

"How can you follow the Gospel better than by listening to Jesus, who demands humility and sacrifice? Can you who honor humility as the highest good, ever have a better opportunity to practise that virtue?—Besides, Francis, don't consider the work of just one day. The form we have given your Order is not a permanent one. We did it in an emergency, overhastily, in order

197

that more Brothers should not leave the Order. We made some mistakes at first, I admit—after all, I'm only human. But I thought it right that you made them leave the house in Bologna, although it belonged to the Church and the Brothers merely had the use of it. And the Ministers did in fact institute the changes too rapidly. Something like that takes time. Yet if you will just have confidence in me, everything will be settled all right. Likewise I willingly admit that it was wrong to oblige Sister Clare to own property. Henceforth she may live in absolute poverty. Also Brother Hat's project will not be approved. We will begin all over again. Your ideal will not be in any way set aside. It will simply be organised. Your spirit must be the soul of the whole movement, as yeast leavens bread. Give me your ideas, and I will have them put into practice in such a way that they will endure. So I request you to write for the coming Pentecost Chapter a new Rule which will restore peace among the Brothers and will make still more flock into the Order. You can do it. The whole country is rejoicing over your return. People will listen to you. Salvation lies in your hands. If you do not sacrifice yourself, then your Order will perish—and so will the world . . ."

There was a pause.

Francis just sat there like a stone. The Cardinal was breathing heavily after his long speech. He began to pace up and down, wiping his forehead. Francis remained motionless, as though not even his heart were beating.

His Eminence found the silence oppressive. He put his pale hand on Francis' shoulder and said: "Francis, you must take a rest. Once I visited the hermitage where St. Romuald lived, in the woods near Casentino. That is the place for you! Rest will bring you health and inspiration. And when winter comes, you can go back to Our Lady of the Angels."

There was another silence, a long silence which troubled the Cardinal.

Francis bent over still further. Then he nodded his head once, slowly. Getting up, he said dully in a sorrowful tomblike voice: "I will write a new Rule . . . And from now on, Peter will govern the Order in my place."

Brother Peter led him to the door. The Cardinal gazed at him with joy and surprise. And before the door closed, Francis turned around again. Holding his hands on the cloth before his eyes, he said: "Your Eminence will be the next Pope."

The Cardinal felt like replying: "Then I will canonise you."

The days he spent in the dark forest of Casentino did his eyes great good, and it was also a good place to forget all the sorrows and suffering of life. Nobody came and disturbed one there. There was nothing but Nature, just as it came from the hands of God. And as time passed, a person became so close to Nature, so united with it, that he almost felt like a flower himself. One lived in harmony with the trees, the moss, the rain, and the animals, and the spirit of the place penetrated deep into one's soul. For instance, there were those great oak trees, age-old yet ever young, firm and mighty, with their enormous roots clamped around the moss-covered rocks. A man's soul could actually listen to their power and their rustling, or to the dripping of a tiny stream that drip-dropped from rock to rock. It went on and on that way for days, months, years, whether someone was there to hear it or not . . . Why? For whom? One's soul listened and heard God. One heard God at work in all things, in the colors, in a rotting leaf —in everything. The soul heard His order, His goodness, His Providence. And it admired and prayed without words.

That was rest. And that was how Francis lived in the woods with Brothers Jack, Juniper, and Leo.

He would sit on a stone near the little brook. And he would sooth his sore eyes with bits of moss which he held under the dripping water. His eyes were a continuous martyrdom. It was as though they were filled with glowing embers. It was enough to make him feel like tearing them out of their sockets with his finger nails. He could not keep them open, and he could not keep them shut. A liquid discharge kept running out of them like juice from a lemon.

Yet he did not complain. What was his suffering compared to that of Jesus—or compared to the pain in his heart when he thought of his Order?

But gradually the purity of that endless silence seemed to lull his anguish to sleep. He forgot to plan the new Rule, and when he did think of it, he put off the job. It all seemed so far from him now, like an indistinct dream. And it all meant so little when one's soul listened to God . . .

He smiled. Through his swollen eyelids he saw Brother Jack feeding some wild rabbits at the foot of the rocks—and far off through the trees rose the rugged top of Mount Alverna. He had already gone there twice to visit Brother Wolf, or rather Brother Lamb. He was indeed a true Friar Minor, a real model Brother.

Juniper came out of the hermitage and clapped his hands: that was the signal for their noontime prayers. Francis went down the path. Suddenly he heard many birds singing deep in the forest. "Brothers, wait a minute," he said. "Listen to our brothers the birds—they are busy praising the Creator! Let us go and sing our psalms over there."

"Fine!"

When they reached the spot, the birds did not fly away, but began to chirp even louder. The four Friars chanted the praises of God, but the birds seemed to sing still louder, so that the men could no longer hear their own voices. Then Francis exclaimed: "Brother Birds, there are hundreds of you, but only four of us. So won't you please be silent a while until we are through?"

The birds immediately stopped chirping and respectfully listened to the chanting of the Friars, until Francis called to them: "Now go on with your singing, little Brothers!" And then the birds warbled and chirped until the air seemed to vibrate with their song, while the four Friars stood hand in hand, respectfully listening to them.

Christmas was near. Snow was falling in great flakes. Around the Portiuncula not a thing stirred. There was nothing but a white silence and the falling snow—and Francis sitting on the threshold of his hut, with his hood over his head, watching the snow. He looked like a hunk of earth. From time to time he murmured: "Brother Snow." Then he held out his thin swarthy hand until a snowflake fell onto it. In his cold palm it melted slowly. He smiled as he gazed at the small white cloud with its thousand tiny crystalline stars that went out one by one until only a droplet of water remained. "How beautiful!" he sighed. "What work Our Lord has put into each one of Brother Snow's flakes!"

His eyes had not yet improved. The salty liquid that constantly ran from them had left a red line along each side of his nose. The door of another hut opened. Out came Brother Caesar, who had come back from Syria with Francis. He was holding a piece of parchment, a pen, and a pot of ink. Francis sighed. They went inside together, and Brother Caesar blew on the little fire that was smouldering on the floor. He put a few dry branches on it and went to shut the door. "Leave it open," said Francis, "so I can see Brother Snow. He is

201

so white. That is to remind us how white our souls must become."

A smile lit up Brother Caesar's blond features. He placed the parchment on a plank on his knees, and he waited with the goose quill in his hand, ready to write.

"How far did we get?" asked Francis.

"That first we must give our belongings to the poor . . ."

"And add that we must keep back nothing, neither books nor—"

"The Cardinal would like the novices to have more clothing," said Caesar very cautiously.

Francis stubbornly shut his mouth and his heart.

"Shall I write 'two habits'?" asked Caesar.

"Write whatever you want," muttered Francis. Caesar wrote 'two habits.' Francis gazed at the beautiful snow and murmured: "God sends Brother Snow onto the earth to protect the seeds in the ground. God provides for the seeds and for everything. But men, with their lack of faith, want two habits!" Suddenly he sprang up and cried: "Write this down: 'In the name of holy Charity, which is God, I bid all the Brothers to set aside every obstacle, care, and concern, so that they may serve God freely and love Him and honor Him with a pure heart and right motive'!"

Caesar wrote as Francis dictated with burning enthusiasm. Then they again came to a point where Francis could use part of the old Rule, and he explained it so marvelously that Brother Caesar forgot to write down his words. But when he had to yield another point, Francis simply could not utter the words. Caesar had to say it. And then Francis immediately added a prayer, an invocation, an outcry straight from his heart which practically annulled the concession.

As Francis sang out the prayers and invocations, here and there doors opened, and the heads of Brothers appeared. They listened with admiration. Caesar could not keep up with Francis and repeatedly had to ask how it went. So Francis sang it over with still more forceful words.

After an hour and a half he could not go on. "We will continue tomorrow, Brother Caesar," he gasped, exhausted, as if he were burnt out. And he moved closer to the little fire and warmed his cold fingertips.

Brother Juniper came up, leading a little donkey. "Come to Mother Clare, Father. You are overdue. Let me see your eyes—yes, they are getting better. She will heal them completely."

"She heals me more by her holiness than by her nursing."

As he held out his arms, Juniper, who was as strong as a bear, picked him up like a father taking up his child, and set him on the donkey.

They left the forest and soon became covered with the falling snow. Juniper noticed how sad Francis was, and he knew why. They all knew why, and they suffered with him. Out of respect for his grief, Juniper did not dare say a word.

Francis felt it. "Sing a little song, Brother Juniper."

"I don't know how to sing, Father. You know it."

"I am no longer your Father. I am a Brother like you."

Juniper began to cry. The big fellow wept. He felt like exclaiming stubbornly: "Still, I will always call you 'Father!'" But he knew that he would hurt Francis if he said something like that, so he kept silent.

"Sing a song, Brother Juniper."

"Yes, Father—Brother . . ." and with tears in his eyes he sang loud and off key: "O Heavens, give forth your dew," and he continued to sing it over and over as they traveled along the silent path. Yet each time there

203

was a lump in his throat. And Francis sang with him—despite all his grief.

When the first violets came out, Francis rode to Rome on a donkey, accompanied by some Brothers on foot, to show the Cardinal the draft of the new Rule. Peter wanted to go with them, but he could not: he had such a severe cold and fever that even in the sun he shook like a reed.

What a difference there was between this trip and the time when they had gone to Rome with the first Rule! Then they had been singing, free, like conquerors, fresh souls with the breath of a new life. Now there was lead in their feet and lead in their hearts.

Everywhere the people flocked to meet them with candles and music. Crowds that filled whole market places knelt before the man who had visited the Sultan of the Moors! The man who could not be killed! Francis had become a hero. Yet this hero was nothing but a little man given to sighing, just a nondescript little fellow with festering eyes.

Lay men and women shouted to him: "Write a Rule for us too!" Everybody wanted to take up his holy way of life somehow or other. Many had already begun by organising groups dedicated to poverty. Rich men had given away their wealth and were earning their living by manual labor. Middle-class citizens were visiting the lepers. Grocers were shutting up their shops and retiring to live in caves. Married couples agreed to live apart. And the poor began to accept their poverty willingly. Such a transformation had never been seen before. It was a spiritual revolution.

"I'll talk it over with His Eminence," said Francis. "He is more learned than I am." He no longer wanted to make decisions. He was no longer able to. He had neither enough strength nor enough courage. Bitter as it was, he surrendered his own will to others. "Besides, they no longer listen to me," he told himself.

Changing the old Rule had cost him much suffering. Now he felt that he was drained dry, exhausted. He had only God left.

"Fine enough to learn by heart," said the Cardinal with mixed admiration and disappointment, after he had read through the new Rule. He crossed out a word here and there. "Submit it to the Chapter."

"As you wish, Your Eminence," said Francis as submissively as a servant boy who has to deliver a message that does not concern him.

Indirectly they came to speak of the lay people who were also asking for a Rule of life. Taking a parchment from a silver box, the Cardinal said: "I have already outlined something like that, in order to spare you the work, Brother. Here is the practical part. Here are the words—now you set them to music!"

And Francis did indeed set them to music. Although at first he did not take much to the job, soon his whole soul sang as he worked at it. Gradually his joy increased as he saw in his imagination all the thousands of persons whom it would help.

With enthusiasm he infused into the dry Rule for the laity a living body by means of prayers, counsels, and invocations that were so beautiful, so pure, and so filled with love for the life of poverty of the Gospels that the regulations no longer seemed necessary. Whoever listened to those prayers with an open heart spontaneously felt like leading a decent life and not bearing arms and not taking part in any war, no matter whom or what it involved.

The Cardinal was satisfied with Francis' version. Francis was as happy as a child. And Brother Jacopa's almond cookies had never tasted so good . . .

The day before he left Rome, the Cardinal sent for

him. "Bad news!" he announced. "I've heard by messenger from Perugia that Father Peter will not recover. Whom do you think you will select as his successor?"

"I leave that to Your Eminence." Again that strong opposition to deciding anything.

"You must make the decision," said the Cardinal. "Even though you are no longer governing the Order, you remain its spiritual leader, its soul, the beacon light by which the Friars Minor steer their course."

He paused for a moment, stroking his sharp chin and looking right into Francis' sick eyes. Then he said firmly, tapping on the table with his finger: "We must have a strong man with a level-headed, clear, and forceful mind; a masterful personality who can control the rebellious Brothers and impose peace between the old and new groups; a man with a perfect reputation and one who respects and loves you . . ."

Francis did not reply. He just gazed at the Cardinal's blue eyes. Yet the way Francis looked at him with his blood-filled red-rimmed eyes was really frightening. For the first time the Cardinal lowered his eyes, as he said: "How about Elias?"

"Elias is a strong man with great intelligence, and he loves me very much, Your Eminence," said Francis. And he began to tremble.

"Think it over."

"I will pray for light, Your Eminence."

On his way back to Assisi, Francis let the crowds in the towns and villages read and copy the Rule for the Third Order of lay persons. And the people wept and embraced one another—rich and poor—just like brothers and children of the same mother.

When Francis saw these children of God rejoicing, he could not help crying and laughing with joy and inwardly thanking the Cardinal. "Yes, yes, he is a wise and understanding man. I am only a child, a little child. I need someone like him. How beautiful—oh, how beautiful! Perhaps he is also right about Elias . . . God help me!"

In his imagination he kept seeing Elias, with his mysterious smile. Who was Elias? Such strange things were being said about him. Francis quickly began to pray: "God, stand by me! Yet just as You will, just as You will . . ." Then he suddenly put his hand over his heart, where he had the Rule. "No matter what they do, they will not touch this, my child, my dear child!"

When they reached the Portiuncula, they learned that Peter had died that morning. The Brothers came running out to meet Francis, lamenting: "Our Mother is dead! Our Mother is dead! Become our Father again!"

"No!" said Francis curtly and sharply.

"If it is not you, then who will it be?" they asked.

Francis replied: "The first Brother who comes out of the Chapel!" and sitting on his donkey, he pointed at Elias, who was just coming out of the Chapel.

Then Francis collapsed from fatigue—and from something else too.

Caesar read the draft of the new Rule before more than three thousand Brothers. Many of the first disciples clasped their hands for joy, but others were displeased. So this was the new Rule? Why, it was nothing but the old Rule cooked up with a new sauce!

Yet poor Francis thought that he had done violence to his heart in making some changes. They put all sorts of tricky questions to him, but Francis, who was sitting on the ground at Elias' feet, cut them short by saying: "Follow Our Lord. Live the way you promised. God wants souls—not fine words."

A Minister with a voice like a trumpet asked: "So we are not allowed to take anything with us? What am I to do with my books which are worth at least fifty pounds?"

With the help of some Brothers, Francis rose to his

feet and cried out indignantly in a hoarse voice: "Brothers—you who want to be known among the people as Friars Minor and Heralds of the Gospel and yet also want very much to own things by the boxload—I have absolutely no intention of sacrificing the Book of the Gospels for your books. Do as you wish, all of you—do as you wish! But I will never let you hinder the other Brothers who want to follow me!" And he collapsed again.

Others intended to ask him more questions, but Elias forbade it. "Enough!" he said. "The Ministers will go over the Rule again with great care. And then it will have to be approved by the Holy See."

But one of the earlier Brothers asked: "Then how are we to live? The old Rule is no longer in force, and the new Rule is not yet adopted."

Elias replied cleverly: "According to the old Rule and according to the Ministers. Next week I will go to see the Cardinal myself. Now we must take up some other matters."

"Carry me to my hut," said Francis.

They carried him away. A young Brother came and kissed his habit.

"Who are you, son?"

"I am Brother Anthony. I became a Friar Minor after seeing the five beheaded Brothers whom you sent to Morocco."

"You are going to become a great light in our Order, Brother Anthony." And he blessed him.

Depressed and lonely, Francis went wandering through the forests and over the mountains, here and there, without rest or consolation, worried and sick—sick in his stomach, his liver, his spleen, his eyes, and most of all sick in his heart.

He felt that his Order was going to ruin and that he was going to ruin with it. Treachery, pride, and hypocrisy were ruining it. It was as though the Lord no longer cared for it. They were planning to erect big monasteries, with fine churches. They had libraries and dainty hands, and they accepted positions of honor among cardinals, prelates, and noblemen, or with the Pope. Instead of being servants, they became advisors, and as such they ate at rich tables. They became important personages. And yet they were capable of giving such a clever explanation of their conduct that they seemed to be more than justified.

Others lost their heads, crept into caves, let their hair grow long, and preached heresies. Others were seen traveling around from town to town, shouting curses and complaints. And those who did not have too much faith to begin with, ran home to their families or got married.

Francis' grief was indescribable. And yet he reproached no one. In his loneliness he cried: "It's all my fault. It's all due to my sins."

He became scrupulous and afraid of himself. He began to punish Brother Ass until at times he could no longer stand on his feet. His soul became filled with doubts and uncertainty. He wondered whether such a sinner, who loved himself more than God, really had the right to found such a fine Order based on the Gospel?

Sometimes the light would return to his heart. Then he would kiss a dewdrop on a leaf or preach to some peasants or sing songs for children. But soon the light would go out again, leaving him in the dark once more. At such times he would climb to a mountaintop and cry out to Heaven with outstretched arms: "Come and take me, O Lord! Come and take me!"

He sought consolation among his true friends, his living Gospels such as Clare, and in the little hermitages with Juniper, Masseo, Angelo, Bernard and others like them. Yet he found no consolation among them. They were as pure as early dawn. Their clear eyes frightened him.

"Why did you give up your authority?" asked Masseo.

"Take it back!" cried Juniper. "You can do it. Drive out the bad Ministers. I'll help you—with my fists!"

"Let them live as they wish," said Francis. "The damnation of a few matters far less than the salvation of many."

They tried to arouse his former fire and fervor. But it did not work. "I do not intend to become an executioner and punish them, but I want to make them better by my own example. Let's just pray and suffer —that is the only way. And let us be joyful, because it seems to me that I am not a Friar Minor if I do not rejoice in all this suffering and humiliation."

A group of young Brothers came and asked him: "How can we best practise holy obedience?"

"Like a corpse," he replied, "without any will to resist, utterly submissive to the will of others."

But a while later a German priest asked: "I want to follow the Rule in all its integrity. Give me permission to separate with some other Brothers from those who do not follow it fully."

"In Christ's name and in mine," rejoiced Francis, "I grant you that permission!"

They reproached him for no longer having a will of his own. Then he would painfully get to his feet—it was a pitiful sight—and he would say: "I will show them! At the next Chapter I will show them how much will I still have!" And then he would weep.

Even Elias bothered him with letters about the guilty Brothers. Francis wrote back: "Try to look upon everything as a grace, even when the Brothers and other men work against you. Practice your charity by not wishing them to be better Christians than you are."

A Brother came and asked him whether he could

study geography. "Suppose you know all there is to know," said Francis. "Well, one devil alone knows more than all men put together, yet there is one thing that he cannot do: be faithful to God."

A young novice begged him to be allowed to have a breviary. He already had his Minister's permission, but he also wanted Francis' consent. Francis took two handfuls of ashes from the hearth and scattered them over the novice's head, crying: "That is your breviary! That is your breviary: humility! Do what your Minister tells you . . ."

The novice was troubled as he walked away. But he was hardly out of the hut when Francis ran after him in the snow, stopped him, kneeled down, and implored: "Forgive me! Forgive me, little Brother novice! He who wants to be a true Friar Minor can own nothing—nothing but his clothes!"

Thus he was torn by inner doubts. The light in his soul flared up and then went out, like a nightlamp. And he kept wandering around, aimlessly, here and there . . .

That winter he came to Gubbio. He met a crowd of peasants on their way to market, yet carrying scythes and flails. "Are you going to mow the snow?" asked Francis.

"No," they said. "It's because of the wolf!" And they told him that an enormous wolf had been running around the region, snatching sheep from the sheds and dogs from their kennels and even attacking horses. "Nobody dares to go out any more. It even runs through the streets of Gubbio. The people there are so terrified they can't sleep!"

"I would like to have a talk with that wolf," said Francis.

The peasants thought that they were dealing with a lunatic, until one of them got a close look at Francis.

211

Then they began to whisper to one another: "It's the holy beggar from Assisi!" And some of them ran off to Gubbio to announce that Little Brother Francis was going to deliver them from the wolf. After all, they had heard so many marvelous stories about him! So the whole town came running out to see him and go with him. They brought along an arsenal of old pikes, cudgels, and swords. One old soldier even had a banner. And the peasants already had their dangerous scythes.

"Are you going to war against the Turks?" asked Francis. "Where is the wolf?"

"Over there in that forest, where the rocks rise up."

"You just stay here—otherwise the wolf will be so scared he will run away." And he set out for the forest.

But the people could not restrain their curiosity, so they went along behind him. After crossing the forest they came to a snow-covered clearing.

There stood the wolf, a great shaggy beast. As soon as he caught sight of them, he rushed toward them. And the peasants ran down the hill, praying to the Madonna. Francis stayed where he was and watched the wolf approach. Then he made the Sign of the Cross toward the raging beast. And all of a sudden the wolf stood still, like a statue.

Francis went up to it. And from behind the trees the crowd saw the animal bow its head and put its right paw in Francis' hand. He spoke to it, warning it with a gesture. And the wolf lay down and licked his bare feet. He stroked it and told it that from now on the people would feed it and that it was to leave all living things in peace.

The wolf nodded, and then ran off into the woods, and Francis went on his way—troubled and depressed and lonely . . .

He came to Bologna to see Brother Anthony, about whom he had heard much: how he had converted whole neighborhoods of heretics, how he had preached to the fishes, and above all what wonderful virtues he had. Brother Anthony was far away on a preaching trip. But Francis encountered Cardinal Hugolin.

The Friars Minor were again living in the fine house from which Francis had once driven them. The Cardinal announced publicly: "This house belongs to the Church. It is not the property of the Friars Minor. They can merely make use of it. So it is not against the Rule."

"That is a mousetrap," said Francis. He felt too weak to argue with the Cardinal. But he took care not to set foot in the house.

Brother Peter Stacia wanted to have a talk with him. Francis refused, saying: "I don't want to lay eyes on him. He was the first to throw out poverty. I put a curse on him, and I will not take back the curse— never! Let me rest."

They let him rest. He stayed in the Dominican monastery with Leo. One day the Cardinal visited him and carefully explained how necessary it was for the Brothers also to have a theology school like the Dominicans'. "No," said Francis. "It leads to pride. The poor Brothers might forget holy simplicity and holy poverty."

"But it is for the fight against heresy," said the Cardinal, staring at him with a piercing eye.

Francis withstood the steely eyes and replied: "They boast that they have converted men by their sermons— but it was my poor Brothers who did it by their prayers."

"We must have prayers and sermons," said His Eminence. "We must not only preach penance but also refute the heretics! They ask tricky questions, and they know the Scriptures. There are even Friars Minor who in their ignorance spread heresies."

"But," sighed Francis, "to state a truth with intense conviction is more effective than to answer tricky questions. A good preacher must first absorb in prayer and recollection what he later gives forth in inspired words. He should have the inner fire rather than utter cold words. That is something one cannot learn in books—only in the presence of God."

"Then how about Brother Anthony?" asked the Cardinal.

"Oh, that fine, splendid Brother!" exclaimed Francis joyfully. "He has the humility and devotion and simplicity of a true Friar Minor!"

"Yet he also has learning and a brilliant intellect," said the Cardinal. "He is such an expert scholar that he defeats the heretics by his genius. They are afraid of him. He is the hammer of heretics. So would you be opposed to having him train young Brothers in his spirit and way of life?"

"Such a school would be a blessing," said Francis. "A school where every teacher would be a Brother Anthony training brother Anthonys, yes—but alas . . ." He sighed, and his sigh conveyed more than words could.

The Cardinal continued: "Give us your consent to found a theology class with him."

"Yes!" exclaimed Francis fervently. "But only with him and no one else! No one else! Brother Leo, take your pen and ink, and write—" Brother Leo unrolled a parchment on his knees and wrote as Francis dictated: "'Brother Anthony, my Bishop, it pleases me that you should give lessons in holy theology to the Brothers, provided that while studying they maintain the spirit of devotion, as the Rule requires.' Please give him this letter when he returns," Francis said to the Cardinal.

Then the Cardinal asked him: "And won't you agree to rewrite the Rule, giving it a legal form, so that the Holy Father can approve it? Until you do so, no order is possible in this confusion. And the Pope wants to have order—otherwise he will abolish the whole Brotherhood."

"I dare not rewrite the Rule, Your Eminence," said Francis. "The Rule comes from our dear Lord. If I changed it in any way, it would be like hurting our Lord. No, no, please, let's not change anything! Let the Holy Father just approve it as it is."

"That is out of the question as long as the Ministers are not in agreement about it. And as you must realise, they will never agree on it . . ."

"Then let's just pray, Your Eminence, that they may come to an understanding. There is nothing else to do but pray and pray—" Suddenly he exclaimed forcefully: "For I would rather see the Brotherhood perish than allow it to drive out Lady Poverty!" Again he collapsed from pain.

And though his suffering made him groan, he smiled at the Cardinal and said: "God is good."

The Divine Refrain

Francis was trying to rewrite the Rule, with Brother
Leo and Brother Bonizio, in a desolate grotto high up
on a rocky mountain, near a fearful torrent. In a sym-
bolic dream God had made him understand that he
must rewrite it. And once God had spoken, there was
no holding Francis back. So he had set out with the
two Brothers for the rocky heights of Fonte Colombo.
Now he was calm, taciturn, serious. The writing of the
Rule had to be done by him and by God, the Eternal
God who hides in the light of billions of stars.

He lay flat on the ground in the depths of the dark
cave, listening—listening with all his soul for what God
would communicate to him in the silence. Brother
Bonizio was listening near the entrance. Leo had placed
the parchment on a rock, and he wrote down what
Bonizio repeated after Francis. Thus the new Rule
gradually crept out of the dark into the light of day. All
three waited. One waited for God, the second for
Francis, and the third for Bonizio.

Now and then a sentence came. Sometimes there
were hours, even days of silence. At night they rested
in sleep. Each evening some kind men from down in
the lonely valley carefully left food for them at the
entrance of the grotto. And so the Rule was written
over. And just as in the former Rule, the divine refrain of poverty came back again and again: "When
the Brothers travel through the world, they may take
nothing with them, neither a sack nor money nor
bread . . ."

That was the core, the soul, the stronghold of the Rule.

Days and nights slipped by in complete solitude and silence up on the rocky hillside. It was an infinite silence, broken only by the deep booming of the mountain torrent. Thunderclouds and lightning came and went. The earth rustled under the rain, and the wind moaned over the rocks. And then they shone again in the sun. The Holy Spirit rustled mystically over the soul of Francis.

When they came back to the Portiuncula with a strange fire in their eyes, Elias ran out to meet Francis. He washed his feet and made him eat right away some porridge sweetened with honey. Elias was always acting like a mother, anxiously taking good care of Francis' body—if only he did the same for his soul! Francis was eager to show him the new Rule. He handed him the little rolls of parchment carefully and reverently, as a Message from Heaven, like the Angel bringing the tidings to Mary.

"All right, all right," said Elias, "I'll read it some time and talk it over with the Ministers." And he carelessly thrust the holy parchment under the cord around his waist.

"It is the Rule as God dictated it to me," Francis warned him.

Elias smiled as though he were bored. "Come," he said. "Let's put the salve on your eyes now—the expensive salve that I prepared for you myself. Your eyes are like fresh wounds."

Francis' eyes—they were important to Elias. The Rule was not. Francis resisted.

"In the name of Holy Obedience," Elias insisted, "I want you to let your eyes be treated!"

Francis yielded. "Good Elias," he murmured.

217

The days passed, filled with sunlight, and the nights filled with the light of the moon and stars. Light by day and light by night. Francis felt a longing for light, the symbol of God. But his sick eyes could not bear the sun. He kept his cowl up and drew it over his head and then even held his hands over his eyes. The light seemed to cut wounds in his brain. Only after the sun had set did his bleeding eyes begin to see, in the twilight of the fading day, and by the light of the stars and of the moon.

At night he often wandered through the woods, which seemed to be shining with light. He would caress a tree where a moonbeam bathed it, or bend over some white flowers that were sleeping in the moonlight. "Sister Moon!" he whispered, awestruck. And after gazing at the moonlight on his hands, he kneeled on the grass and said: "Thank You, O Lord, for Sister Moon, by whom God illumines the dark."

He listened to the grasshoppers. And he watched the rabbits frolicking. And he heard a frog croaking in a pond. He could feel the mysterious forces of nature at work. And when the sun rose amid heavenly colors in the eastern sky, he pulled his cowl down over his head again and covered his eyes with his hands and said: "Thank You, O Lord, for Brother Sun, whom I will never be able to see again—but that does not matter, because You did not create him just for me."

Elias brought him a little wooden bowl filled with fresh strawberries which he had picked himself. Elias would do anything for him, for he felt insecure. Francis had been waiting a long time for news about the new Rule. He had expected that Elias would soon run to him and exclaim enthusiastically: "Thank God for this Rule!" But Elias said nothing. He brought Francis food, nourishing food, and fruit, and salves and medicines for his spleen, stomach, and liver.

Francis continued to wait, but still no one mentioned the Rule. Now all of a sudden he grasped Elias' wrist and asked: "What do you think of the Rule, Father Elias?"

"The Ministers with whom I have discussed it do not consider it good. It is still the same thing in different words."

"Not good? But it comes from God Himself! God dictated it to me up there in the dark cave! Give me the Rule, Elias! Show me one line that is not inspired by God!"

Elias kept staring at him with his twisted smile. "What is the matter?" cried Francis, his voice rising.

Elias did not like noise. "Francis, dear Brother, I should have told you long ago—but I didn't dare to, because I did not want to hurt your health . . ." He did not dare to look at Francis. The strawberries fell out of the bowl. "The Rule has been . . . lost—lost due to carelessness or oversight. I don't know how it happened . . . I really don't know how it happened . . ."

Francis moaned. That was all. His purple lips opened, but not a word came out. Elias stole a glance at him. He saw Francis' large bleeding eyes and his sore flesh. But in his eyes he saw no reproach and no accusation, nothing but an ocean of grief. Elias let the bowl drop. Then Francis fell over—Brother Leo just had time to catch him.

"Quick! Some vinegar!" Elias shouted to the Brothers outside. "Francis has fainted!" And as they did not fetch it fast enough, he went to get it himself.

Finally Brother Juniper brought the vinegar, but Elias did not come back.

Francis went right back to the grotto of Fonte Colombo with Brothers Leo and Bonizio, to rewrite the Rule. They slipped away without anyone knowing it. Francis did not ask that God should dictate to him a

219

second time—that would be expecting too much. They would manage all right by themselves. There were three of them, and one would remember what the other had forgotten. One does not forget a song that has penetrated so deeply into one's heart.

All three sat side by side, and Brother Leo wrote it down. At times they were stuck and had to stop. Then, sometimes for hours, they were quiet, thinking and praying. And bit by bit the lost Rule was remade. It was like restringing a broken pearl necklace.

Winter was approaching. November brought rain and fog and cold winds. The mountain torrent became swollen and seemed to make the rocks shake. At night the howling wind struck at the rocks and rushed up the mountain and broke down trees. One day when the world was drowned in a thick mist, they were working at the entrance of the cave. Suddenly, unexpectedly, like an apparition of ghosts in a nightmare, a large group of Brothers appeared before them. It was the Ministers, led by Elias. Throwing back their cowls, they approached like wolves, until they filled the entrance of the cave.

Francis sprang up and exclaimed: "Why have you come here?"

Elias stepped forward and looked down at him in a domineering way. "At last we have found you! So what we thought is true: you are rewriting the Rule. But I tell you, on behalf of the Ministers and thousands of Friars, that we will not live according to that Rule. You can write such a Rule for yourself only—not for us!"

Francis was trembling with indignation, and he shouted into Elias' smiling countenance, with forceful gestures: "This Rule is from God. There is nothing of mine in it. It is all from Him. And He wants it to be followed literally—literally—literally! Without interpretation! Without interpretation! Without interpretation!

And anyone who does not want to do that can leave the Order!"

He was shaking, standing on tiptoe. He looked them straight in the eye, one by one, with his bloodshot eyes. And like leaves of grass falling under a sickle, they lowered their eyes under the fiery power of his look, which not even a devil could have withstood.

Elias made a gesture and was about to speak. But Francis sprang toward him as if he had been bitten and shouted, waving his arms: "Without interpretation! Without interpretation! And anyone who does not want to do so can leave the Order!"

Threateningly he advanced toward them. And step by step they fell back before the power of his will blazing out of his red eyes. And suddenly, just as they had appeared, they vanished into the mist. Francis stood gazing at the place where they had vanished. With his left hand he grasped a broken pine tree. Against the background of the mist he looked like some wild and mighty elemental being, like a sentinel of the Lord, vibrating with a consuming inner fire . . .

"Like the holy Angel Michael," Leo whispered to Bonizio.

Then Francis went directly to Rome with the Rule. There were three of them: he and Leo and a little lost lamb which they found on the way. Brother Leo carried it in his arms like a child. And sometimes Francis also carried it, but he became tired too quickly. "Poor little Sister Lamb," he said as he stroked its silky wool, "I'll bring you to a place where they will take good care of you, dear little sister." They begged milk for it along the road.

When they reached Rome, they gave it to Lady "Brother Jacopa," who was very happy to have it. And she said that she would spin a habit for Francis from its wool. Again he ate some of her delicious almond cookies. He enjoyed them so much that he licked the last crumbs from his fingertips.

One evening while he was staying at the Cardinal's residence, when suppertime came, a fine dinner table was ready for a number of noblemen and important personages who came to hear Francis. But he did not show up, so they sat down at the table without him. Suddenly he came running in with a nearly empty sack on his back. He emptied the sack onto his plate after sitting at his place next to the Cardinal. Out fell some stale day-old bread, some hard and crusty slices of bread which he had hastily begged from door to door. He made the Sign of the Cross over them and then gayly and rapidly went around the table, putting a piece on each plate.

"It is charity bread," he said as he came back to his place and began to eat it as if it were cake.

The distinguished guests looked at one another, not knowing what to do. Some considered themselves fortunate to receive the bread, and they ate it with respect. Others kept theirs as a relic. Still others kept theirs too, but they did it with insincere ostentation.

During the meal Francis spoke about the angels who have nothing else to do but praise God, and said that that should also be our aim. Afterward the Cardinal took him aside and said: "Brother, you really have humiliated me!"

"I have honored you," replied Francis. "I brought angels' bread to your table. Bread obtained by begging is angels' bread."

A few days later he began to go over the Rule with the Cardinal. There ensued an intense conflict between them, the fiercest conflict in Francis' life. He felt that dying would be nothing compared to it.

The Cardinal was an intelligent man. "The world will not always stay the way it is," he said. "Everything changes: customs and usages and kingdoms. But the Church ever remains over it all, like a light in the dark. And your Rule must be the lamp that illumines the Church from within. But then it is not satisfactory as it is. First you must be able to forget yourself and these times and me—everyone. The Rule must be good for all times."

"God dictated it to me as it is. God wants it to be followed literally, without interpretation. God told me so."

"That's just it: God is in it—otherwise I would put down my pen." And the Cardinal set aside his pen. "But the form is not right."

"The form is nothing but words, Your Eminence. God dictated it to me as it is."

"Words are the shells of truth. If God inspires the same thing in two men, each one will write it down differently, even though the spirit is the same. This form is not right—not right for the future. And that is what counts. Your Order must continue to sustain the Church. It must! It will! But it can only do so with a strong, clear Rule, a plain broad road. For instance, it is wrong for the Rule to state that the Brothers, if they should find the Blessed Sacrament in neglected Tabernacles, must admonish the priests. That is bad—it would cause arguments and conflicts between the clergy and the Brothers. If a Brother sees such a thing, he can do it on his own initiative. But don't write it in the Rule, for then they will abuse it, will they not?"

Francis said nothing. The Cardinal crossed out the sentence about the Blessed Sacrament. "There has to be a novitiate. You know why."

"Did Our Lord require a novitiate for those who came to Him?"

"The Church baptises anyone who wants to be a Christian, even the greatest heathens. But a religious Order is different."

Silence. The Cardinal took his pen and added a note concerning an obligatory novitiate. Thus they weighed and shaped point after point. But the sharpest conflict arose over the passage in the Gospel: "When the Brothers travel through the world, they shall take nothing with them, no sack, no money, no bread . . ." There was a real duel between Francis and the Cardinal over that.

"A Friar Minor may take with him nothing but his harp," said Francis. "His soul is his harp, with which he constantly praises God."

"I ask nothing better," exclaimed the Cardinal slyly. "Yet everyone cannot do that all the time. Each individual is different."

"Then let them enter another Order!" cried Francis just as fervently. "Let them not come and spoil our Order!"

"Exactly. That is why I have stressed the novitiate so strongly: so that they can be tried and tested. Your Order must also be ready to accept everyone who feels drawn to it."

"Let them come! A novitiate is not necessary for that. The bad ones will fall away by themselves."

Thus they argued keenly, sometimes for days.

Francis kept insisting on the divine refrain of poverty. He refused to give it up. "I cannot! I cannot!" he would cry. "The Order is based on that. That is its soul, its light! Take that out and the Order will collapse."

"I am not taking it out. I am putting it differently. I am putting it in such a way that Brother Anthony may take with him on his preaching tours his books, in which he finds additional inspiration for the fight against the heretics. To possess something does not mean anything if one is not attached to it."

"Whoever lives in plenty enjoys plenty."

"The desire for plenty can also exist in poverty.

Come, Brother Francis, suppose we write: 'The Brothers may own nothing as their personal property, neither a house nor a residence, not a single thing; and as pilgrims in the world they shall serve the Lord in poverty and humility.' If we write that they may go around begging alms with confidence and without shame; if we write that this is the summit of perfect poverty; that the Brothers must be satisfied with poor patched clothes and that they cannot accept money; if we write that wherever they come they must say, 'Peace be to this house,' and that they must always be meek and humble; if we write that the uneducated ones must not be anxious to become learned, and that they must always pray for their enemies—is that not the Gospel? Is not all that to be found in the Gospels?" The Cardinal's hands were trembling. His whole body was trembling.

Francis said quietly: "God dictated the old Rule to me."

"The Pope is the Vicar of Christ."

"Long live the Pope!"

"Then listen to him!"

"The Pope cannot refuse us the Gospel."

The Cardinal was discouraged and at his wit's end. "I have had enough of this," he cried. "It has been going on for years. It has got to stop now! Do whatever you want. Go ahead and live according to the Gospel. The heretics claim that they are also doing that. They are always talking about the Gospel. Within a year your Order will be a nest of heretics!"

"We will pray," said Francis. "We will pray that that does not happen."

"Do you or do you not believe in the divine wisdom of the Church? If you do, you must heed it. If you do not, you do not belong here. 'Whoever is not with Me is against Me.' In that case we have nothing more to say to each other."

Francis was weeping like a child as he asked: "Why can the Church not accept the Rule as God gave it to me?"

"Because in its wisdom the Church must distinguish between the person and the law." The Cardinal took Francis' hand. "Brother, it is really the same thing. I am merely expressing it in a more sober and realistic way. Are you going to let your Order fail because of a personal attachment to the other form? Then think first of your thousands of Brothers, however divided they are! After all, they came to you with good will, did they not? Unite them again! Think of the Brothers who will come long after we are dead! Think of the centuries ahead! Be a symbol of reconciliation!"

The Cardinal was holding his hand firmly. Francis freed it and kneeled down. He remained there as still as a statue, with his sore eyes closed. He was listening for the voice of God within, in his heart . . .

The Cardinal watched him with his pale blue eyes while waiting for an answer. A long time passed. The Cardinal's hands began to tremble as he waited.

For Francis, it was like martyrdom. For him and for his Brothers, his Rule was shattered into splinters—the Rule that was the book of their life, the hope of salvation, the marrow of the Gospel, the way of the Cross, the state of perfection, the key to Paradise, and the foretaste of life eternal—that beautiful Rule for which he had lived and suffered—that beautiful Rule by which he had attracted others, like butterflies around a fire. And now it was splintered into tiny pieces. He shuddered.

"For the sake of peace among your little Brothers," the Cardinal begged. "For the sake of peace!"

Then Francis opened his eyes, and raising his hands he cried: "May Our Lord forgive my weakness—it is for the sake of my Brothers . . ."

The Cardinal went to his desk and drew a thick black

line through the refrain of the Gospel: "When they travel through the world, they shall take nothing with them . . ." Then he ran his hand through his long white hair. And a shiver passed over his pale features.

The New Grass

When Francis left Rome, in a rain storm, it was really as if he were fleeing. "From now on," he said to himself, "I have nothing more to do in this world but to be an example. No one can find any excuse to fall away on my account. I want to be an example of the true Friar Minor. And beside that, I desire nothing but God. And now let's go and celebrate Christmas at the hermitage of Greccio!"

On the day before Christmas, deep snow covered the world. The little hermitage of Greccio, which was merely a few huts made of matted rushes, was situated on top of a high rock in a dark oak forest. There was a striking view from up there. Crag after crag seemed to stand shoulder to shoulder. Down below in the valley where the village of Greccio lay, a black river cut through the snow like a crevasse. And on the other side of the valley another mass of peaks and crags reared up into the sky. Deep and spotless snow blanketed the whole scene.

As night came on, big stars began to shine way, way up above the mountains. The silence and the cold made the stars seem still bigger. Then, here and there in the dark, tiny lights appeared in the valley. Bit by bit the number of lights increased. And they were all coming up the mountainside. It was the people of the valley who, carrying a torch or lantern, were coming to spend Christmas Eve at the hermitage.

Francis had planned a wonderful surprise for them. In the oak grove there was a grotto. And in the grotto the Brothers had arranged a little crib. On one side of the crib there was a live white ox with a pink muzzle and yellow horns, and on the other side a little ass. "It's like the Stable of Bethlehem!" exclaimed the children in awe and admiration. Just above the crib, an altar had been set up for Mass.

Brothers from the other grottoes and hermitages of the region had come too. The children were allowed to stand near the crib, and their wide-open eyes eagerly sought out the Infant Jesus. Their mothers were deeply touched. And the peasants with their flint-like features and eyes flashing like pearls folded their big dark hands in prayer.

Everybody was gazing devoutly at the little crib, in which there was only some straw. It was biting cold. Their ears throbbed, and the children's little red noses were running. The light of the torches which had been stuck in crevices in the rocky walls flickered on their faces and danced in their eyes. There was a reverent silence, as everyone was waiting for something wonderful to happen. Then a little bell tinkled. And from behind the altar came a Friar vested for Mass, with Francis as altar boy.

The Mass began, and everybody knelt down. They all watched Francis. He followed the Mass with the closest attention, but from time to time he looked at the crib and smiled a heavenly smile. At the Gospel, Francis took the holy book and sang the verses that told about God becoming a poor human being in a little stable—the most beautiful story in the world. Tears ran from his sore eyes. Then he fervently kissed the book, and went to the crib and stood before it on tiptoe. Stretching out his arms, he gazed at the empty crib and sighed with longing. And he felt a mystical inspiration come over him, as before in Bethlehem. Again he had a vision of the Nativity. And it made his soul melt with tenderness. He felt crushed by an excess of love—

flooded and suffused with holy bliss. For the Baby Jesus was lying there before him.

Francis saw Him lying in His little crib, a tiny lightsome being. The Babe held out His arms toward him. And Francis bent down, and with his bony fingers he caressed the rosy cheeks and curly golden locks. Then very carefully he took up in his arms the radiant little Infant and clasped Him to his face, close to his stricken eyes. And the Babe fondled Francis' tough beard and his pale hollow cheeks.

By a marvelous grace a devout man among those present actually saw the Babe in Francis' arms. The others saw Him too, but only in spirit, not with their eyes. Gently he put the Infant back in the crib and remained half-kneeling beside it, gazing at the Little Jesus and smiling at Him. And then Francis began to speak.

From time to time he looked up at the people and into the wondering eyes of the children. He spoke about the beauty and the infinite goodness of the Babe —of God who had become the child of poor human beings. And with his strong, sweet, clear voice, his beautiful voice (as the old chronicles describe it), he spoke slowly and feelingly, as though he were being accompanied by a harp. Every word he said radiated light, like a star. Every word was vibrant with joy. And every time he said the word "Bethlehem," he said it more with his heart than with his mouth. And he imitated the gentle bleating of a little lamb, and the word sounded as sweet as the bleating of a young lamb

And every time he said the words "Little Jesus," the flame of his love coursed through his blood, and he was almost overcome with intense joy. He drawled the word long and clearly, like an organ tone, and then he passed his tongue over his lips in order to taste fully the sweetness and blessing which the word had left on them.

The torches shone on the amazed faces of the peo

ple. And tears, like beads of light, ran down the cheeks of the children and of the grownups.

The next day, Christmas, the sun was shining dazzlingly on the snow. Francis stood on the edge of the woods, looking out into the distance. He called Brother Leo, who came to him. "Little Lamb of God, come and look: Nature herself has put on her finest clothes. See how beautiful it is to honor God! This is the Feast of Feasts! Today God became a baby and fed on the milk of woman!" And he embraced Brother Leo.

A flight of crows were croaking in the trees. "Our little pitch-black sisters have come to beg," exclaimed Francis. "Quick! Go get a lot of bread from Brother Cook!"

And then he cried out: "If I should ever happen to meet the Emperor, I would ask him to issue a decree to the world that everyone who could, should be obliged to throw a lot of seed along the roadsides on Christmas Day, as a treat for our little sisters, the birds. Oh, Brothers, on such a wonderful day the rich should have to invite the poor to a sumptuous feast, and today the oxen and donkeys should be given more hay than usual."

During the Brothers' meal, they again spoke about the holy Feast of Christmas. Francis listened. Among them there was an old Friar who talked very movingly about the Nativity. He described very vividly how poor Joseph and Mary had been: they had had no tablecloth, no spoons to eat with, no pitchers to drink from . . .

Suddenly Francis began to weep. Standing up, he took his bread and cheese from his plate and sat down on the bare ground. "What is the matter?" they all asked together.

"I do not want to be better off than Mary and Joseph," he said, and they all joined him and ate out of their hands.

231

He had gone preaching among the peasants down in the valley, and he was coming back up the mountain by a short cut through the woods. For three days the snow had been melting, but the day before, the cold had returned with fog, and now everything was covered with a glazed frost. And that had a magic effect in the forest. Each tree was white from top to bottom, including the tiniest twigs. They were like trees made of porcelain. And where the earth had formerly been hidden under the snow, now that the snow had melted, it revealed the old grass and millions of ferns that had turned white, as though the fog had breathed on them, making them utterly white, tender, fragile, marvelous, like crystal flowers on a windowpane. They had ennobled the forest.

Francis stepped carefully and reverently so as not to damage a single fern, and he pulled up his habit in order not to crush their delicate beauty. And he hummed a song. During the two months that he had been in Greccio, light had returned to his soul. He had enjoyed the solitude and wild nature, the company of some of his true and model Brothers and of the simple peasant people down in the valley, who were satisfied with bread and goat's milk. Simple people and simple things.

The presence of God had again blossomed in his soul. He could feel it blossoming. He felt God's limitless power, and he sensed that something very marvelous, filled with light and shadow, was going to enter into his life. Would it be the death of something? Of what?

He awaited it every day, spending most of the time alone, constantly absorbed in prayer. He lived on other planes. Things around him seemed very remote. He saw only the spirit of God in them. It was with regret that he consented to eat and to sleep. He was more of a soul than a body, even though his body was aching with pain. But he would not do a thing to heal it. He used a small block of wood as a pillow. He had forgotten his own body—yet now in the forest he raised his habit so as not to crush the beautiful embroidery of the frost-covered ferns.

In that very moment the presence of God blossomed anew in him, and it intoxicated him. From time to time he cried: "Jesus! Jesus!" and the echo sent the words back to him through the white forest.

He felt an ardent longing for the sufferings of Christ on the Cross. "The Cross! The Cross!" he shouted. He wanted to say beautiful things, but he found only scraps of words. He wanted to sing, but he had no voice. He wanted to dance, but he could hardly stand on his feet. Oh, if only, in such a moment of ecstatic love, he could make some music! Some music worthy of Jesus and the Cross!

He picked up a stick, broke it in two on his knee, and held one end under his chin, using the other piece as a violinist's bow. He played on a violin made of two sticks. And yet he heard music.

He swayed like a virtuoso, in that white forest where nothing could be heard but the rubbing of one stick against another. Yet he heard the song of his heart, the song of his Brothers, the song of humanity, that hymn of thankfulness and longing which, amid the darkness of sin, rises silently to God, to the bleeding Christ on the Cross.

He continued to play that way, swaying from side to side, like a reed in the wind, and Heaven opened its gates and sent forth its angels to stand around him and listen to him . . .

Once more the winter was gone and forgotten. Young green moss appeared on the ground and between the cracks in the rocks. The buds on the trees were just waiting for a mild night to open up their green hearts. Fine weather was ahead.

Yet up on the heights the air suddenly turned much colder in the evenings. Francis was shivering, so they made a little fire in the refectory, where they sat around after meals, talking about heavenly subjects. Francis closed his eyes on account of the brightness of the fire.

The twelve Brothers fell silent. They listened to the crackling of the firewood and the sighing of the spring wind outside in the trees. No one spoke. And in that silence Francis said softly: "The perfect Friar Minor must remain true to poverty like Bernard. He must be courteous like Angelo, intelligent and ready to help like Masseo. He must keep his thoughts directed toward Heaven like Brother Giles. And his prayer must be like Rufino's, who prays all the time, whether he is awake or asleep, because his heart is always with God. He must be patient like Juniper, strong in body and soul like John, filled with charity like Roger, and like Lucidus he must not be attached to any one place, for our home is Heaven. And the true Friar Minor must . . ."

Here Francis paused and said to Leo: "Go out and see if it is raining."

He who never cared what the weather was like, was suddenly interested in whether it was raining—they all thought that was strange. But Brother Leo, with his short white beard, went out to see if it was raining. And meanwhile Francis said quickly: "A true Friar Minor must be pure and simple like Brother Leo."

Leo came back and reported that it was not raining.

Then Francis spoke with the highest praise about Brother Anthony, that holy bee, and Countess Elisabeth of Hungary who was living the life of a poor Minor Sister in her castle in Germany.

There was a knock at the door, and two Brothers who had left the hermitage a year ago for Spain entered. Everyone was glad to see them. Another log was put on the fire.

Then, holding some buttered bread in their hands, the two Friars explained—both speaking at once—how wonderfully the Brothers in Spain were getting along: how they were living in perfect poverty, in reed huts, and how they relieved one another at work, so that the others could pray—and many similar examples of simplicity and humility.

Francis was so moved that he stood up and went outside and made a great Sign of the Cross in the direction of Spain, as a blessing for his distant Brothers. Then he came back to sit around the fire and hear some more, when all of a sudden, without anyone knowing how it happened, his habit caught fire!

All the others sprang up and tried to extinguish the flames. "Water! Water!" they shouted.

But Francis just sat there calmly. "No," he objected, "leave Brother Fire alone," and as the flames rose higher, he smiled at them.

In desperation a Brother threw his cloak around Francis' legs and thus put out the fire. "What a pity!" said Francis, gazing at the scorched spot. "Why did you take Brother Fire's prey away from him?"

They were speechless with awe. To them Francis was really no longer a man but an angel, a second Christ almost. They sat around the fire in silence. Francis' face was raised, and the firelight played on it. He was smiling at something up there. Then he slowly covered his face with his cloak. The Brothers quietly tiptoed out of the room, with their fingers on their lips.

Brother Leo whispered to one of the Friars who had returned from Spain: "He is praying! God is with him now!"

They did not dare witness something like that.

They were preparing to celebrate Easter. They went

and borrowed some fine tablecloth from the mayor, and they set the table in the hermitage as in a rich man's mansion. And for the meal they made some soup and several other courses.

But Francis' place remained empty after they had all sat down.

There was a knock at the door, and there stood an aged bent-over pilgrim with a staff in his hand, wearing a dusty cloak and a broad hat. In a trembling voice he quavered: "A poor sick pilgrim begs an alms for the love of God."

They looked at one another. They knew that voice. Yet no one dared say who it was. "Come in," said the Father Guardian anxiously, motioning him toward Francis' seat.

The pilgrim went to it, but instead of sitting on the stool, he took his plate and bread and sat on the ground. No one felt like eating a bite of food.

He quietly ate what was on his plate and gave it back to the Brother Server. The latter took it and said: "Thank you, Father Francis."

Francis took off his hat and said, sadly and plaintively: "I at least am sitting here like a Friar Minor. When I saw that beautifully set table, I could not imagine that I was living among poor Friars Minor who have to go and beg from door to door in order to stay alive."

While he was speaking, at a brief but clear sign from the Guardian, the serving Brothers were already taking away the crystal glasses and porcelain plates. And another Friar Minor folded up the linen tablecloth, and then put his piece of bread on the humble white wood of the table.

The Mirror of God

His whole soul yearned for God, and in his heart there was an intense longing for Mount Alverna. In August, when the corn was bending under the weight of the ears, Francis and Leo went up there to spend the fast before St. Michael's Day. On the way Angelo, Masseo, Silvester, Rufino, and Bonizio joined them. So all seven Brothers traveled across the country together.

When Francis could not walk any farther, they went and asked a peasant whether he would take Father Francis up to Mount Alverna on his donkey.

"Francis of Assisi?" asked the peasant.

"Yes," they replied.

And the peasant ran over to him. "Are you Francis of Assisi?" he asked.

"I am," said Francis.

And the fellow exclaimed: "Well then, take care to be as good as they say you are, because many people have put their trust in you. So I beg you never to do anything that will destroy our faith and hope!"

The Brothers were highly indignant, but Francis kneeled down and kissed the peasant's feet, saying: "Thank you for this warning!"

At last they reached the top of the mountain, three thousand feet high. They knocked on the door of the tiny hermitage, and it swung open all by itself: no one was there. But behind the trees someone was singing with a rich voice like a trombone. And then Brother Lamb came into view, tall and dark, bent under the weight of a leather sack filled with water. He looked somewhat like St. Christopher, with a long beard and hair so thick it almost got in his eyes. He burst into joyful laughter, dropped his sack, and kneeled in front of Francis. And when he heard that they had come to spend St. Michael's fast there, he laughed still louder, like a horse neighing. After kissing the tattered hem of Francis' habit, he suddenly sprang up and shouted: "Have a drink! And I'll wash your feet!"

They drank the fresh water which he had brought from the stream hundreds of feet below, and Brother Lamb washed their feet in a small wooden tub. That great big fellow who could knock all seven of them down with one blow, who killed bears with his club, and who lived on crows and raw fish, acted like a bashful servant boy, like a tame little pet dog. He was the guardian and caretaker of Mount Alverna. But he was only happy when from time to time a Brother came to say Mass and spoke to him about Francis. Then he would cry.

He lived all alone like a bear. And when there had been silence for too long, just to hear something he would begin to sing, and he would sing for hours on end as loudly as he could. Or he would imitate the howling of the wolves and the cries of wild animals. Or he would ring the little chapel bell for half a day at a time. That was the way he was: powerful and good and proud —like a wolf with the heart of a child. If ever he met someone who spoke against Francis or made fun of him, he would have smashed the man's head. He even wished he could meet a devil in order to beat him up— but he never had such luck.

Proudly he showed Francis how clean and neat he kept the little hermitage, and how well he had kept the small hut under the linden tree from rotting. Francis patted his long hair, and the big fellow groaned with pleasure.

238

The good peasant left his donkey with them and went home. They promised to bring it back to him later.

The tired Brothers enjoyed gazing at the distant horizon as the sun went down in a mass of gold and red clouds. Francis stood up and said: "Lord, stay with us. Night is coming on."

He stood there like a statue bathed in red light. Down below lay the towns, villages, and hamlets in which he had preached. Down there lived human beings with souls like stars in their bodies. How many stars had he made to flare up? While he thanked God for such results, he felt sorry for those who remained in the dark, wrapped in the fog of sin and confusion, and he thought of the Brothers who could not give themselves completely to God.

"Lord, have mercy on those who come after me!"

The golden light faded away. Only the Apennines still glowed a bit. Somewhere in the distance a light appeared.

"Lord, stay with us. Night is coming on!"

He thought of his mother, and he held out his hands toward Assisi. Then he said, with a tremor in his voice: "Brothers, I am not going to live much longer. My song is ended. So I would like to be alone—in order to immerse myself in God and weep over my sins. Brother Leo can bring me some water from time to time, whenever he wants to. But he must let no one else come near me. And Brother Masseo will see to it that meanwhile you pray a lot here." Then he blessed them and went to his little hut under the linden tree.

The Brothers shuddered with fear and clustered together.

Each time Leo came back, after bringing him some food, they went and stood around him, questioning him with the look in their eyes.

"Beautiful—beautiful!" he would whisper. "He

kneels there in a heavenly light and talks out loud, but I don't dare listen. I have to struggle not to listen. He is so absorbed in prayer that he does not even hear me."

The Brothers sighed with delight.

One night Brother Lamb got up very quietly and thrust his head out of the half-open door. He was not moved by curiosity. His joy and veneration and love made him long to see that light and hear that voice. But because of the rule of obedience, he did not dare leave the hut. He saw and heard nothing. The night wind was blowing through his beard. He felt his heart thumping in his chest with anticipation. And he stayed there all night, until the first light of dawn fell on the tops of the Apennines. Then he went back inside.

The very next day, the eve of the Assumption of the Blessed Virgin, when Brother Leo brought his food, Francis told him to go and stand at the door of the little chapel, and said: "Each time I shout, 'Lamb of God, do you hear me?' then you must answer as loud as you can, 'Yes, I hear you.'"

Francis went deeper into the woods, turned around, and called: "Lamb of God, do you hear me?"

"Yes, Father, I hear you!" he heard from way off through the trees.

Francis went farther—up over piles of rocks. Then he called again. The answer came as softly as a sigh. Francis went still farther, though he had to struggle through the underbrush, until suddenly he stood before a precipice about ten feet wide and at least three hundred feet deep. No reply reached him there.

"I am going to live on the other side of this chasm," he decided.

When he told his companions, Brother Lamb was heartbroken. "It's my fault," he thought, "he knows that I tried to spy on him last night." And so he was ready to do anything in order to get back into Francis' favor.

He carried up the great beam all by himself—and what a beam it was! He nearly collapsed under it. The veins on his forehead swelled up like cords. And he looked pleadingly at Francis as if to say: "Just see what I can do for you and how I love you."

They placed the plank over the chasm. There was not much room on the other side. A little farther on, the rocks again dropped right down, so that Francis was on a sort of island. They built him a tiny hut under some oak trees. And toward evening when it was finished, Francis said to the Brothers:

"Now go back. No one can come to visit me. Only Brother Leo must bring some bread and water once a day, very quietly, and also at night at the hour for Matins. Brother Leo, you must put the bread at the beginning of the bridge, and when you reach it, call out, 'Lord, open Thou my lips!' And if I answer, 'In order to sing Thy praises,' then come over the bridge and we will chant Matins together. But if I do not answer, then go back!"

When Francis was alone, he kneeled down and murmured: "Lord, I am ready."

But then the Devil appeared on the scene and injected fear into his prayers, saying: "Elias! Elias! The house in Bologna! Brothers at the University of Paris! Comfortable monasteries! Magnificent churches! That is what you have achieved with that phantom of yours, Lady Poverty! You have always tried to grasp phantoms: knight, poet, nobleman, troubadour, saint! Just between ourselves, admit that you were born crazy. But you certainly made those dupes believe your lies. And yet that is nothing. But how many of them have you driven into confusion or sin? You are going to pay for that! The Pope is going to condemn you, and your name will become a curse. Your Order is breaking up— it is already ruined! You persuade yourself that God is

241

with it—what proof have you? Elias has the proofs. God has abandoned your Order. And He is right!"

Sweat dripped down Francis' face, and he kept crying: "Jesus is my only light! Jesus is my only light!"

Then physical suffering came over him in waves. His muscles cracked over his bones from pain and anguish. This lasted for many days. Once when he answered Leo's call and Leo went to him, Francis embraced him and sobbed: "If you only knew what I have been suffering from the Devil, how the Brothers would have pity on me!"

And while Leo reverently wiped the sweat from his brow, Francis added: "But when I think of the sufferings of our dear Lord, then my pains are but fleabites. And when the temptations have gone, thanks to patience and prayer, then I have such wonderful experiences, Brother Leo! Then Heaven comes down to me. Only the day before yesterday, a beautiful luminous figure suddenly stood before me, holding a violin. And then he drew over the strings a bow that was as bright as a sun-beam, and filled the air with a sound that was so supernaturally lovely that all the beauty of Heaven seemed to have been fused into that one note. My soul vibrated with such intense joy that it nearly escaped from my intoxicated body. If the Angel had touched the strings once more, my soul would have broken loose and soared up to Heaven. When I had come back to myself, I cried out: 'Just let me suffer and renounce!' And I say it again: I can stand it now. If I can enjoy such bliss while I am still dust and flesh, what will it be like when my soul has left this miserable sack?"

And he caressed a falcon, a new friend that awakened him by its call every night for Matins. "Brother Falcon," he said, and the bird preened its powerful and handsome head.

"Listen, Brother Falcon," and Francis hummed: "Te Deum laudamus . . ." Leo hummed the melody with him, and Brother Falcon reverently spread out his wings.

Leo called in the moonlight. As usual, there was no answer, but this time he had a strange foreboding. Suppose Francis was lying there dead! Then, after a moment's hesitation, motivated by a good intention, Leo carefully crossed over the plank. The moon was shining brightly, and not a leaf stirred.

He intended to look in the hut, but then he caught sight of Francis, kneeling, his face and his arms raised toward heaven, and Leo heard him say in a muffled voice: "Who art Thou, my dearest Lord—and who am I, a miserable worm and useless servant?" The moonlight fell directly on his features, and his cheeks seemed like two cavities. Leo was so deeply moved that he had to hold onto a tree.

Suddenly a great flame appeared and hovered above Francis' head. And out of the flame came a Voice that Leo could not understand. He trembled. He felt ashamed to be spying on such a holy event, and he silently retreated, without taking his eyes from Francis— until a branch cracked under his foot!

Francis sprang up and cried out sharply: "In the name of Jesus, who is there? Stand still! Don't move!"

Francis approached. Leo was so frightened that he crouched down and put his hands over his face. Francis stood right before him and said: "Who are you?"

Then Leo timidly arose, weeping, and begged forgiveness, explaining what he had done. Francis took his trembling hand. "Leo, I was absorbed in the light of contemplation, and in it I saw the infinite depth of God's beauty in contrast with my own miserable self." Francis took the Lamb of God into his arms. "I don't know what it will be," he exclaimed, "but God is going to do such great things to me on this mountain as have never happened to any living creature. And now go to

243

the chapel and fetch the Book of the Gospels. That is where God will show me what I must do."

Later, in the bright moonlight, Leo came back, holding the book. Blindly, haphazardly, he opened it—to the Passion of Christ. The second time—again the Passion. The third time—again the same.

"Now I know," said Francis, and he turned as white as chalk, while cold sweat ran over his face. And with his eyes closed, he murmured: "To be like Him in His suffering and torment, before death comes! Lord, be merciful to me!"

Leo went away anxiously, with the Book of the Gospels under his arm.

"O my God, Jesus Christ! On this Feast of the Holy Cross, I ask for two things before I die: that during my short life I may feel Your sufferings and Your love in my soul and in my body!"

Francis was kneeling outside his hut. His prayer quivered in the silence of the night. Dawn was near. It was bitingly cold, and the stars were shining brightly in the sky. And then, as the first glimmer of light appeared in the dark, what he had lived for all his life happened.

All of a sudden there was a dazzling light. It was as though the heavens were exploding and splashing forth all their glory in millions of waterfalls of colors and stars. And in the center of that bright whirlpool was a core of blinding light that flashed down from the depths of the sky with terrifying speed until suddenly it stopped, motionless and sacred, above a pointed rock in front of Francis. It was a fiery figure with wings, nailed to a cross of fire. Two flaming wings rose straight upward, two others opened out horizontally, and two more covered the figure. And the wounds in the hands and feet and heart were blazing rays of blood. The sparkling features of the Being wore an expression of supernatural beauty and grief.

It was the face of Jesus, and Jesus spoke.

Then suddenly streams of fire and blood shot from His wounds and pierced the hands and feet of Francis with nails and his heart with the stab of a lance. As Francis uttered a mighty shout of joy and pain, the fiery image impressed itself into his body, as into a mirrored reflection of itself, with all its love, its beauty, and its grief. And it vanished within him. Another cry pierced the air. Then, with nails and wounds through his body, and with his soul and spirit aflame, Francis sank down, unconscious, in his blood.

The Singing Wounds

"Live in peace, little brothers—and goodbye! My body is leaving you, but my heart will stay here. Goodbye to all of you—and to you too, beautiful Mount Alverna, good holy mountain, mount of angels—goodbye! Goodbye, trees, plants, rocks, and birds, especially Brother Falcon, my awakener and companion—goodbye! Goodbye to the rock before which I prayed! Goodbye to the little chapel! O Mother of God, I entrust the Brothers and the mountain to you! I will never see you again!"

He was sitting on the small donkey, with his hands and feet wrapped in bandages through which seeped the blood from the nails planted in his feet and hands. What heavenly joy and pure bliss those wounds brought him—and what inhuman torture!

He gave his blessing to his Brothers. Then Leo led the little donkey forward. But instead of going down, they went up higher, from one summit to another. It was as though Francis could not tear himself away from these sacred heights. And the Brothers who had to stay up there seemed to be drawn after him, for they followed him at a bowshot's distance.

When the travelers finally came down into the valley that evening, Francis tried to get off the donkey alone, despite all his pain. He had to be extremely careful, with the nails and bent nail tips projecting from his hands and feet. Dropping onto his knees and turning his face toward Mount Alverna, he cried: "God bless you, Holy Mount where God revealed Himself! God bless you!"

Before they had traveled another hour, Brother Lamb had impulsively told the inhabitants of the first village about the miracle of the wounds. And from there the news spread along the road like a prairie fire. The trip became a series of triumphal celebrations such as had never been seen before. It was a trip marked by miracles and divine marvels.

"The saint! The saint is coming!"

Mothers held out their babies. The crowds came from far and near, by wagon and on foot. The sick and the cripples and the blind stood in rows along the hedges by the roadside, as if all the hospitals in the region had been left empty. But Francis did not notice it. He lived with his mind still turned inward, in that heavenly ecstasy filled with bliss and suffering. Two hours after they had left the celebration in San Sepolcro, he asked: "When will we get to San Sepolcro?"

"We passed it two hours ago," replied Leo.

He lived absorbed in his inner life. Yet every step hurt him. His pain was so great that they stayed in a little mountain village for a whole month. Later they were snowed in for a while. It was only in mid-November that, escorted by everybody in Assisi, they reached Our Lady of the Angels.

Everywhere people spoke of Francis as like a second Christ.

Though he seemed to be nothing but skin and bones, in his bleeding, dark-circled, sunken-in eyes there was a look of such gentle kindness and love that it made men and women kneel down and cry. His father and mother came to see him every day and found him lying on his straw bed.

One evening the Brothers were sitting around the fire with Francis. Elias and Leo were next to him. Leo told them about the miracle on the mount. Tears sparkled on their cheeks in the light of the flames. Francis kept his wounds covered, but a small pool of blood spread around his feet.

Elias listened proudly to Leo's account, and his great eyes seemed to be peering into the future: this was fine for the Order, he thought, now it will more easily conquer the world. He was concerned only with the external glory and fame of the Order—the rest did not matter to him.

Brother Bernard and many of the first Friars who had joined Francis were also present. When Leo finished his report, the Brothers sat there with clasped hands, entranced by the heavenly beauty of the miracle. Then Elias, who was holding Francis in his arms, said: "Now you will have to rest, Brother. You must rest up well all winter."

Francis reacted as if he had been stung. "No!" he cried, holding out his hands with their bloody bandages. "No! I will not rest! I must begin to work right now! Nothing has been accomplished yet. The great task must begin now! I want to go out again and preach and take care of the lepers and again be despised by the world."

Brother Juniper, who could not stand Elias, laughed triumphantly at Elias, as if to say: "What a difference between you and him!" And Elias scornfully shrugged his shoulders, as though he had understood.

It was a hard winter. Yet Francis worked hard. Seated on a little donkey, accompanied by Leo and sometimes by Elias, he rode from village to village. He would even preach in three villages on the same day, no matter how bad the weather was. He could no longer walk, for the points of the nails extended beyond the soles of his feet. He felt a constant searing pain. Yet through all his suffering flamed his love for Jesus, and he wanted everyone to share it. He even sang, and he visited Clare and her Sisters, and he could still laugh over Brother Juniper's clowning.

Juniper had just been to Rome. The people must have known that he was coming, for everybody had heard of his great simplicity. A large crowd went out to welcome him. When he saw them, Juniper wanted to run away. But they surrounded him. Suddenly he caught sight of some children seesawing on a plank over a tree, and he ran over to them.

"Can I play with you, boys?" he asked.

"Yes! Yes!"

So he sat on one end of the plank, while about seven children climbed onto the other end, in order to make it balance. And then they all seesawed up and down, up and down, with the Friar laughing and shouting.

The crowd was shocked.

"Is that Brother Juniper, the best friend of Francis?"

"He is an idiot!"

"He is not sober!"

"Just look at him seesawing there—it's a disgrace!"

"I'm going home!"

"So am I!"

And when the crowd had left, Juniper went on his way.

"Good for him!" laughed Francis. "Good for him!"

His fervor increased every day. But his strength ebbed away with his blood, which kept flowing all the time. At the end of the winter, he again lay sick in his hut—exhausted and spent and half blind again. Leo had to hold the first violets under his nose. Francis could still smell their fragrance, but he could hardly see them. His stomach was bleeding from ulcers. He was bleeding all over. He reeked with blood.

"I should have died long ago," he said. "Once when I was in the mountains with Elias, he dreamed that a priest in white vestments came and told him that I had only two more years to live. I always thought that he mistook 'one' for 'two.' But it must have been two after all. What a pity—otherwise I would already be up there!"

People said that Elias knew how to make gold, that he was an alchemist, and that he had learned the art from the Arabs. They even said that he was a sorcerer. But no matter what anyone thought of Elias, he did love Francis, and he wanted him to get well. He wanted it so much that it would not let him rest. So he wrote to the Cardinal, who was spending the summer with the Pope in Rieti, for he had good doctors.

Elias wanted Francis to go there. But Francis said: "When God gives me the suffering which I have begged from Him, it would not be polite to obtain relief from it."

But after another painful night, Elias went to his bed and declared, in a voice like a trumpet: "As your Father Superior, I command you, in the name of holy obedience, to let us take you to Rieti!"

Francis moaned: "Under holy obedience, I will go to Rieti."

He set out the next morning with Leo and a few others. He rode on a strong donkey, but at each step he had to stifle a cry of pain. They advanced only step by step, and after every ten steps they rested. It was afternoon before they reached St. Damian, which was not even an hour away. "Let's rest here a bit," said Francis, "and visit Clare, that angel, for God knows whether I will ever see her again . . ."

He was still there a month later. He lay, blind, in a little wattle hut in the tiny vegetable garden behind the small church. Clare herself had made the hut. Many flowers and three tall cypress trees grew there. There was a fine view over the fertile valley.

Everything there was so youthful, so beautiful, and

so peaceful that it was like Sunday every day. Except at night! Then the rats and mice made an infernal racket as they squeaked and shrieked and scampered over his body, sniffing at his wounds, scratching at the reeds, and falling down from the ceiling onto his face and chest. There were also swarms of mosquitoes and moths and horseflies. And the summer weather was heavy with storms that did not break.

Nevertheless he did not want anyone to watch by his bedside at night. So he lay there in his blindness and suffering, in that beloved St. Damian where his spiritual life had begun. During the day the Brothers often came to pray at his side. But he preferred to be alone or still more to be with the silent, holy Clare. She nursed and refreshed his wounds, his pains, and his heavy heart.

"Clare—Sister," he sometimes murmured when she was treating his eyes and the scars on his hands and feet. Only Leo took care of the wound in his side. He alone had seen that sacred wound. How movingly he described those holy roses of blood!

Clare's complexion had become luminously pale, the color of the top of a burning candle. It was as though a flame were shining through, behind her forehead. She was thin, but there was not a single line in her face. And her large blue eyes were always filled with a beautiful light, filled with hope. Francis' veneration for her had become immense. He felt that he was still so utterly human that he considered his sufferings a remedy against temptations. But she no longer needed physical suffering. She had come on earth like a morning star, lovely and brilliant, straight from heaven. The light of God shone through her.

When Francis greeted her, he greeted God in her. When she was with him and they prayed together, he felt so good that he could bear his sufferings and afflictions. But when he was alone, then gloom descended upon him, and his old sorrow over the Order began to prey on his soul—especially at night, when the rats and mice prevented him from even dozing a bit.

"Little Brother Rats and Mice," he sometimes begged, "please go away and play somewhere else. You make my life sad. And when I am sad, my Brothers are too. Yet we should be joyful and see the sunny side of everything. So go play elsewhere, little fellows."

Just then dozens of them dropped onto his body, and hundreds of rats slid over his legs like one enormous monster. "It's the devil who sends them to me, to humiliate me. But I will not give in—not for all the money in the world!" Then, sitting up straight in his bed, he began to pray, and he prayed until the Sisters rang the bell for Matins. Minute by minute he maintained patience and fought bravely for his love of God.

As a result of Clare's gentle nursing, at last a slight glimmer of light opened in his sore eyes, and he could see again. Holding his hand in front of his eyes, he glimpsed some of the summer light, the shadows of Clare and the Brothers and a bit of the colors among the flowers. But then he could also see the rats and mice. And the sight was so terrifying that it made him wish he were blind again.

It was too much for one human being. One night when his wounds and his sickness and the animals were all afflicting him together, he cried out: "O Lord, have pity on Your poor little beggar! Dear God, I beg of You —I cannot stand it any longer . . . It's not that I ask for less pain—oh no, give me still more! I deserve it. But just give me a little patience to bear it!"

He had hardly finished speaking when he heard a sound like an organ which became a human voice, and it told him that he would gain Heaven through his suffering and that he should rejoice in it and even sing! "Then let it come—no matter how terrible it is!" he shouted, and as he did so, a cloud seemed to lift from his soul. Everything was fresh and fine again. And the light in his heart flowed into his body and its pains.

When morning came, his spirit had revived, like a dew-drenched flower, white and sparkling, and he saw the blossoms, the mist over the plain, the trees, and the rich beauty of the dawn and of the great red sun. He held out his hands toward the light. And dragging himself to the entrance of the hut, he called: "Brothers! Brothers!"

They came running. Clare too came at once. He told them that they should no longer be sorry for him: "Because last night Heaven was promised to me! Let us sing! Let us rejoice! Let us admire God's creation—how all things have sprung from one Love—how we are brothers with all things, with the light and fire and water! They are our brothers and sisters. And for the praise of God and the consolation of men, I want to sing about those brothers and sisters that we use every day and cannot live without, and yet that we unfortunately misuse so much that thereby we offend God!"

In an ecstasy of inspiration he stood up and went out, leaning on Clare and Leo. Then he began to sing to a lovely melody of his youth, accompanying himself with gestures as if he were playing a harp:

"Most High Almighty Good Lord!
Yours are the praises, the glory, the honor, and all blessings!
To You alone, Most High, do they belong,
And no man is worthy to mention You.

Be praised, my Lord, with all Your creatures!
Especially Sir Brother Sun,
By whom You give us the light of day,
And he is beautiful and radiant with great splendor!
Of You, Most High, he is a symbol!

Be praised, my Lord, for Sister Moon and for the Stars!
In the sky You formed them bright and lovely and fair.

253

Be praised, my Lord, for Brother Wind
And for the air, and cloudy and clear and all weather,
By which You give sustenance to Your creatures!

Be praised, my Lord, for Sister Water,
Who is very useful and humble and lovely and chaste!

Be praised, my Lord, for Brother Fire,
By whom You light up the darkness!
And he is beautiful and merry and mighty and strong!

Be praised, my Lord, for our Sister Mother Earth,
Who sustains and governs us
And produces various fruits with colorful flowers and
     leaves!

Praise and bless my Lord, and thank Him
And serve Him with great humility!"

After a moment of silence and holy recollection,
Brother Leo sighed: "You have made our lives more
beautiful!"

Francis was happy. He looked around at the Brothers. They all nodded, admiringly and joyfully.

Then he looked at Clare, and she said: "I want to
recite that song every day with my prayers."

"I owe that song to you—to your prayers," he said,
and taking her small hand in his two bandaged ones, he
looked deep into her eyes. Then, as if speaking to
Heaven, he exclaimed: "We must go all over the world
with that song, like singing birds! Brother Pacifico, the
king of poets, will again go around singing with us.
Someone must go get him today. Brothers, first you will
preach a bit and then sing that song! Singing softens
and enlightens men's souls. And you will say to the
people: 'We are the minstrels of God, and we ask for
no other reward but that you do penance and thus learn

to live a life of pure joy.' Come—let's sing the song together until we know it!"

He sang the first verse. And the others, including Clare, sang it after him. In the end all the Sisters were there too, and they joined in the praises of that song of reverence and gratitude for life.

Francis' gloom was forgotten. Elias, Bologna, Paris—all were forgotten. He was reliving his days as a troubadour, with his new Knights of the Round Table, the singing beggars, the larks of the Gospel, of Lady Poverty, and of Jesus Christ.

At the end of the summer he went to Rieti on foot. He wore sandals which Clare had made for him from cord and wool, with a little hole in the middle of the sole, so that the bent tip of the nail had free play and did not touch the ground. They walked slowly, as though following a procession, and they sang the Canticle of the Sun. All along the way, people came down from the hills and from beyond the mountains, in order to see him and touch him and even to kiss the ground on which he had stepped . . .

After a few days he perceived some rocky cliffs in the distance and then Rieti way at the end of a long valley, and behind it in the sunset the snow-covered peaks of the Sabine mountains.

The people ran out to welcome him with flags and banners, leaving their towns empty. The church bells kept ringing all the time. Cardinal Hugolin and all the prelates of the papal court came out to meet him with great pomp, and they conducted him to the palace where the Pope was awaiting him.

It was simply impossible to change Francis' mind: he insisted on living in the humble home of a converted Moslem. He lay there in a tiny room. Celebrated physicians came with their salves, plasters, and drugs. But nothing helped him. It only made him worse.

Maybe some music would make him feel better. He called in Brother Pacifico, and said to him: "King of poets and my Brother, go borrow a mandolin and sing to me about our dear Lord, in order to relieve my Brother Body that is suffering so much."

"Gladly, Herald of God," Pacifico replied. "But what will people think of me if I sing while you are sick?"

"Perhaps you are right," sighed Francis, "though I would so much have liked to hear some music, even just one little melody . . ."

During the night he woke up. "What do I hear?" he asked himself. Beautiful singing—like a choir of a thousand angels—filled his room. He recognised the voices. They seemed to float down from above, like a cloud sparkling with crystalline harp and zither notes. Yet it was all so delicate, so soft, so far and so near, that it seemed like the scent of various singing flowers.

Francis lay there sobbing and weeping, flooded with happiness and overwhelmed by the beauty of God which had thus been expressed in sound . . .

Every day he received many visitors, rich and poor. Cardinal Hugolin himself came and asked Francis whether he would give his cloak to the very noble and saintly countess Elisabeth of Hungary.

"Gladly," said Francis with a smile. "For the world will become more beautiful when counts and princes wear the cloak of poverty."

He lay there in misery, nursed by Leo, who came every morning and soaked away the bandages adhering to his wounds, and replaced them with new ones, and washed his poor eyes, those sore eyes of his.

A doctor said: "I could certainly heal them if you did not cry so much. It is the salt in your tears that keeps inflaming the sore tissues. We will have to isolate the tear glands."

"Yes, doctor," said Leo, "he cries a great deal—from pain and from joy."

"And I want to keep on crying!" exclaimed Francis. "Tears are the blood of the soul, as St. Augustine said, they are the pearls of the soul! What have I to offer to God besides my tears? Don't stop up that holy stream that flows from the soul and blesses and ennobles Brother Body! What do I care about light, which flies can also see, if thereby I darken my soul?"

Naturally the doctors did not touch the sacred wounds, and no one mentioned them. But otherwise they gave him compresses and salves and whatnot—but without any results.

The doctor scratched his head behind his ear and said: "Our medicines cannot help you if you do not cooperate. You are sick, and consequently you must not bother about scruples of conscience. Whether it happens to be a day for fasting or not, you must eat, and eat well and a lot, and the best foods. You must dress warmly, even if you have promised to wear nothing but a habit. You must do what we say."

"That's right, Father Francis," added Leo. "You act ungratefully toward your Brother Body. He has always served you well, but you do not give him his due reward. That is not fair . . ."

This line of argument impressed Francis. "Yes," he murmured, shivering, "that is true. Brother Body has always served me well," and suddenly he cried out, speaking to himself: "Listen, Brother Body! I ask you to forgive me for all that I have made you suffer! But rejoice, Brother Body, from now on I will be your servant, and I will humor you in all your wishes!"

But Brother Body no longer had any wishes. It was as though a prisoner who had not been allowed to say a word for forty years were told: "Now talk as much as you want." The prisoner has nothing to say. He cannot

257

remember any words, and besides, his tongue has grown stiff.

He began to wear a lambskin inside his habit. "But you must also sew one on outside," he said. "Otherwise people will not know that I am warmly dressed, and I want to appear as I am!"

Now he was also given good food and delicacies, sweetmeats, trout, and jam—but he hardly touched it. And they gave him a soft feather pillow. But never again! Brother Body could not sleep all night. It was as though he had been thrust into a smoking chimney. "Away with that pillow!" Francis said. "The devil is in it. Give me quickly back my good little block of wood."

Day and night he longed for the solitary little hermitages. "That is where I will get well," he told them. "There the air is clear and pure!" They were willing to do anything to help him. So they carried him up to the cave of Fonte Colombo, where he had twice rewritten the Rule. But the doctor followed him, with his assistants and a whole arsenal of instruments: an iron brazier, pincers, irons, and medicine boxes.

"In order to heal your eyes," announced the doctor, "we must draw the pain into another part of your head. We have to pass a red-hot iron over your forehead . . . It is a drastic remedy. And it might kill you."

"For all that concerns my body, I submit to Elias and to the Cardinal," said Francis calmly. "I no longer have any will of my own concerning it. It is in their hands. And if the burning is good for Brother Body, then go ahead."

While he waited, he looked down into the valley where the houses and trees and everything was so small. Then he looked back at the young assistant who was stirring up the fire. The doctor was planning the operation.

The Brothers were becoming nervous. This preparation for the martyrdom was taking too long and was a real martyrdom in itself. Their mouths were dry. They wandered up and down. Finally the doctor grasped an iron bar with a flat end and placed it on the glowing embers of wood. From time to time he drew it out to see whether it had turned white-hot.

Francis smiled at Brother Fire. Still, he was somewhat frightened by its untamable power. "Brother Fire," he said, "you who are the most useful of all creatures, be kind to me, for I have always been good to you. Each time I blew out the lamp in the evening, I did it unwillingly. I have always respected you, for love of Him who created both of us. Now be good to me too. Come, Brother Fire!"

The doctor drew the iron out of the embers. It was white-hot. Quickly he walked over to Francis, who held his head forward. When the glowing iron came in contact with his flesh, there was a hiss, a nauseating odor, and some smoke. The Brothers ran off, shocked and terrified. Francis' forehead and temples were nothing but a single dreadful wound consisting of bare flesh and white blisters. "Let us hope that it will help," said the doctor, who had to turn away, he was so horrified.

One by one the Brothers hesitantly came back. But they ran away again when they heard Francis say: "If it is not yet roasted enough, then just put it back on the spit, for it does not hurt."

His martyrdom was not over. A few days later they pierced his ears with burning needles, and then they applied leeches to the veins on his temples. And they gave him salves, pastes, oils, and bandages. And they made him swallow medicines that were so bitter they made his hair stand up straight.

He let them do whatever they wished, while he hummed a tune. He was feverish with pain—and yet he

259

still sang. Again he felt as industrious as a bee, as in the beginning of his vocation. He wanted to take care of the lepers, to go out preaching once more, even to go back to the Moors!

Poor Francis. Brother Body was nothing but a rag now.

He rode on a little donkey to the hermitages of the district, and he preached a bit to the peasants. After he had been in a church for only ten minutes, it would be filled to bursting. "You think I am a saint," he said. "Yet during the whole of Advent I did not fast but ate all sorts of delicacies." He simply could not stand that they should have a falsely based good opinion of him. But he could not go on preaching. The ground on which he stood became moist with the constantly dripping blood. And after a quarter of an hour he would collapse.

While traveling with Leo from one hermitage to another, he dictated to him some beautiful letters for Elias, for the Superiors, for Countess Elisabeth, and for all Christians. He sang many hymns in honor of the Blessed Sacrament and the Virgin Mary. Leo had to write them down, with the music, and send them to Clare, to whom they brought great joy.

Thus they spent the winter, and when the good weather returned, the Cardinal sent word to Francis that he should go to Siena, where the spring air was like a tonic and where there resided a doctor who was famous for curing eye troubles.

"Let's go," said Francis.

Then the doctor from Rieti came over and stood before Francis.

"Why are you crying, Doctor?" asked Francis.

"Well, I am not married. And I have been so stirred by your actions and by your way of living that I would like to join your Order!"

"God be praised that you prefer the balm of prayer to the one in your little jars! Come along with us, Brother Doctor!" and they went singing through the spring-scented country to Siena. Astride his donkey, Francis often sang songs.

While resting on the way, he wrote this note to Clare: "I, Brother Francis, want to imitate the life and poverty of the Most High Lord Jesus Christ and of His Most Blessed Mother. And I will persevere in it until the end. I beg you, dear Sisters, and I hope that you will remain firm in that holy way of life and in that poverty. And take good care that you never depart from it in any way whatsoever by the advice of others!"

To Clare this note was like a mighty fortress. She replied that she was guarding the document as if it were the Tables of the Law of Moses in the Ark of the Covenant.

In a little monastery in a poor section of the town, Francis was again confined to his bed, despite the excellence of Siena's air and the ability of the city's famous doctor. He was spitting blood, and they thought he was going to die. "No," he smiled, "I want to die and be buried in Assisi."

So once more they traveled across the country. But this time Elias was with them. Leo, Angelo, Rufino, and Masseo carried Francis on a stretcher, for now he also had dropsy in the lower half of his body. Francis held Elias' hand firmly. And now and then he said: "Thank you for coming to get me so quickly. I want to die in my Assisi, so that Brother Body may become just a piece of its earth—out of gratitude."

And, thought Elias, so that we may erect a magnificent basilica over your tomb. This idea made him cautious. He obliged them to take a long detour through the woods and hills, because the inhabitants of Perugia might decide to keep the saint in their city in order to have him buried there—such a relic would be a blessing for a city for all time! To be quite safe, Elias had some soldiers come from Assisi as an escort. They were armed to the teeth, about a hundred of them, just to protect Francis' body.

Traveling over a lonely mountain path, they reached Assisi in August. The people went wild with joy, especially since they had heard a rumor that the Perugians had planned to kidnap Francis. Some of them even climbed onto roofs and showered him with flowers as he passed by. His Excellency the Bishop, who had formerly covered Francis' nakedness with his cloak, left his palace in order to welcome him and to kiss his habit. And he said: "Let him live with me. Let me have that honor," so they carried Francis into the Bishop's palace.

"No! No! To Our Lady of the Angels!" Francis begged. "I want to die where I began."

"Of course," said Elias. "But not right now. The crowd will not let you leave the town, for fear of the Perugians. First an agreement will have to be made with the city council of Perugia, and then . . ."

Francis was carried to a fine room in which there was a small altar, and they laid him in a fresh bed.

When the Mayor heard about it, he was angry and jealous. The Bishop had excommunicated him because he had forbidden the people to have anything to do with the Bishop—all because of a quarrel over a few square yards of real estate.

Gilded leather—tapestries—bed curtains! Francis could not help laughing. Brother Body would rather be lying on some leaves in a hollow tree. "Now listen," he said to Leo and Angelo, panting. "While I was thinking about this unfortunate quarrel between the city officials and the Bishop, I composed another verse for our Canticle of Brother Sun. Listen."

And he sang feebly:

"Be praised, my Lord, for those who forgive for love of
    You
And endure infirmities and tribulations.
Happy are those who accept them in peace,
For by You, Most High, they will be crowned!"

And when he had sung the verse, he said: "Add it to the Canticle of Brother Sun. Learn it by heart. And then go and give my greetings to the Mayor and to the rich citizens of his party, and tell them to come to the palace. And when they are face to face with the Bishop, then begin to sing the Canticle of Brother Sun and add on the new verse. And I'll send Masseo to the Bishop."

The next day Francis heard a great clamor outside. "Lord, this beautiful, this good town is torn by a quarrel over a little handful of ground," he prayed. "Let the Canticle melt their stubborn hearts!"

In the palace too Francis heard more noise than usual, and he wondered how it was going to turn out. Masseo stood watching through the checkered window-panes, and described to Francis what was going on. He opened the window a bit and said: "Here comes the Mayor with all the rich men!"

The crowd cheered and yelled.

"That's for the Mayor," said Masseo. "But now they are quiet! His Excellency the Bishop is coming to meet them. He is wearing his finest vestments, and all the cathedral clergy are with him."

Again the people raised a great cheer.

"Why has it suddenly become so quiet?" asked Francis.

"They are face to face now . . . There are Leo and Angelo . . . Leo is saying something and pointing this way . . . The whole crowd is looking in this direction . . . Listen! They are going to sing . . . !"

The city square had become as quiet as on an ordinary summer afternoon. And in the silence they heard the beautiful voices of Leo and Angelo singing the Canticle of the Sun. Their voices sounded like two bells, one deep-toned and the other light.

"Look! The Mayor is kneeling down! And the Bishop is raising him up and saying something to him . . ."

Francis could not hear the rest of Masseo's words because of the mighty roar of the cheers that beat against the walls of the buildings. He knew what the cheering meant. And joining his hands he murmured: "Thank You, O Lord, for the peace that You have brought to my good town!"

Peace! But no recipe existed, no song had been composed that would bring peace to the Brotherhood of Poverty. Day in and day out he heard from the Brothers what was going on. Sometimes he said: "They are waiting for my death. Then they will spring—like wolves!"

He often said to his faithful companions: "Brothers, we should be able to begin all over again now, with men who want nothing but poverty and who consider themselves below the least human beings. If only I could begin again! If only I could go to the Chapter again! But it is too late for that. Maybe it's my own fault. I should not have handed over the reins to others. Perhaps I counted too much on God. Perhaps I did not cooperate enough myself. Was it cowardice on my part? When someone is drowning, can I say, 'God will help him,' instead of pulling him out myself? Was I lazy? Or selfish?"

At night when his fears and suffering increased with the dark, at times he would sit up in bed, and lifting his arms toward heaven, he would cry: "Where are those who have taken my little lambs from me?"

When his parents and his brother visited him, he managed to repress his groans and sighs so well that it seemed as though he were lying there for his own pleasure.

The new doctor, a clever little fellow whose name was John and who was an old friend, had just examined Francis again. His diagnosis was: dropsy, stomach ulcers, intestinal colic, inflammation of the spleen, abscesses in the eyes, etc.—enough to fell a Goliath. The doctor was speechless.

"What do you think of it, John?" asked Francis.

"If God helps, you will get well."

"I know that as well as you do." Suddenly Francis grasped his wrist. "How long have I still to live? Tell me! You know I am not a coward. I am not afraid of death."

The doctor hesitated, but Francis did not loosen his grasp. "Well, until the end of September or the beginning of October . . ."

With a sigh of relief, Francis sat up straight, and raising his bandaged hands, he sang with great joy: "Welcome, Sister Death!"

Then Masseo said: "Father, your whole life has been a light and a mirror. Now rejoice and be glad that your death may, like your life, be a holy memory to men!"

It took someone like the kingly Masseo to speak so frankly and so clearly. All anxiety left Francis. He no longer had to think of his failures. His life was over. Nothing was left but death, beautiful liberating death. Meekly he gave himself up to it and to God. He asked Angelo and Leo to sing the Canticle of the Sun, and he listened with gratitude shining in his eyes.

As soon as they finished, he held out his arms and sang, resignedly but very distinctly:

"Be praised, my Lord, for our Sister Bodily Death,
From whom no living man can escape.
Woe to those who die in mortal sin.
Happy are they who find themselves in Your most holy will,
For the Second Death will not be able to harm them."

And in the mighty radiance of his soul, all things took on a new beauty: life, the world, creatures, and death. He welcomed death with a song.

The moon was shining brightly in the silence of the hot summer night. Beggars were lying asleep near the fountain. Two sentries were pacing up and down before the Bishop's palace, for fear that the Perugians might dare to come and kidnap Francis.

Suddenly in the silence of the night a voice sang:

"Be praised, my Lord, for Sister Moon . . ."

"There he goes again, that saint of yours," said one sentry to the other, as they passed each other.

"At any rate you get your money's worth of music here. He won't let us fall asleep."

"I don't mind it, but people think it's very queer for a man to lie there dying and sing that way."

"I think it's beautiful!" said the other sentry. "That fellow must be brave! For that alone I think he's a saint. So long." Each went his way again.

Francis was silent a while. Then from his open window could be heard the voices of Leo and Angelo, repeating the song. A beggar who was unable to fall asleep sat up and joined in the singing. After all, he had heard the song every night for a week! Next Francis sang again. One after another they took up the refrain, alternating sometimes with a psalm or a hymn to Mary. And they continued singing that way while the moon climbed into the sky, until morning.

Little wine carts drove by. A fish seller shouted his long call. Women came to fetch water at the fountain, and the life of the small town began again, though with occasional velvety silences through it all.

Then suddenly they would start to sing up there. At twilight—in the evening—at night—they were always singing.

"I'm beginning to be fed up with it!" said the first sentry. "Now I know why the Bishop went off on a pilgrimage. Everybody is saying that this singing is disgraceful—even the Mayor, and—"

"—and everybody is complaining, I know," said the other. And each went his way again.

One dark night a moving lantern appeared. Two Brothers came into the square, a tall one and a short one. The latter carried the lantern. As they stopped opposite the palace, Francis' voice sang:

"Be praised, my Lord, for those who forgive for love of You!"

The two Friars listened. Suddenly the tall one seized the lantern and went toward the entrance. The sentry challenged him. "I am Brother Elias. Has this been going on every night?"

"Yes—it's enough to drive a man mad, Reverend Brother!"

But the other sentry interrupted: "It's enough to make a man begin to pray!"

Elias quickly went in. He knew his way around the Bishop's palace. Going up the stairs, he entered Francis' room without knocking. A little vigil light was burning. Leo and Angelo were standing in front of the small

267

altar, singing, while Francis was listening devoutly. Even Elias was moved. But he suppressed his emotion and said: "There are some sentries outside, and they do not believe that you are a saint when they hear a dying man sing. Certain respectable citizens have made complaints!"

Francis had already yielded far too much. It was due to his yielding that so much confusion had come into the Order. Now that he was soon going to die, his former strength came back to him and made him feel firm, young, and brave. So he said to Elias, cheerfully, resolutely, and courteously: "Brother, by the grace of the Holy Spirit I am so closely united to my God in my soul that I cannot help rejoicing and being happy with Him."

Elias tried to explain his opposition. It did not matter whether Francis sang. He himself admired the singing. But it might hurt Francis' reputation as a saint. And to Elias the reputation of Francis and the Order was everything! But without paying any more attention to Elias, Francis gave a signal, and all three began to sing again.

The Lark of Christ

Perugia promised not to interfere, so the Mayor of Assisi gave Elias permission to take Francis to the Portiuncula to die, on condition that his body be buried in Assisi. This condition suited Elias' plans. He had already selected the site where the basilica would be built, at the farthermost corner of the town, like a challenge in the face of Perugia. All this for Francis, who wanted nothing but a piece of ground and a little cross over Brother Body . . .

It was the end of September, when the whole countryside seemed to lie under a kind of powdery sunlight and when everything was very quiet and peaceful. The sun wove gossamer cobwebs in pale blue mists, and the earth was submerged in a light that was like golden wine. One morning four Brothers carried Francis on a stretcher down to Our Lady of the Angels, while many Friars and a great crowd followed them in a devout procession.

"It seems to be fine weather again," said Francis. He could hardly see anything.

"Very fine," said Masseo, who was helping to carry the stretcher. "The scenery is like a royal cloak, and everything is covered with dew that sparkles in the sunlight."

"In gratitude for this favor of his, let's sing about Brother Sun once more," Francis requested.

They sang the Canticle of the Sun. Francis smiled.

He had changed a great deal. His eyes were like two red flames in his lean ivory-colored face. They sang as they walked to the place where he was going to die.

The grapes were ripe, and the vineyards were full of large clusters of grapes, hanging ready to be gathered. The path wound through the fields. When they reached the little old chapel of the lepers, Francis asked: "Aren't we at the chapel now?—Ah, good! This is where I first mastered myself, when I kissed that leper. There is a beautiful view of the city from here—I still remember it. Turn me around with my face to Assisi. I will not see it again. I want to give my blessing to my town, my beautiful, my good town."

They turned the stretcher around. Leo and Masseo helped him to sit up. His eyes sought Assisi. And he saw it—not with his eyes, but with his heart. Up there on the hill his town lay white in the sun.

As quickly as a flash of lightning, he saw his life unfold before his mind's eye: his years as a troubadour . . . his turning to God . . . the lepers . . . his friend . . . the cave . . . the Crucifix . . . the little priest . . . his mother . . . He saw himself singing . . . building . . . preaching . . . He saw Clare . . . the Brothers . . . their work . . . And that indescribable feeling of love for one's birthplace which makes a person both happy and sad, overwhelmed him. He trembled. Tears ran down the red grooves on each side of his mouth.

Then, making a great Sign of the Cross toward the East, he gave his blessing to his town, saying: "O Lord, formerly godlessness dwelled in Assisi. But You were merciful. And You had pity on her. Your goodness alone founded our little mother house here, whence the glory of Your Name and the fragrance of Your holy life and of the true Gospel are spreading over the whole of Christendom. I implore You, Jesus Christ, Father of Mercy, do not consider our ingratitude, but remember the immense kindness that You have shown to this town. Let it be the place and the home of those who acknowledge You and who honor Your Name, Your praiseworthy and glorious Name! For ever and ever. Amen."

The sun was shining above Mount Subasio and shedding its light on the white town of Assisi. The Brothers were kneeling, and the crowd was kneeling, facing Assisi. Francis fell back, exhausted and happy. Carefully they helped him to rest comfortably. And after turning the stretcher around again, they carried him onward, singing as they went.

He had blessed his town. There was a smile on his pale features. And many of those present took another look at Assisi, as though something great and beautiful had come over them and over the town.

While lying on his little mattress made of leaves, he could easily see into the small Chapel and thus attend all the ceremonies with the others. Brother Juniper and Brother Jack were praying before the altar, and sometimes they would look around at him, like little children toward their mother.

Autumn had turned the oak forest golden. The yellow leaves hung drenched in sunlight. The sun penetrated into the tiny hut and fell on his body. Brother Sun was doing what he could to console and to please his friend.

On a small table were some melons, fish, fruit, and cakes—little delicacies for Brother Body. But when Francis put them in his mouth, he could not taste anything. So they remained on the table. Brother Leo was sitting beside him, reading a prayerbook. And Brother Elias was searching among the medicine bottles for something to soothe Francis' pain. Now and then a Brother passed by and looked in, reverently and anxiously. It was the deathwatch. It would not come right away. But there was no more oil in the lamp. There was nothing but the wick, still burning itself out . . .

Rufino came in and sat down beside Francis. Again he had brought greetings from Clare, and he asked what answer he should take back to her. Rufino bore the latest reports to Clare every day. And each time he promised her that Francis would come and visit her again.

Francis drew his bandaged hand from his sleeve, and with his wax-pale forefinger on Rufino's dark-skinned hand, he said: "Write to the holy Sister that I will not see her again, that I give her my blessing, and that I absolve her from every transgression that she may have committed against the commandments of God or against mine. Tell her that she must set aside all grief and sorrow. She cannot come to see me any more. But before she dies, she and her Sisters will see me and will obtain great comfort therefrom . . . When I am dead, I must be taken by St. Damian."

Rufino left.

Then Francis said: "Leo, go get Angelo, and sing the Canticle once more."

When he was not suffering too much, he dictated his will to Angelo, who wrote it down on parchment, while the others listened in silent recollection. It was the story of his soul, his love for the Gospel, his devotion to the Blessed Sacrament, his longing for purity of heart, his attachment to the Rule, and his prayers for the Order, for peace, poverty, and love. It was his gospel.

At each new line the Brothers looked at one another with joy. They felt that it marked a new dawn in the Order in the days ahead. It was like the waters of a clear spring from which they could drink their fill—or like a pure light in which their souls could again soar freely! There was only one among them who did not stir. He stood as stiffly as a wooden pole: Elias.

Francis woke up when the stars were already out. "Angelo!" he called. "Sit beside me and write to Lady Brother Jacopa that I am soon going to die and that if she wants to see me again, she must hurry. And ask her also to bring along my shroud and some of those good almond cakes that I enjoy eating so much."

While Angelo was writing near the little lamp, Brother Juniper came in and said: "Father, a rich lady is here with her two sons and many noble persons, and she says she is Brother Jacopa, about whom you have told us so many fine things. But as Lady Brother Jacopa is a woman, I have not let her come in."

"Brother Jacopa!" Francis exclaimed joyfully. "Let her come right in. This woman is a Brother. No women can enter here, but this woman is Brother Jacopa."

The hut rapidly filled with noblemen, to whom Elias bowed and smiled very politely and obligingly. Then Brother Jacopa came in, dressed in black silk. Angelo raised the little lamp above Francis' face. When she saw him, she started with fright—then kneeled down and reverently kissed his hands and feet. Her tears dropped onto his bloody bandages.

"I had just written you," said Francis.

"And I dreamed that you wanted the little cakes and the habit made from the wool of that young lamb you gave me."

"Sweet Brother Jacopa!" And he smiled as he looked at the habit and shroud in which he was to be buried.

And he laughed when he saw the cakes which she took out of a small leather box. He took one in both hands and ate it. But it did not taste like before. Brother Body's palate could no longer taste anything. Brother Body was dried out. So Bernard had to eat the cakes.

"I am going to die, Brother Jacopa. You must stay

273

here at Our Lady of the Angels until I am dead. But it will not take long now. Brothers, let's sing the Canticle of the Sun for Brother Jacopa!"

And they all sang it together, with the welcome to Sister Death.

Elias did not join in the singing.

Then Francis gave his blessing to all the Brothers who were there, and especially to Brother Bernard, his first follower. And he said: "When you see my last moments approaching, lay me naked on the bare ground—that is how I want to die . . ."

He asked for some bread, took it reverently in his hands, kissed it and blessed it. He wanted to break it, but he was too weak. Masseo did it for him and gave a little piece to each Brother.

It was a quiet October evening filled with the fragrance of dying nature.

Saturday was radiant with sunshine. When the doctor came in, Francis asked: "When will the gate of Heaven open for me?"

"Today," replied the doctor.

Then Elias sent word to Assisi that Francis was dying. The people came running. They left their work in the vineyards. Shoemakers left their lasts. And innkeepers stopped up their hogsheads.

The sun was low on the horizon. The shadows were lengthening. A blue haze appeared in the distance. It grew dark in the hut. The trees seemed to be listening. The light of the two candles beside Francis became brighter. Once more he looked around at all the Brothers, very lovingly and very joyfully. Then he joined his hands and nodded once.

They understood. They undressed him and laid him naked on the bare ground. He covered the wound under his heart with his left hand. He lay there in utter poverty, clothed only in the bandages on his hands and feet, through which blood was seeping.

"Throw ashes on my Brother Body," he said.

The Brothers strewed ashes over him.

"Now sing," he said, and Angelo and Leo sang once more about Brother Sun.

The Brothers and the people who were on the other side of the hedge kneeled down. Then there was silence again. Death was coming now. In such a silence death must come.

Suddenly Francis opened his eyes wide. He sat up, leaning on his right elbow and keeping his left hand over the wound in his side. Then he began to sing with extraordinary strength, with his rich young voice, as he used to sing when alone in the mountains:

"With my voice I cried unto the Lord.
With my voice I implored the Lord . . .
Thou art my hope and my portion in the land of the
    living.
Take my soul out of prison, that I may praise Thy Name!
The just wait for me, until Thou reward me!"

An echo in the hut. Then silence. His elbow bent, and he lay back with a smile on his purplish lips. His red eyes slowly closed in their dark blue sockets. And an ashen pallor spread over his thin features. Then his hand fell away from the wound in his side. The wound was like a beautiful fresh red rose.

The Brothers remained on their knees, sobbing and praying . . .

Suddenly, outside on the roof, arose the loud warbling of hundreds of larks, and as if at a signal, they all soared triumphantly up into the sky.

The first stars began to twinkle. The dying rose-tinted twilight hovered above the white town of Assisi

in the distance, with its dark cypress trees. The sun
had glided down like a goldfish.

*That is the way I visualised these events after I
had read the books which the scholars have
written about his beautiful life. I saw the scenes
unfold that way. And I dedicated these little pic-
tures to my wife and my children, to the Reverend
Father Giuseppe Pronti of Assisi, and to some
plain people who live on our street, in honor of
St. Francis.* Lier, 1931.